IN THE COMPANY OF PREACHERS

By the Faculty of

AQUINAS INSTITUTE OF THEOLOGY

Charles Bouchard
Thomas Brodie
Louis Brusatti
Harry Byrne
Joan Delaplane
Mary Catherine Hilkert
Mary Margaret Pazdan
Frank Quinn
Edward Ruane
Benjamin Russell
Carla Mae Streeter
Samuel Torvend
Edward van Merrienboer
Ronald Zawilla

Editors: Regina Siegfried
Edward Ruane

Preface by Walter J. Burghardt, S.J.

A Liturgical Press Book

THE LITURGICAL PRESS
Collegeville, Minnesota

Cover design by Ann Blattner

Cover illustration: "Dominic Preaching to the Nations" by Albert Carpentier, O.P.

1 2 3 4 5 6 7 8 9

Library of Congress Cataloging-in-Publication Data

In the company of preachers / by the faculty of Aquinas Institute of Theology, Charles Bouchard . . . [et al.] : editors, Regina Siegfried, Edward Ruane.

p. cm.

ISBN 0-8146-2091-4

1. Preaching 2. Catholic Church—Liturgy. I. Aquinas Institute of Theology. II. Bouchard, Charles. III. Siegfried, Regina. IV. Ruane, Edward.

BV4211.2.I56 1993

251—dc20 92-32646

CIP

Dedication

For Joan Delaplane, O.P.,
our colleague whose commitment to preaching
the word has enriched and inspired our
Aquinas community as well as
the Christian community.

Contents

Preface vii
Walter J. Burghardt, S.J.

Acknowledgments x

Introduction 1
Regina Siegfried, A.S.C.

Section I: *Liturgical, Biblical, and Historical Theology*

Chapter 1: Liturgy: Foundation and Context for Preaching 7
Frank C. Quinn, O.P.

Chapter 2: Hermeneutics and Proclaiming the Sunday Readings 26
Mary Margaret Pazdan, O.P.

Chapter 3: John's Gospel: A Model of Preaching 38
Thomas Brodie, O.P.

Chapter 4: Preaching the Liturgy: A Social Mystagogy 48
Samuel E. Torvend, O.P.

Chapter 5: The Spiritual Exegesis of Scripture and Contemporary Preaching: Claiming Sacred History as Our Own 66
Ronald J. Zawilla

Section II: *Systematic Theology*

Chapter 6: Religious Language and Preaching 89
Benjamin J. Russell, O.P.

Chapter 7: The Role of Theological Communication in the Act of Preaching 102
Carla Mae Streeter, O.P.

Chapter 8: Revelation and Proclamation: Shifting Paradigms 113
Mary Catherine Hilkert, O.P.

Section III: *Pastoral and Spiritual Theology*

Chapter 9: The Living Word: An Overshadowing of the Spirit 141
Joan Delaplane, O.P.

Chapter 10: The Spirituality of the Preacher 151
Edward M. Ruane, O.P.

Chapter 11: Preaching and Pastoral Care 165
Harry M. Byrne, O.P.

Chapter 12: Preaching the Social Gospel 176
Edward J. van Merrienboer, O.P.

Chapter 13: Authentic Preaching on Moral Issues 191
Charles E. Bouchard, O.P.

Chapter 14: The Primordial Word: Preaching, Poetry, and Pastoral Presence 210
Louis Brusatti, C.M.

Contributors 227

Preface

Over two decades ago, a remarkably learned French Dominican, Yves Congar, penned a startling sentence: "I could quote a whole series of ancient texts, all saying more or less that if in one country Mass was celebrated for thirty years without preaching and in another there was preaching for thirty years without the Mass, people would be more Christian in the country where there was preaching."[1]

That observation, from a circumspect scholar, should be scotch-taped to every rectory refrigerator. For, despite Vatican II's insistence that "priests . . . have as their *primary duty* the proclamation of the gospel of God to all,"[2] despite the flat confirmatory assertion of the Bishops' Committee on Priestly Life and Ministry, "The other duties of the priest are to be considered properly presbyteral to the degree that they support the proclamation of the Gospel,"[3] the view from the pew is discouragingly critical. All too consistently, our people are not confronted with a word that nourishes while it challenges, heals while it bruises. The criticism is further fueled by an increasingly educated populace no longer silent before homiletic pap and bromides, and by articulate Catholic women who are even more thoroughly convinced of their calling to the pulpit when they must submit to our contemporary constipation of thought and diarrhea of words. And all the more eloquent is the mute witness of untold thousands of "ordinary folk" forsaking our liturgy for the impassioned preaching of the Pentecostals.

My experience across the country indeed reveals priests in large number seriously committed to effective preaching despite extraordinary obstacles. On the whole, however, relatively few priests seem to see preaching as their "primary duty." A ceaseless refrain from workshops on preaching—"I do not have time to prepare"—clearly implies that something else is primary. Priests without natural gifts for communication rarely imitate leaders in industry who seek professional help for their deficiencies. And, tragically, there are those who "don't know what to say" from Sunday to Sunday—for any one or all of three reasons. God's Word is not the air they breathe; theology is an abstraction, not the Church's ceaseless search for Christ; they fail to see that their homilies are all around them, in their daily experience of people and newspapers, film and music, hospital beds and homeless shelters—in their experience of Eucharist, of

God. All too few homilists do what Ralph Waldo Emerson expected of a "true preacher" back in 1838: "that he deals out to the people his life—life passed through the fire of thought."[4]

It is in this context that *In the Company of Preachers* comes to a timely birth. Fittingly, from the Order of Preachers, founded to further Christ's salvific work by preaching the gospel. It is an uncommonly comprehensive volume—understandably so, since it stems from a theological faculty in constant dialogue. As such, it is not bedtime reading; it calls for concentration, challenges the mind. In a sense, it is a contemporary, updated, high-level course in homiletics rarely if ever provided in a seminary. It is not to be read at a single sitting. I recommend a meditative reading of a single chapter each week, followed by several days of reflection.

My warmest recommendation of this ambitious venture is my own experience. After a decade of teaching homiletics and a half century of preaching, I have learned much from it. I have seen with fresh eyes preaching as a sacramental act, integral to our central act of worship. I have been forced to reflect again on different ways of interpreting God's Word. I discovered how shifting paradigms in the theology of revelation have influenced homiletics, how a Christian theology of preaching will incorporate both the Reformation insistence on the Wholly Other and the Catholic stress on the mysterious link between the divine and the created. I delighted in the affirmation that the art of preaching is the crown of theological reflection and articulation, its most powerful and effective form. I was genuinely instructed by the five purposes of preaching on moral issues—how to reveal graced personhood and a graced lifestyle, how to blend scriptural text and moral topic into an imaginative homily. I was compelled to confront again a realization fundamental for the preacher: religious language can be valid only as analogous language. Each time I use a religious word, it refers to realities more dissimilar from than similar to our experiences.

More importantly perhaps, I have been stimulated. In John's Gospel I discovered human life surrounded by a personal loving presence. I now see the RCIA as a model for preaching. With my love for the Church Fathers, I find provocative the thesis that the "spiritual senses" of Scripture are a way of claiming biblical history as our own. I am confirmed in my conviction that through preaching an entire community can be empowered to share in the ministry of compassionate care: healing, sustaining, guiding, and reconciling.

In line with my own project *Preaching the Just Word*, I found fresh stimulus in the chapter on preaching the "social gospel," including the three models for social preaching (informational, dialogical, action) and the need to respect the social context of the congregation. And with that, the challenge of martyred Oscar Romero: "A church that doesn't provoke any crisis, a gospel that doesn't unsettle, a word of God that doesn't get under anyone's skin, a word of God that doesn't touch the real sin of the society in which it is being proclaimed, what gospel is that?" I found myself profoundly moved by the presentation of the poet-preacher, to whom is entrusted the primordial word, Rahner's "words that evoke the blinding mystery of things," and its incarnation in the story of cancer-ridden Stephen. I suspect that only a woman could write, as intimately and passionately as we read here, of preaching as a work of the overshadowing Spirit. For homiletic spirituality, I needed the affirmation that "it is the preacher's life in the midst of the church that is the acid test of whether the message proclaimed is ideology or genuine praxis."

For this experience I am profoundly grateful to the Aquinas School of Theology and the fourteen pastoral/scholarly authors. I can only pray that a host of preachers actual and potential, clergy and lay, women and men, will be graced with a similar experience. I would be especially delighted if professors of homiletics and students of theology were to immerse themselves in this treasure. It is "deep stuff"; but, as a Trappist in Graham Greene's novel *Monsignor Quixote* put it to an inquiring skeptic, "I think you know, professor, that when one has to jump, it's so much safer to jump into deep water."[5]

Walter J. Burghardt, S.J.
Manresa-on-Severn
Annapolis, Maryland

Notes

1. Yves Congar, O.P., "Sacramental Worship and Preaching," in *The Renewal of Preaching: Theory and Practice* (Concilium 33; New York: Paulist, 1968) 51–63, at 62.
2. Decree on the Ministry and Life of Priests, no. 4; italics mine.
3. Bishops' Committee on Priestly Life and Ministry, National Conference of Catholic Bishops, *Fulfilled in Your Hearing: The Homily in the Sunday Assembly* (Washington, D.C.: USCC, 1982) 1.
4. Ralph Waldo Emerson, "Divinity School Address," in Jaroslav Pelikan, ed., *The World Treasury of Modern Religious Thought* (Boston: Little, Brown, 1990) 253.
5. New York: Simon and Schuster, 1982, at 207.

Acknowledgments

When the faculty of Aquinas Institute of Theology agreed to undertake "the book" project in August 1989, we were fortunately and blissfully unaware of the hours of labor that would be involved beyond those our own research and writing would require. As the calendar sheets turned, we met monthly, sometimes twice a month, to discuss, critique, and evaluate each other's chapters. These sessions proved to be challenging, supportive, and creative. Each of us left with ideas and suggestions for a much better, stronger manuscript. An unexpected benefit of the hours of discussion was our growing awareness of each other's disciplines, methods of research, and commitment to scholarship.

We thank the faculty for its devoted diligence, good-humored and good-natured endurance, and toleration of our sometimes nearly Gestapo urging to get the work accomplished. This project would be complete, but not with its competent computer editing, if we had not relied on the professional expertise of Kim Waterman. In addition to her computer skills and meticulous proofreading, Kim's fine theological background was a valuable asset for our project.

Diane Kennedy, O.P., assumed her position as academic dean in August 1990. Arriving at Aquinas Institute a year after our book project began, she immediately and consistently, generously and enthusiastically encouraged and promoted our undertaking. The faculty hopes that its gratitude for her leadership and presence matches her support. She and our president Charles Bouchard, O.P., model the collaborative style from which this book grew.

Edward Ruane, O.P. Editors
Regina Siegfried, A.S.C.

The Lord gave the word:
great was the company of the preachers.

How beautiful are the feet of those
who preach the gospel of peace,
and bring glad tidings of good things.

Their sound is gone out into all lands,
and their words unto the ends of the world.

Handel's "Messiah"

Introduction

REGINA SIEGFRIED, A.S.C.

The contemporary cry for quality preaching in the Catholic tradition is the seed from which this book on preaching grew. It is one response to a critical pastoral need. The faculty of Aquinas Institute of Theology, steeped in and dedicated to teaching and preaching the word in a multitude of ways and from a variety of disciplines, joined their efforts to collaborate on this work.

More than a book about preaching, this volume is itself a fine example of the power of the word. It is the fruit of combined efforts and a modeling of what a theological faculty can do. Just as the authors of the chapters were in constant conversation with each other when the work was in progress, so also is the book itself a dialogue among the academic disciplines represented in a school of theology. Each faculty member contemplates and explores what preaching the word means from her or his discipline. The result is a multi-faceted, multi-disciplined yet integrated approach to walking in the company of preachers whose words go "unto the ends of the world."

Arranged in three sections of "Liturgical, Biblical, and Historical Theology," "Systematic Theology," and "Spiritual and Pastoral Theology," each chapter offers a unique perspective on preaching the word. The reader will notice that the chapters within the sections expand upon, correlate, and respond to each other's ideas. For example, Joan Delaplane's chapter focuses on the presence of the Spirit; the other chapters in that division amplify that word in a spiritual and pastoral context.

The "Liturgical, Biblical, and Historical Theology" section ranges from liturgy to John's Gospel as a model for preaching. Frank Quinn's chapter, "Liturgy: Foundation and Context for Preaching," examines the liturgical foundations for preaching, demonstrating that preaching, indeed a part of the liturgical act, is itself sacramental in nature. Quinn's insights broaden our understanding of the many kinds of liturgical preaching and those events that are not limited to the ordained as preachers called to proclaim the word. His section on the Lectionary and preaching accents the role of the non-ordained in preaching.

Samuel Torvend's contribution parallels Quinn's in its focus on liturgy. With the RCIA as a model, Torvend poses this question: "How does the preacher evoke, clarify, and enlarge the meaning of sacramental initiation so that all the baptized might experience a more profound conversion to the grace of Christ symbolized in the liturgical action?" Preaching on the mysteries is a "form of preaching on the multi-faceted presence of grace in the life of the individual and community," he concludes.

Mary Margaret Pazdan guides the readers through six hermeneutical methods, judiciously balancing the strengths and weaknesses of each. She writes that "preaching involves a hermeneutical process of mediating a personal symbolic world with a textual symbolic world." The chapter concludes with an application of the methods to the readings for the Thirteenth Sunday of the Year—Cycle C.

Directly complementing Mary Margaret Pazdan's chapter on hermeneutics, Thomas Brodie's chapter highlights John's Gospel as a model of preaching through a careful explication of literary and sociological themes found in the gospel. Brodie concludes that the central theme of the gospel is God's unifying Spirit.

In his chapter on the history of preaching and the history of biblical exegesis, Ronald Zawilla, using a sermon of Thomas Aquinas for the Second Sunday after Trinity as a text, points out that spiritual exegesis, properly understood, is historical and must be rooted in the literal exegesis of the text. His chapter does much to redeem the anagogical approach and indicates how the method can still make a contribution.

Section two has three chapters devoted to systematics and preaching. Benjamin Russell's chapter cautions that, because the use of religious language is complex, the preacher must be aware of the problems and implications this complexity offers. After exploring three basic kinds of word usage, Russell discusses the creative force of religious language. The language which the preacher uses creates reality for the hearers. "The world which the Christian preacher creates in the minds, hearts, and intellects of the hearers must be in accord with the best available understanding of the Scriptures and with the general theological tradition of the church," Russell writes.

In distinguishing preaching from theological teaching, Carla Mae Streeter clarifies the difference between theology and religion. Streeter maintains that theology needs to communicate with other disciplines, needs to be "transposed" for the "common man and woman on the street," and be adaptive to the forms of the media. Preaching is the mature fruit of theological communication.

Mary Catherine Hilkert's chapter identifies the shifting paradigms in revelation and proclamation from both the dialectical imagination of the classic Reformation tradition and the sacramental imagination of the Catholic tradition. No one theological perspective can adequately explore the mystery of how God is made known to humanity or how the mystery of the human person and community is to be understood. A fully Christian theology of preaching will incorporate the truth of both perspectives, Hilkert writes.

The third section considers preaching from the viewpoint of spiritual and pastoral theology. These chapters move from Joan Delaplane's which explores the necessity of the role of the Spirit, to Edward Ruane's which examines the spirituality of the preacher, to Harry Byrne, Edward van Merrienboer, Charles Bouchard, and Louis Brusatti's chapters which discuss the pastoral dimensions of preaching the word.

Joan Delaplane writes of the overshadowing of the Spirit and the role of the Spirit as vital to the preaching endeavor. In four sections, Delaplane explores the critical role of the Spirit in forming and transmitting the word, the preacher, the hearers, and society. Jesus' promise of the presence of the Spirit strengthens the preachers to "trust that promise and that gift to be present as [they] give birth to the word anew for a people and a world so in need."

The spirituality of the preacher grows from five inter-penetrating dynamics, writes Edward Ruane in his chapter on the spirituality of the preacher. The grace of preaching, always God's gift, may be described as present when a person, "having been touched by grace in the midst of the Church, possesses a sense of urgency for the sake of the world to effect a hearing of the ineffable word of God."

Harry Byrne, after situating preaching in its liturgical context, offers another perspective, namely that preaching provides a primary means of pastoral care. The pastoral voice and tone of this chapter mirrors the message that "preaching is an essential form of pastoral communication in the ministry of the Church."

An essential and necessary, but sometimes overlooked aspect of preaching is its social justice dimension. Edward van Merrienboer provides insight into preaching the social gospel by raising the two concerns of the complexity of social issues and the witness of the preacher to the values preached. After analyzing four social values in the preaching of Jesus, van Merrienboer moves the discussion into the social arena of the parish and outlines models of social preaching.

Because little has been written on moral preaching, Charles Bouchard's chapter provides a valuable perspective on the subject. After describing different ethical systems, the use of scripture in moral theology, and the relationship between liturgy and morality, Bouchard offers a method of moral preaching and provides examples from several contemporary moral issues. Like van Merrienboer, he situates moral preaching within the parish context.

Louis Brusatti's chapter models the theory and practice of preaching with emphasis on exploring the power of the poetic word to move and transform its hearers. The poet-preacher crafts "sacramental words, pointing to and revealing, while shrouding and concealing." The life, dying, and death of Stephen, one of Brusatti's students, poignantly and sensitively portrayed in the last section of the chapter, is the pastoral, poetic voice reflecting the process of theological reflection that crafted the message of the homily.

Even a cursory exploration of the table of contents of this book points out the interdisciplinary approach of its chapters. The role of the preacher is to answer the cry for a life-giving word heard throughout the land. This book is a response to that cry, a response to those who preach and who also cry for a word that will give them a solid theology of preaching.

Section I

Liturgical, Biblical, and Historical Theology

Chapter 1

Liturgy: Foundation and Context for Preaching

FRANK C. QUINN, O.P.

Introduction: Preaching as Integral to the Liturgical Act

> And on the day called Sunday an assembly is held in one place of all who live in town or country, and the records of the apostles or the writings of the prophets are read as time allows. Then, when the reader has finished, the president in a discourse admonishes [us] to imitate these good things. Then we all stand up together and send up prayers.[1] When we have ended the prayers, we greet one another with a kiss.[2]

The earliest evidence for the liturgy of the word as we know it today, is found in the testimony of Justin Martyr, ca. 150 C.E. He witnesses to the structure so familiar to us, especially after its post-Vatican II restoration: proclamation of the word, preaching on that word, and intercessory prayer.[3] Of particular interest is the intimate connection between liturgical preaching and scripture text. Preaching is scripture's bridge to the contemporary world; through preaching, we are taught how to put the scriptures into effect in our daily lives. The first (ritual) indication of our intention to "imitate these good things" is the assembly's corporate intercessions. Thus, liturgical preaching is integral to, and part of, the liturgy of the word: God's word, proclaimed in the assembly, is brought into contemporary life, continued in corporate prayer, and lived in daily life.

From the beginning, then, liturgical preaching has been a constitutive part of the liturgy, an element of what we today speak of as the liturgy of the word, itself most often part of a larger sacramental action such as the eucharist. Such preaching, liturgical preaching, is independent neither of scripture nor liturgy. Instead, successful liturgical preaching serves the Church's scriptures and enables the assembly to worship in a more meaningful and committed manner.

In the following pages we shall first examine the liturgical foundations for preaching. Here it will be noted that preaching is indeed part of the liturgical act as well as sacramental in nature. In the second section of this chapter, liturgy as the context for preaching is explored. Here, we will first look at liturgical structures and how preaching is both part of them and influenced by them. Next, we will consider other liturgical factors which have a profound effect on preaching, such as the liturgical year, the use of a lectionary for proclaiming the scriptures, and the location of proclamation and preaching in church buildings.

I. The Liturgical Setting for Preaching

Liturgy is a corporate action whereby the *ekklesia* or assembly gives praise and thanksgiving to God for salvation achieved and offered. Such praise and thanksgiving centers on remembering (*anamnesis*) God's intervention in human history, especially in that climactic event which created us a Christian people, the paschal mystery of Jesus Christ, and petitioning or invoking (*epiclesis*) God to continue to remember us by favoring us here and now in this grace-filled moment. Praise/thanksgiving, memorial, supplication, these three elements are found in all Christian liturgies, no matter how diverse.

In the liturgy of the word we remember God in the proclamation of our "story" and *intercede* with that same God for favor here and now. In sacramental action we also commemorate God's mighty works in our prayer, such as in the great prayers of thanksgiving and praise over bread and cup, or over the waters of the baptismal pool, or over those to be ordained or married. And in our prayer and ritual actions, we also beseech God to send the Spirit to transform us so that we may be "members of Christ who is Priest, Prophet, and King."[4]

Preaching is part of the liturgical action of commemoration, supplication, and thanksgiving. The preacher realizes that liturgy is not simply a dramatic recalling of the story of our redemption in Christ Jesus, although it is that as well. It is also a corporate celebration of our common story, which is as much present as past. Jean Corbon reminds us of this:

> In the liturgical celebration, the Church remembers all the saving events which God brought about in history and which had their climax and fulfillment in the cross and resurrection of Christ. But the paschal event, which occurred only once in history, is contemporary with each moment of our lives, for now that Christ is risen he has broken through the wall of mortal time. . . . We do the remembering, but the reality remembered is no longer in the past but is here: the Church's memory becomes a presence.[5]

It is the task of the preacher both to engage the members of the assembly in such a way that they realize their role in that which they celebrate and to exhort and encourage them to continue to live out that story here and now in their daily lives. It would seem that in our contemporary world preachers need to be especially immersed in the scriptures so that they can speak of Christian "history" intelligently and with feeling and conviction. For it is a fact that, despite the numerous bible study groups which have sprung up throughout the land, many Catholics are not attuned to their scriptural heritage, to either the Jewish or Christian testaments, due to a lack of scriptural formation.

II. Preaching: a Sacramental Action

God encounters us and we experience God in and through the created order. Such encounter was brought to full visibility in the incarnation, in the word becoming flesh. Though long removed from the actual experience of the historical Jesus, Christian worship not only centers on the incarnate one, but allows encounter with him. It is in the gathering of the Christian assembly that Christ is "really" present to his body[6] through the Holy Spirit poured out upon them and who is repeatedly invoked in liturgical worship.

Christian worship is, therefore, a "doorway" to the sacred, the "link" between God and humanity. In other words, Christian worship is "sacramental." It mediates the encounter between the baptized and their God through the risen One, Jesus the Lord. He is both God and human, worshiper and worshipped, the priest with and through whom we offer prayer and the one who is enthroned at the right hand of the Almighty who accepts these prayers. Every act of worship, every element of the worship act, is sacramental, symbolic of and mediating God's favor and our response. Whether it be prayer or action, music or speech, all the symbolic elements of communication which are part of the human repertoire and which make up the worship act are elevated in worship to be bearers of the transcendent, enablers of the divine-human encounter, agents of spiritual transformation. Of course, this ability of created reality to operate not only symbolically but even sacramentally is due to God, not to us.

Preaching, as one of the symbolic actions of liturgy, is also a sacramental action within the larger context of the entire liturgical act. As communication it is an art form pertaining to the rhetorical areas of explanation and exhortation and dependent on human preparation and oral skills. In the community's worship it both remains a means of verbal communication and, at the same time, is more than that. By the very fact of being part of the Christian assembly's worship, preaching is also God's word to us.

The vehicles of such divine/human encounter are quite fragile, however. Though due to God's enabling of created reality and human arts to be vehicles of the transcendent, still such mediation of divine presence does not do away with human freedom and the possibility of human repudiation, or even corruption, of such means of encounter. Sacraments, as symbolic actions, are open to human abuse.[7] Rather than being a door to the sacred, preaching, as any other sacramental and symbolic action, may be a veiling rather than an epiphany of the divine. The potential danger of engaging in sacramental activity is that we may say more about God's absence than God's presence. In terms of preaching, this could mean that the one commissioned to preach God's word instead perverts that word by preaching him or herself or by misinterpreting the word through ignorance, lack of preparation, or carelessness for that treasury which belongs to the people of God, the divine scriptures. By naming preaching as sacramental we claim for it not only a more important task but also one which demands much more from us and from our community, the church.

III. Liturgy: Context for Preaching

In the Catholic Church, liturgical preaching is not an isolated event. It is part of a larger whole, the entire liturgical act which provides not only the context for preaching but also specifies its particular character.

A. PREACHING AND THE WORSHIP ACT

The Church's worship is the matrix for liturgical preaching. As such, liturgy is much more than a simple occasion for preaching. Preaching is one element in an integral act of worship. This factor affects preaching in two fundamental ways: (1) in terms of the location of preaching in worship, where preaching is always related to, and follows, the proclamation of the scriptures and (2) in terms of the worship act itself, since there are many different types of liturgy, each with its own particular structure and purpose. Think, for example, of the difference between the eucharistic and the baptismal liturgies.

Recognition of the manner in which preaching is part of Catholic worship will, from a practical pastoral point of view, prevent ministers from treating their role in the liturgical act as having nothing to do with other aspects of worship or other ministries involved in worship. If the preacher is someone other than the presider, recognition of the priority, structure, and character of the entire community action we call liturgy will prevent the minister of the word from treating preaching as if it is *the* event for which the worship of the assembly exists.

B. THE PLACE OF PREACHING IN THE LITURGICAL STRUCTURE

As part of a particular liturgical action, preaching is found at a specific point in that action and has a particular dynamic and purpose. Preaching is conditioned and shaped by the liturgical structure of which it is a part. In turn, it is the task of preaching to make the act of worship a reality in the life of the worshiper here and now. There are three primary liturgical structures in Catholic worship of which the preacher should be aware, the service of the word, the service of praise, and the service of the word as part of a sacramental action.

1. PREACHING AS AN ELEMENT IN THE SERVICE OF THE WORD

Where preaching is part of an independent service of the word it forms, along with the gospel, a climax in the proclamation of the word. Preaching, or even the reading of scriptures, is not *the* only important element in this type of worship. But certainly the main part of this service as well as the longest is the proclamation and preaching of God's word. Traditionally, the word read and preached is concluded by intercession, a corporate putting what we have heard into immediate practice by way of insistent prayer, itself symbolic of how we will live and act in the world as the body of Christ. The fundamental structure of the word service the preacher needs to be aware of, as well as take account of in homily preparation, is then the proclamation of the revealed word with its extension into everyday life through preaching, all of which leads to intercession, the immediate community response to the word and the preaching.

This structure of word and intercession reveals the relationship between God and God's people. Ours is a revealed religion in which God sets up a dialogue with the faithful. This encounter is ritualized through proclamation (scripture and preaching) and response (intercession). Preaching could be said to constitute the bridge between God's call and our response. A simple structure, yet a profound reality: God speaks, initiating the offer of grace and we respond, accepting God's offer in praise and intercession, acknowledging our need for God and our willingness to live out the gospel in our ordinary life. By our image of bridge we mean to say that preaching enables us to hear the word of God not as something addressed to our forebears but as something alive and active among us here and now.

Such a simple structure of word and prayer may be amplified and focused both through the number of scripture readings and also through song, procession, ritual movement and gestures. But its heart is the hearing of God's word in scripture and preaching and response in intercession.

One might object that although the service of the word is clear as to its structure it is not particularly important as an independent rite since the "bible vigils" recommended by the *Constitution on the Liturgy* fell on deaf ears[8] and few, if any, use such celebrations as occasions for bringing back the music of the past as promoted by *Musicam Sacram.*[9] And yet all we need do is study the reformed rites to discover the importance of the service of the word in contemporary liturgy. We cite but a few examples: (1) The first of the three major funeral liturgies is a service of the word, entitled "Vigil for the Deceased."[10] (2) The *Rite of Penance* includes a number of penitential services in its appendix which are structurally services of the word.[11] (3) A final example is that of the recommendation of the celebration of the word of God during the period of the catechumenate found in the *Rite of Christian Initiation of Adults.* This is not simply an occasional service but *the* regular manner in which catechumens are to be formed by the word of God and its extension in preaching during the entire formation period of the catechumenate.[12] Moreover, catechumens experience Sunday liturgy as a service of the word since dismissal of this group from the assembly takes place before the eucharist begins.

These examples point out, then, that by recovering the service of the word, even outside of its use in sacramental rites, we reclaim a precious element of the Church's worship life and also challenge ourselves to view scriptural preaching in a wider framework than simply that of Sunday mass and occasional sacramental rites.

2. PREACHING AND THE LITURGY OF THE HOURS

The liturgy of the hours provides us with a structure quite different from the service of the word. In contrast to the latter where God "speaks" to us in the proclamation of the scriptures and in the homily, in daily prayer we speak to God even though we normally use God's word, especially the psalms, to form the means whereby we who are always being called by God respond to our maker in praise, thanksgiving, and intercession.

It would be a mistake to think, as some evidently do, that the Roman Catholic daily prayer of praise and intercession focuses primarily on readings and preaching and is the same as the service of the word.[13] In doing so we ignore another series of rites which challenge the preacher to become thoroughly immersed in the question of time and the praise of God.

As presently revised, the liturgy of the hours, particularly morning and evening prayer, maintains several of its traditional characteristics, particularly the focus on praise and intercession. Although the scriptures are read in daily prayer, outside the office of readings which was never seriously intended for parochial usage, scripture reading has a relatively minor role to play. Two other elements predominate: (1) praise, realized in hymnody, psalms, and canticles, and (2) petition, realized in the intercessions and Lord's Prayer. It could be said that the brief, topical reading acts more as a kind of pause along the path of praise and intercession.

This does not mean, of course, that daily prayer, especially morning and evening prayer, may not be expanded through lengthier readings on special occasions. Nor does it mean that preaching at these hours should be avoided. But it would seem to indicate that the assembly's praise is not simply introductory to the reading of scripture. Rather, the heart of daily prayer *is* praise of God. When we look to the origins of this kind of prayer we discover that in parochial settings our tradition speaks of the elaboration of morning and evening prayer more in terms of ceremonies of light and incense and through movement and gesture than through concentration on the "listening" element of daily prayer. In other words, it is a prayer which involves the assembly in singing and response, in movement and bodily position, in sights and smells, all of these centering attention on Jesus Christ. Rather than an emphasis only on hearing the word, the assembly itself sings and speaks God's word in hymns and songs of praise. Even though the hours are celebrated in different ways, depending upon the group celebrating, still this type of prayer originates in the assembly; it is not directed *to* the assembly as is the service of the word.

Having said this, it is also necessary to reflect on the nature of preaching at daily prayer, since it not only should happen, but will most likely increase as this type of prayer becomes more common in our parishes. One example of such preaching is at an hour of morning or evening prayer in a parish where the absence of an ordained minister precludes a eucharistic celebration. When this is a Sunday celebration the readings appointed in the Sunday lectionary will ordinarily be proclaimed. In this case, the importance and number of the readings will give the hearing of the word and preaching on it a much greater emphasis than when dealing with regular morning and evening prayer.

In the latter situation both reading and preaching are relatively brief.[14] Even more important is the nature of the preaching. The character of the hour of prayer must engage the sensitivities of the preacher; the (brief) reading is but part of a larger whole which serves as inspiration for preaching. It is a mistake to preach at morning or evening prayer as if the time of day and meaning of the particular hour of prayer make no difference. In reality, they provide the context and motivation for effective preaching. We may say then that the liturgy of the hours presents the preacher with a quite different challenge than does the analogous service of the word.

One way of imaging this type of preaching, especially outside of those festal occasions where preaching receives more attention, is to think of it as "meditative" preaching or "reflective" preaching which flows from the community's offering of praise and thanksgiving. Such preaching acknowledges the time for prayer, whether in the morning where there is the call to sanctify the coming day and where emphasis is placed on light, praise, and the resurrection of Jesus Christ, or in the evening where we are called to repentance and reconciliation, as we give thanks for the redeeming sacrifice of Christ. The focus on Jesus and his paschal mystery is given special weight on Fridays, dedicated to the remembrance of the passion, and on Sundays, where the journey of Christ from his obediential "emptying" of himself to become one like us (Phil 2:7, the New Testament Canticle at Evening Prayer I) to his victory at God's right hand (Ps 110 and the Canticle of the Lamb, Rev 19:1-7, at Evening Prayer II) gives structure to the Christian Sunday.

One final point: preaching at morning or evening prayer does not lead to intercession, but to the continuation of, and climax of, the assembly's praise and thanksgiving in the gospel canticles, the song of Zechariah in the morning and that of Mary in the evening. Intercession flows from praise and thanksgiving, then, not directly from reading and preaching. In sum, the preacher at daily prayer will find inspiration in the particular hour of prayer, its location in the morning or evening, the day of the week it occurs, and in the hymns and psalms as well as the reading. It goes without saying that a knowledge and appreciation of the psalms will aid any who are charged with preaching in the liturgy of the hours.

3. THE SERVICE OF THE WORD AS PART OF A MORE COMPLEX LITURGICAL ACTION

In speaking of the word service, Justin Martyr treated it as part of a larger liturgical whole, the eucharist. After the intercessions and the kiss of peace, he continued his description of the service as follows:

> When we have finished praying, bread, wine, and water are brought up. The president then prays and gives thanks according to his ability. And the people give their assent with an "Amen!" Next the gifts which have been "eucharistified" are distributed, and everyone shares in them, while they are sent by way of the deacons to those absent.[15]

It is at the eucharist that most Catholics experience liturgical preaching, even though there are many other occasions for preaching, as we have already indicated. But other sacramental rites also include the liturgy of the word as an essential part of their structure. In all these cases the occasion for preaching will be governed by the particular sacramental event.

What does this mean? Preaching as part of a larger ritual unit, such as a sacramental event, is not independent of that event. Neither scripture nor homily are ends in themselves. Although the liturgy of the word has the same structure whether or not it is part of a larger liturgical action (entrance, prayer, reading and response, homily, intercessions), when joined to a sacramental rite such as a baptism or an ordination or the eucharist, scripture and preaching instruct us but also prepare us for and lead us into the particular sacrament being celebrated. In other words, the liturgy is not simply the occasion for preaching, even though experience tells us that this seems to be the situation with some preachers. Preaching is part of a particular liturgy and fulfills its function by acknowledging its role in that liturgy.

For example, preaching at eucharist must not end in such a way that the community cannot go on with the eucharist. Rather, it should be of such a nature as to lead the community into a *more* fruitful celebration of the eucharist. To preach the word with authentic effect in the eucharist enables the assembly to offer more fitting praise and thanksgiving to God in the eucharistic prayer and to dine on the bread broken and the cup poured out for our salvation.

It should be self-evident that the character of the liturgical or sacramental event of which reading and preaching are a part will lend a special color to preaching. Think for a moment of preaching at the funeral liturgy or at a funeral vigil liturgy during the period of the waking of the body. The age of the deceased and the conditions of the death, as well as the liturgy and scriptures, influence the preacher both in preparation for preaching and in the words finally spoken. The various rites of Christian initiation, in which the service of the word and preaching is directed to entrance into the catechumenate, or to election for the sacraments of initiation, or to the *traditio* of the church's rule of faith (the creed) or its rule of prayer (the Our Father), or to the sacramental moment of baptism-confirmation-eucharist, determine the content and direction of preaching as well as the choice of scriptures. Any sacramental event, in other words, enters into the preaching act, and preaching has as one of its goals the calling of the community to effective sacramental celebration.

C. OTHER ELEMENTS WHICH SHAPE LITURGICAL PREACHING

Liturgical preaching is not only shaped by the liturgical structures of which it is a part but also by other aspects of liturgy which (1) situate the assembly in a particular moment of its paschal life, the liturgical year, (2) provide a method for hearing the word of God in a more complete and meaningful fashion, the lectionary, and (3) locate preaching visually as an authoritative ministerial act, the ministerial center where reading and preaching take place.

1. THE LITURGICAL YEAR

In Justin Martyr's day, the liturgical calendar was quite different from today. However, the major temporal observance which he notes as essential to Christian life, the Sunday,[16] is once again urged as the heart of the liturgical year for contemporary Christians:

> The Church celebrates the paschal mystery on the first day of the week, known as the Lord's day or Sunday. This follows a tradition handed down from the apostles and having its origin from the day of Christ's resurrection. *Thus Sunday must be ranked as the first holyday of all.*[17]

Sunday, always for Christians the day of Christ's victory over death, continues to be for us *the* day to assemble in order to hear the word proclaimed and preached and to gather around the table of the Lord. It further reminds preacher and people that all are engaged in the enterprise of living out their baptism into Christ's death in order to one day share in his resurrection both individually and corporately.[18]

As in the past so now, the Sundays of the year all celebrate the same event, the paschal mystery of Jesus Christ. Still they take on different colors because of the way liturgical time has come to be organized. Any knowledge of the history of the liturgical year will aid the preacher in realizing that the way Christians celebrate is not simply by taking a walk in the past with a long dead Jesus, but by corporately "remembering" the Jesus who is Christ, the one who was and is and is to come. This remembering focuses now on one facet, now on another, of that one mystery which gives life to all, that very mystery which in liturgical celebration is present in grace and power. The moment of preaching and celebration is always "now." "Now" the mystery of God in Christ unfolds before us; "now" is the time for our entrance into and transformation by that mystery; "now" is the time to corporately respond in prayer and sacramental action to the gifting of the baptized assembly with the Holy Spirit.

The original feastday of Christians, the Sunday, receives a special focus on one particular Sunday of the year, when the entirety of the paschal mystery of Jesus is recalled. This is the Easter vigil, the extension of one Sunday of the year by an all-night preparatory vigil. All the Sundays of Easter which the Easter Vigil leads to are, as one early writer put it, one "great Sunday"[19] in which the death and resurrection of Jesus figure prominently in word, preaching, and worship. Easter Vigil and Sundays of Easter are themselves prepared for by the season of Lent which originated as a period of final preparation for those elected for sacramental initiation at the Vigil. It is our good fortune that Lent in our own day has once more been restored to its original purpose with the recovery of the Rite of Christian Initiation of Adults.

Emphasis on Christ's incarnation and birth provide us with another tonality for the fall and winter season[20] of the liturgical year. The four Sundays of Advent celebrate the full meaning of God becoming human in terms of its implications at the end time (second coming), its intersection with human history in a particular time and place, and its call for decision on the part of not only those with a special mission (Mary) but also all who call themselves Christian. With the celebration of the nativity of Jesus on the solemnity of Christmas, the succeeding Sundays continue with the various epiphanies or manifestations of Christ which explore the mystery of God-made-flesh-for-us.

Those Sundays of the year which are not part of special seasons occur after the feast of the Baptism of Christ and after the solemnity of Pentecost. They are governed, relative to special meanings, more by the particular lectionary readings assigned to them than are the Sundays of Lent-Easter and Advent-Christmas.[21]

The rich and variegated liturgical year, with its constant manifestation of the Christ mystery, even in the celebration of the saints, who are witnesses to how Christ shaped their lives, provides the context for liturgical celebration and is ignored by the preacher at his or her own peril. We are all creatures of time and history, yet redeemed within time and history because the God who acted in the past acts here and now among us through Jesus Christ and in the Holy Spirit. This is the "message" of the liturgical year as it is also the "message" of our preaching, a word of liberation for those captive to time, a word of freedom for those bowed down by the woes of the present world.

2. THE LECTIONARY

The lectionary is a book with assigned scripture readings, organized according to certain principles of selection and covering the entirety of the liturgical year. The major principle underlying the post-Vatican II Roman Catholic lectionary is the demand that the scriptures be heard by the people of God in as full a fashion as possible. A lectionary provides a convenient way of accomplishing this demand. This is especially important for those who claim scripture as necessary for their faith. A lectionary is another difference Justin Martyr would notice if he attended one of our contemporary liturgies. In his time it would seem that the scriptures, especially the Hebrew scriptures, were read in course. But, of course, in his time the canon of Christian scriptures was not yet complete.

In the Roman Catholic Church readings are assigned to every Sunday of the liturgical year according to a three-year cycle. Weekdays of the year have a two-year cycle for the first reading. The guiding principle in choosing Sunday lessons, especially for those Sundays outside of the Advent-Christmas and Lent-Easter cycles, is the reading in course of the three synoptical gospels. One of the synoptics is read for each of the cycles A, B, and C. Thus, instead of presenting the assembly with a selection of gospel pericopes from the four gospels, in effect harmonizing the gospel story, the gospel writers are allowed to speak of Jesus Christ as they understood him. The Gospel of John is not provided with its own year. Instead, it is read on many of the Sundays of Lent and Easter and is used in ordinary time to fill out the relatively brief Gospel of Mark.

The first reading, ordinarily taken from the Old Testament except during Easter time, is chosen so as to reflect the gospel. The second reading is a more or less continuous reading from the epistles.

In the two great cycles of Advent-Christmas and Lent-Easter the principles of selection are different. Appropriateness of readings is one reason for the lessons provided. Tradition also plays a role in the assignment of some books of scripture and even special readings to special times, e.g., of Isaiah to Advent, of the Gospel of John to the later Sundays of Lent and Eastertide, of the Acts of the Apostles to Eastertide, and even of special gospel pericopes to the third, fourth, and fifth Sundays of Lent because of the liturgical scrutinies celebrated on those Sundays.

The major principle in the selection of readings for the feasts of Christ, of Mary, and the feasts and solemnities of the saints is also the appropriateness of the reading to the event or saint celebrated. Finally, a series of readings is proposed for various sacramental rites, from which specific readings *may* be chosen for any particular celebration.

Although Roman Catholics are used to a lectionary arrangement, some other Christians are not and would claim that lectionaries go contrary to the spirit of the gospel. Why a lectionary, then? One clear reason, already mentioned above, is commented upon in the Introduction to the *Lectionary for Mass*, the desire to provide the faithful with a rich scriptural fare:

> The present order of Readings for Mass, then, is an arrangement of biblical readings that provides the faithful with a knowledge of the whole of God's word, in a pattern suited to the purpose. Throughout the liturgical year, but above all during the seasons of Easter, Lent, and Advent, the choice and sequence of readings are aimed at giving the faithful an ever-deepening perception of the faith they profess and of the history of salvation. Accordingly, the Order of Readings corresponds to the requirements and interests of the Christian people.[22]

Another reason for not leaving the choice of readings to the individual preacher is because the scriptures are not subject to the whim of the individual. They are the cherished possession of the Church. To really possess the scriptures they must be *heard* by the Church since the scriptures come to life in proclamation. That proclamation takes place in particular liturgical celebrations and is occasioned by the specific period of the liturgical year in which the reading is done. In other words, the scriptures play a primary role in the liturgy of the Church, as does the liturgical preaching based upon them.

The importance of the scriptures for liturgical action and the liturgical year is a contemporary rediscovery, mandated by the Second Vatican Council. Honored more by neglect in the past, the revised lectionary testifies to the demand that Catholic Christians become people of the bible, including both Hebrew and Christian scriptures:

> The treasures of the Bible are to be opened up more lavishly, so that a richer share in God's word may be provided for the faithful. In this way a more representative portion of holy Scripture will be read to the people in the course of a prescribed number of years.[23]

With a recovery of a richer scriptural fare the Church has rediscovered liturgical preaching as preaching on the scriptures:

> By means of the homily the mysteries of the faith and the guiding principles of the Christian life are expounded *from the sacred text* during the course of the liturgical year. . . .[24] (italics mine).

So important has the proclamation of scripture become in Catholic worship that although it would be false to say that the liturgy exists *because* of the scriptures yet it may be said that it is based upon them:

> The many riches contained in the one word of God are admirably brought out in the different kinds of liturgical celebrations and liturgical assemblies. This takes place as the unfolding mystery of Christ is recalled during the course of the liturgical year, as the Church's sacraments and sacramentals are celebrated, or as the faithful respond individually to the Holy Spirit working within them. For then the liturgical celebration, *based primarily on the word of God and sustained by it*, becomes a new event and enriches the word itself with new meaning and power[25] (italics mine).

There is reciprocity then between liturgy and scripture. Each enriches the other. Scripture allows the assembly to enter more fully into sacramental acts through hearing God's call in a specific manner. Liturgy provides not only the occasion but even the reason for hearing the word of God. In order for this to happen, a method for choosing which scriptures will be read at any one time, that is, a lectionary system, is extremely convenient.

The preacher hears the same word of God as does the assembly and preaches from that word. This is a significant difference from choosing the scriptures in order to fit a preaching schema for the year as occurs in some communions. In the Roman Catholic Church the preacher is indeed servant to the word. That word, in turn, is a word conditioned by and proclaimed in and as part of a liturgical event.

One final caution might be in order. A lectionary system provides us with a convenient means of hearing and preaching on the scriptures rather than limiting ourselves to a few well-known passages. But it is the scriptures that are inspired, not the lectionary. Although the new Roman lectionary is in many ways one of the finest results of the demand for a renewal of liturgy, it is not perfect. It is a great gift to the church because it restored the scriptures to Roman Catholic liturgy, a consequence of which was the restoration of liturgical preaching to the church. Furthermore, at the ecumenical level it has had a profound impact. Many other churches have chosen the Roman lectionary as a foundation for their own efforts at lectionary reform.

Yet the lectionary is not perfect and certainly can be modified to make it more effective for future use. One of the strong criticisms of the Roman lectionary is the use of the Hebrew scriptures, especially in Ordinary Time. Instead of allowing the scriptures to speak on their own, there is the feeling that too often they are simply accommodated to the gospel of the day; moreover, too many readings are taken from the prophets rather than the books of the Torah and the later historical books, seemingly as a way of indicating that the prophecies have been fulfilled in Christ![26] Even the criticisms of the Roman lectionary, however, indicate its importance. The number of homiletic aids which have appeared, based upon the lectionary and intended for homily preparation, testify to the rediscovery of the homily in the course of the past twenty-five years.

3. THE LOCATION OF THE MINISTRY OF THE WORD

As has already been indicated, a number of things have changed since Justin's day. In his description of word and preaching, there is no distinction between the ministerial center or place for the presider, and the area where preaching occurs. In our day we designate not only the ministerial center, the eucharistic center, the baptismal center, etc., but also the center for the word and preaching.

> There must be a place in the church that is somewhat elevated, fixed, and of a suitable design and nobility. It should reflect the dignity of God's word and be a clear reminder to the people that in the Mass the table of God's word and of Christ's body is placed before them.[27]

As we have symbolic objects in the other centers, such as the altar-table in the eucharistic center, so indeed we have a special piece of furniture in the center for the word and preaching, the ambo or reading desk. However, unlike the altar-table, the ambo is not in itself symbolic of the word.

Rather, it is symbolic of the place from where authoritative proclamation and preaching take place. The authentic symbol of the word of God is the scripture itself, in the form of lectionary or epistolary or evangelary. The reason for reading and preaching from a special location with the scriptures lying open on the ambo is not so that one may hide behind a poorly designed lectern but so that it may be clearly seen that reading and preaching are from the word of God and not simply one's personal invention.

In the time of Justin, as the description above makes clear, preaching was the task of the presider, even more than reading, and so took place at the chair of the preside. This custom, symbolizing teaching authority, continued through the ages (think of Augustine sitting and preaching with authority while the people stood) and even now is the preferred alternative to preaching at the ambo or lectern.[28] Such a practice indicates the official nature of preaching, that it is the task of the Church's ministers and that it is for all the people. But preaching at the ambo even more clearly associates preaching with the scriptures which lie thereon.[29]

The task or ministry of preaching has been broadened since the time of Justin. In his day the minister who preached would have been like our bishop. But the right to preach was gradually extended to others, such as presbyters. In our day it has been extended to many deacons. In a number of dioceses bishops have authorized the non-ordained to assume the ministry of liturgical (and, in particular, eucharistic) preaching. Do the separation of the two ministerial centers of presiding and proclamation/preaching provide us with a symbolic reason for the extension of the ministry of preaching? Might this establishment of two different ministerial centers argue for an even greater sharing of the task of liturgical preaching?

The chair in the ministerial center symbolizes the authority of the preside. Preaching at the ambo, with the scriptures open before the preacher, symbolizes fidelity to the word of God. Might not the one at the chair preside over preaching even when, on occasion, that person is not actually preaching? Even as one can preside over baptism by having others take a ministerial role in it, so might not we understand presiding at eucharist in a broader fashion, so that although ministry at table is closely associated with ministering the word at the ambo, still a number of ministries occur in any liturgical act under the leadership of the one who enables the prayer, the presider. May not one of these ministries be that of preacher?

At any rate, today the center for the word and preaching is one of the major liturgical centers for the Christian assembly.

Conclusion

The importance of liturgical preaching for the contemporary church cannot be overemphasized. Its rediscovery in our century and its gradual recovery will mean that Christians once more can be truly nourished by the word of God. The task of liturgical preaching is not an easy one. It is a sacramental act, demanding living faith from the preacher, careful preparation, reverence for the scriptures, and humble realization that ultimately it is the Holy Spirit who effects change in the hearts of the hearers of the word. And yet the glory of the task of preaching is the belief that as sacramental act the preacher is partner with the Spirit in proclaiming the Lordship of Jesus over all of creation.

In this chapter we have explored the nature of liturgical preaching. It is a preaching flowing from the word of God. It is a preaching which is done at the mandate of the church, because it is a preaching in which both preacher and listener engage the word of God, the possession of the entire church. Such preaching occurs in different types of liturgical actions. It takes place in the course of a liturgical year which helps shape its direction. Liturgical preaching's importance is indicated by the reading and preaching center in our churches.

Although we have focused to a great extent on the Sunday proclamation of the word, the climax of the church's liturgical life, we have also attempted to indicate the wide variety of preaching which is liturgical and which is found at many other times than on Sunday. Although liturgical preaching, because of its character as preaching in the name of the church, demands some kind of mandate, this does not mean that it is limited only to the ordained, especially as we rediscover those many types of liturgical preaching which do not engage the entire community, as preaching at Sunday eucharist does.

Perhaps the most important truth about liturgical preaching, however, is the realization that this is how the scriptures, the word of God, are brought more fully alive in our liturgical assemblies. This is a realization that is at the same time both thrilling and humbling.

Notes

1. Justin Martyr, *First Apology*, 67.1.
2. Ibid. 65.1.

3. In Justin Martyr all of this was sealed by the kiss of peace. Although the original location for this ritual act, the kiss of peace was kept in its later position—in the communion rite—in the *Ordo Missae* of 1969.

4. The Roman Ritual, *Rite of Christian Initiation of Adults*, Approved for Use in the United States of America by the National Conference of Catholic Bishops and Confirmed by the Apostolic See (Washington: NCCB, 1988), *RCIA*, Prayer during the first postbaptismal anointing. Hereafter, cited as RCIA.

5. Jean Corbon, *The Wellspring of Worship* (New York: Paulist Press, 1988) 5-6.

6. Vatican Council II, *Constitution on the Liturgy* (Sacrosanctum Concilium), 4 December 1963, par. 7: "[Christ] is present . . . when the Church prays and sings, for he promised: 'Where two or three are gathered together in my name, there am I in the midst of them' " (Mt 18:20). For the text see *Documents on the Liturgy 1963-1979* (Collegeville: The Liturgical Press, 1982) 6, 7. Hereafter, cited as DOL.

7. It goes without saying that such abuse may be due to human carelessness or laziness, i.e., lack of preparation, lack of interest in preaching, even lack of faith. Occasionally these seemingly ordinary foibles may have their basis in convictions about sacraments which are foreign to authentic Catholic tradition. On this confer Tad Guzie, *The Book of Sacramental Basics* (New York: Paulist Press, 1981) 124-128, where the author speaks of the two "fallacies" we are open to in our approach to symbols and, perforce, to sacraments: (1) the concretist fallacy in which symbol and reality are identified and (2) the reductionist fallacy in which symbols lose all their multivalent power and become but "reminders of things we already know and grasp in a rational way" (125). The first view leads to magic, the second to the destruction of the very notion of sacrament as a mediator of divine mystery.

8. Paragraph 35.4 (DOL, 1, 35).

9. SC Rites, Instruction *Musicam Sacram*, on music in the liturgy, 5 March 1967, no. 46: "Musical pieces that no longer have a place in the liturgy, but have the power to touch religious feeling and to assist meditation on the sacred mysteries are very well suited for use in popular devotions and especially in celebrations of the word of God" (DOL 508, 4167).

10. The Roman Ritual, *Order of Christian Funerals*, Approved for Use in the United States of America by the National Conference of Catholic Bishops and Confirmed by the Apostolic See (Washington: NCCB, 1989), I:l,. "Vigil for the Deceased"; II.7, "Vigil for a Deceased Child."

11. The Roman Ritual, *The Rite of Penance,* Approved for Use in the United States of American by the Conference of Catholic Bishops and Approved by the Apostolic See (Washington: NCCB, 1975.) Confer Appendix 2.

12. RCIA; see "Celebrations of the Word of God," nos. 81-89. Note that these numbers simply outline the service of the word since, being a constant feature of the catechumen's worship life, a structuring of individual rites could fill several volumes. Probably because these numbers simply provide an outline of the rites those involved in the formation of catechumens and candidates have not always recognized that the service of the word provides the context for catechumenal gatherings of many different kinds. One addition that could be made to the outline suggested in nos. 81-89 is the conclusion of the rite by intercessions, surely a most fitting conclusion to the service of the word.

13. I say Roman Catholic because there is no doubt that both Lutheran and Anglican daily prayer, with their greater emphasis on readings from scripture, a reformation addition to ordinary morning and evening prayer, have a somewhat different structure, more closely related to the service of the word than is the Catholic Liturgy of the Hours.

14. Note that the reading provided for morning and evening prayer in *Christian Prayer* is much too truncated for liturgical celebration. Even though the reading should be relatively brief, it need not be that brief. Such readings as those printed in the book of hours are so short that they are over before the assembly is even prepared to hear them.

15. Justin, op. cit.

16. "And on that day called Sunday an assembly is held in one place of all who live in town and country. . . ." *First Apology*, 67.1.

17. SC Rites (Consilium), *General Norms for the Liturgical Year and the Calendar*, 21 March 1969, no. 4 (italics mine). (DOL, 442, 3770).

18. Confer Romans 6.

19. Athanasius, *Epist. fest.* 1; see *General Norms for the Liturgical Year*, par. 22 (DOL 442, 3788).

20. For those living in the southern hemisphere the Advent-Christmas cycle occurs during the summer months.

21. I do not mean to deny, however, that the scriptures always play a role in every eucharistic celebration. But there is no doubt that liturgical seasons play a greater role, even in the selection of readings, in some periods of the year than in others.

22. The Roman Missal Revised by Decree of the Second Vatican Ecumenical Council and Published by Authority of Pope Paul VI, *Lectionary for Mass*, "Introduction," Second *Editio Typica* (1981) (Washington: ICEL, 1981) 60.

23. Vatican Council II, *Constitution on the Liturgy*, Sacrosanctum Concilium (4 December 1963), 51 (DOL, 1, 51).

24. Ibid. 52 (DOL, 1, 52).

25. *Lectionary for Mass*, 3.

26. Much is being written on the lectionary today, a testimony to its influence. Two recent articles which spell out the attempts to develop a common, ecumenical lectionary and which provide a sound critique of the Roman lectionary are found in the book *Shaping English Liturgy* edited by Peter C. Finn and James M. Schellman (Washington: The Pastoral Press, 1990): Horace T. Allen, "The Ecumenical Impact of Lectionary Reform," 361–384, and Eileen Schuler, "Some Criteria for the Choice of Scripture Texts in the Roman Lectionary," 385–404.

27. *Lectionary for Mass*, 32.

28. SC Divine Worship, *General Instruction of the Roman Missal*, 4th edition (27 March 1975), 97 (DOL, 208, 1487).

29. And is the only option suggested in the new Introduction to the revised *Lectionary for Mass*, 32.

Chapter 2

Hermeneutics and Proclaiming the Sunday Readings

MARY MARGARET PAZDAN, O.P.

Essential for each preacher is a realistic assessment of learned theories and praxis in biblical hermeneutics, resources and time available to prepare for preaching. An occasional appraisal effects the level of probable involvement in exegetical methods and its relationship to the formation of the preacher. Consider the possibilities of these professional goals:

1. Recognition of what method/s various commentaries, monographs, etc., employ as a basis for interpretation.
2. Competence to discriminate the quality of resources based on methodological considerations.
3. Proficiency in one or more methods to shape preaching according to the text's interpretive perspective.

While it is important to know one's competence in exegetical methods, the choice of method/s is also a decision based on the genre of the text/s within the context of the liturgical year. No less important is the *Sitz im Leben* of the community and the preacher.

Most readers are familiar with critical biblical commentaries or homiletic resources to prepare a homily. Others have studied basic methods of exegesis, but have not had the opportunity to apply the methods to texts selected for preaching in various contexts.

This chapter presents a description of major interpretive methods and examples of how they were utilized for the lectionary readings of the Thirteenth Sunday of the Year, Cycle C.[1] Next, it assesses the values and limitations of the methods for preaching. Finally, the chapter considers the role of hermeneutics in the life of the preacher.

Biblical Methods and Texts[2]

Patristic interpreters used allegorical exegesis to uncover the hidden, deeper meaning suggested by the literal sense of the biblical words, e.g., Jerusalem refers to the church of Christ. Building on allegory, medieval commentators added three types of interpretation: literal, e.g., Jerusalem is a Jewish city; anthropological, e.g., Jerusalem indicates the human soul; and eschatological, e.g., Jerusalem represents the heavenly city. Literal exegesis contained historical significance while the allegorical, anthropological, and eschatological exegesis provided assistance for belief and conduct.[3] From the impact of the Renaissance and Reformation, confessional exegesis developed in the sixteenth and seventeenth centuries. Its emphasis was to locate passages in the Bible which authenticated one's doctrinal position, i.e., proof-texting.

The pre-critical methods utilized for over fifteen hundred years had developed from particular religious, philosophical, and cultural worldviews. With the rise of rationalism and the Enlightenment in the eighteenth century, a critical mode of inquiry for linguistics, natural sciences, and historiography had profound implications for biblical interpretation. The creation of the historical-critical method and responses to it constitute the variety of critical methods available today. While exegetes continue to use the historical-critical method, many link it with literary methods or with liberation theology. A brief description of each method follows.

A. HISTORICAL-CRITICAL METHOD

The intention of historical-critical pioneers was to apply the new standards of historical studies to reclaim for the bible its prominence which had waned during the Enlightenment. The interpretive procedures were a radical change from previous exegetical studies. Based on scientific, objective criteria, the historical-critical method seeks to reconstruct the event to which the text refers. It employs a *diachronic* perspective which goes back *through time* via the text to the basic event. The text is a window for the process which traces the history of the pericope through its various stages, beginning with the event and through its traditions and their use by the community. It moves from preliterary to literary composition and redaction.

Historical-critical exegesis includes four major points of analysis:

1. Textual Criticism is an analysis of copies of the original text, since there are no autographs.[4] Text critics collect, study, evaluate, restore, classify, and describe a history for manuscripts in order to establish a reliable text. (Since biblical texts were written and copied by hand from dictation as well as from other manuscripts, there were errors, e.g., copying the same word twice, omitting words and phrases, hearing different words.)

For this analysis one can rely on an authoritative translation of the bible whose notes indicate any variation in manuscript traditions by reference to other ancient authorities. For example, the Oxford Annotated Bible distinguishes two *additions* in Luke 9:51-62 (See Appendix): *as Elijah did* after "come down from heaven and consume them" (v 54); *and he said, "You do not know what manner of spirit you are of; for the Son of man came not to destroy men's lives but to save them"* after "he turned and rebuked them" (v 55).[5]

2. Source Criticism investigates the literary relationship of the text to other documents. It categorizes the types of traditions (oral and written) which were used to formulate the text. For example, according to most synoptic scholars, Luke used Mark, Q, and special material. A comparison of Luke 9:51-62 with Matthew and Mark using a *Synopsis* or *Gospel Parallels* attests to similarities and differences with their traditions.[6]

3. Form Criticism identifies how the structure of a text is related to its function. The form which represents a particular genre and its characteristics indicates how it was used in the life of a community. For example, 1 Kings 19:16, 19-21 (See Appendix) is a legend with a nucleus of historical fact which is told for edification.

4. Redaction Criticism investigates the distinctive perspective of an editor (redactor) who has reshaped sources and forms of traditions. For example, compare Luke 9:51-62 with the Matthean and Markan parallels (See *Synopsis*). The analysis specifies how Luke reshaped the common tradition of Jesus' decision to go to Jerusalem and his sayings on discipleship (Q) by introducing Lukan motifs, i.e., Jerusalem (v 51); Samaritans (vv 52-56); and another saying on discipleship (vv 60b–62).

B. LITERARY METHODS

The historical-critical method considered literary aspects of a text, e.g., its source, form, and redaction, to reconstruct the event which the text narrates. The text is the vehicle for a diachronic perspective which seeks to know the basic event. In contrast, literary critics employ a *synchronic* perspective which regards the text in its final form at the *present* time. In non-contextual approaches, e.g., structuralism, the focus is the text. In contextual approaches, e.g., sociology, art, analogy, the focus is the readers who engage the text as a mirror to enter into its own world. Although not a contextual literary approach, the theological perspective of liberation engages the reader and the text.

1. Structuralism defines language as an ordered system of signs whose meaning is derived from its interrelationships and differences. It analyzes a text for its levels of meaning.[7] A. J. Greimas' model of narrative relates six persons or spheres of action which function as *actants*:

a.) *Sender*, a communicator of a message or action;
b.) *Object*, what is communicated;
c.) *Receiver*, one to whom communication is sent;
d.) *Helper*, whatever assists the sender;
e.) *Subject*, agent who facilitates communication and deals with the opponent;
f.) *Opponent*, force which opposes communication.

Three axes function in the model:
*Sender——>Object—— Receiver
**Helper——>Subject<——Opponent
***

The axis of *communication* (*) is the sender communicating an *object* to the *receiver*. The axis of *power* (**) is a *helper* assisting the *subject* to communicate in view of the *opponent*. The axis of *volition* (***) is the plot where the *subject* assists the communication.

For example, in 1 Kings 19:16, 19–21 (See Appendix) the *actants* may be plotted out:
*Lord——>anoint prophet—Elisha to succeed you
**Elijah—>Lord through Elijah< -hardships of leaving home (Elisha)
***

Analysis of a narrative according to three axes (communication, power, volition) discloses *how* and *why* the text moves from its inception to a climax. It illustrates characters, plot, conflict, and resolution.

2. Sociological analysis examines social worlds and dynamics as referents for interpreting the text.[8] Sociological exegesis applied to 1 Kings 19:16, 19-21 (See Appendix) can be richer if the entire discourse unit (1 Kgs 17:1–19:21) is examined.[9] The analysis includes:

a.) Describe social facts (environment and basic activities). The rural life of Elisha from a wealthy family (note twelve yoke of oxen) and providing a banquet for his people is contrasted to Elijah's mission of anointing Elisha to succeed him.

b.) Indicate the social history (political, economic, cultural, and religious events). The historical situation of the divided kingdom attests to the wealthier, schismatic status of the Northern Kingdom where the major conflict is the king and prophet. The Baal cult which competes with worship in Jerusalem is a focus of Elijah's zeal. The cult focuses on fertility rituals.

c.) Identify the social position of the community. It held a minority status as the Deuteronomic traditions were edited by Jerusalemites.

d.) Describe the social situation within the community. Its conflict was how to reconstitute the community in a post-exilic situation when neither prophet or king, nor appeal to covenant were sufficient.

e.) Identify the "social strategy" of the text. It *confirms* the present situation through the call to follow and be faithful to God via the prophets. It *adjusts* to the present hostile situation by repeating the injunction to fidelity.

f.) Describe the relationship between the social situation and the text. The cloak and anointing rituals assure community of God's fidelity and individual's acceptance and response.

3. As a work of art a text is a representation of feeling. In some measure, it is a response to religious, social, economic, or political tension by integrating the "rational/ logical/ analytical with the intuitive/ feeling."[10] The basic question of analysis is: What feelings are expressed in this text? For example, Luke 9:51-62 (See Appendix) evokes many feelings from its images and gestures: not welcome (v 53); call down brimstone from heaven to destroy them (v 54); reprimands (vv 55, 60, 62); no place to call home (v 58); not paying final respects to a parent (vv 59-60) or farewell to relatives before following Jesus (vv 61-62).

4. Analogy is the hermeneutical contribution of Paul Ricoeur to identify, distinguish, and bridge the distance between the ancient worldview of the text, e.g., words, concepts, and realities, and a contemporary reader's worldview.[11] His interpretation theory is based on analogous experience:

a.) Recognize the first naivete which occurs when a reader does not question the worldview, language, or imagery of the text.

b.) Arouse a critical consciousness by acknowledging distinctive historical and cultural realities which distance the text from the reader.

c.) Appropriate the language and symbolism of the text vis-a-vis personal understanding.

In applying Ricoeur's theory to Reading II: Galatians 5:1, 13-18 (See Appendix), one can use L. Dornisch's (unpublished materials) model which outlines an exegetical process to incorporate his theory:

a.) Choose a small text (one or two verses): "remember that you have been called to live in freedom—but not a freedom that gives free rein to the flesh" (v 13).

b.) Study the words by consulting different translations of the verse/s, concordances, and biblical dictionaries. Then, underline the significant words: called, live, freedom, flesh. The exercise initiates a critical consciousness.

c.) Locate the unit in its immediate context: a pastoral warning.

d.) Locate the unit in a larger context (of Galatians): an exhortation which concludes Paul's defense of the gospel he preached to the Gentiles.

e.) What worldview is revealed in the unit? Personal freedom means serving one another in love.

f.) Check research with secondary literature. Use several commentaries, monographs, and journal articles. This step confirms and extends the critical consciousness of distancization between the text and the reader.

g.) How does the worldview of the text relate to personal worldview? For example, what gospel do I proclaim when confronted by threatening situations?

h.) Proclaim the text to contemporaries. The reader can rephrase the verse/s in personal language. For example, remember you are baptized to live freely in mutual love.

C. LIBERATION

The perspective of liberation theology is included here because it engages the reader with the text. Some important liberation themes are:

1. The conviction that God's fundamental activity is liberating persons from oppressive situations.

2. God's bias is toward the poor.

3. Oppression often results from a political and economic system. Although not strictly an exegetical process, its focus is reading a text to understand God's words and activity for the destitute who are politically, economically, and socially oppressed. This type of reading is a contrast to the reading of the powerful and privileged who read the Bible to confirm their identity and activity.[12]

In applying this perspective to Galatians 5:1, 13-18 (See Appendix), these questions may be used:

a.) Does the text presuppose awareness of an oppressive reality to which it is directed? Yes, the hostile attitude of the Jews toward Paul's gospel of salvation.

b.) How is the oppression manifest in the situation? From Paul's warning to the Galatians: "It was for liberty that Christ freed us. So stand firm, and do not take on yourselves the yoke of slavery a second time" (v 1).

c.) Did the community addressed by the text participate in the situation as oppressed or oppressors? If members harassed Paul and his followers, they were oppressors. If they believed his gospel of freedom in Christ, they were oppressed by other community members and missionaries.

d.) What is the message of the text to the oppressor? to the oppressed? The message has multiple nuances. For the oppressor it includes the conviction that the yoke of slavery is to reassume burden of law if Jews or to assume it for the first time if Gentiles. The genuine yoke is to place oneself at the service of one another in love. To the oppressed it is a call to the freedom of Christ which is possible with his spirit.

Values and Limitations of Methods for Preaching

An evaluation of how contemporary methods offer particular values as well as limitations for the preacher follows.

A. HISTORICAL-CRITICAL METHOD

One value is that no text is a neutral statement of an individual or a community. As a representation of a particular *Sitz im Leben*, it indicates historical, religious, and cultural manifestations which are analyzed through source, form, and redaction. Another related value is its process which confirms learning a distinctive worldview of the text.

One limitation is the presupposition that the truth of the text *is* its historical components. Another is that its scientific, objective criteria do not embody a presuppositionless interpreter; rather, it often conceals an unawareness of motives which leads to the "worst possible subjectivism—the worst, because it is invincible."[13] Elisabeth Schussler Fiorenza concurs: "the world of historical data can never be perceived independently from the linguistic conceptualizations of the interpreter. It also denies the relationships of power inscribed in its own discourses."[14] The power of the predominant male voice heard in exegetical method in the church and the academy fosters "oppression and vilification of the subordinated 'others'."[15]

It is important that the limitations of the historical-critical method be considered seriously, since it is the one method which has found virtually universal acceptance and use in the church and academy for the past two hundred years. In particular, papal documents since 1941 have encouraged Roman Catholic biblical scholars to investigate critical exegesis. The historical-critical method has been evaluated, and many Roman Catholic scholars confirm its limitations. In the pastoral ministry of preaching and adult education, however, the method has often caused concern and confusion. In addition, resources for pastoral ministry do not reflect a plurality of interpretative theories and praxes.

B. STRUCTURALISM

One value is the search for the different levels of meaning in the text. Another is its analysis which includes the characteristics of the author's faith and how they are disclosed in the unit (See above, steps 5 and 6). Several questions which can be limitations about the method are: Is the biblical text a source of divine revelation? How is the revelation disclosed? What is the role of the community? Another limitation is the sparse resources which delineate the method. Currently it appears as a sophisticated process which is quite challenging to many interpreters and preachers.

C. SOCIOLOGICAL ANALYSIS

A value is the broad analysis of the social phenomena which constitute the community. It is related to the historical-critical method by indicating a specific worldview of a group quite diverse from the contemporary reader. Another value is interest in the symbols which give a community identity and purpose. One limitation is that modern constructs are imposed on ancient texts. In addition, the theological insight of a community is often identified with its social behavior. Again, the questions posed to structuralist interpretation may be examined here.

D. AS A WORK OF ART

Its value is in incorporating the symbolic, multi-faceted reality of art when speaking of a biblical text. However, aesthetics applied to a text does not exhaust its meaning. The method may be used in correlation with others.

E. ANALOGY

A significant value of Ricoeur's theory is his focus on bridging the distance between the text and the contemporary reader. There are related values in the exegetical process wherein the interpretation does not collapse the distance between text and reader (first naivete); rather, it unmasks the illusion that the distance does not exist. It also calls for critical inquiry which does not diminish a believer's activity (critical consciousness). By encouraging a comparison of the worldviews of text and reader, the method invites a synthetic insight which is integral to appropriating the significance of the text. Another value is communal participation in the process to substantiate the "surplus of meaning."

F. LIBERATION

A value in this theological approach is that additional voices are welcomed as necessary. They are the voices whose worldviews provide characteristic contrasts to the authoritative voices of other interpreters. A related value is the explicit connection between the liberation/oppression of the biblical text and contemporary communities. Justice is the unifying factor. One limitation is that liberation theologians often work with themes rather than one text (or a set of texts) with which the preacher struggles. Another is the assumption that the questions posed by first and second world interpreters about liberation and oppression authentically represent the experience of third world persons. Again, communal participation in the method with a variety of persons would enhance the experience.

The Preacher and Hermeneutics

A preacher is rooted in a particular worldview whose symbols have been shaped by years of experience and reinterpretation. Initially, the horizon of a preacher predicates being in relationship to God, others, and self as independent perspectives. Gradually, the horizon expands in a fusion of those relationships whose power unifies its political, social, and religious symbols. While it is difficult to determine which symbol is primary, each one is operative in a preacher's proclamation of the Word for the community. It is somewhat easier to identify an emotional response to a pericope, i.e., a point on a trajectory between fear/trembling and recognition/joy. Relationships, symbols, and emotions are often juxtaposed as the foundation for the hermeneutical process which offers guidelines to engage a personal symbolic world with the textual symbolic world.

To dismiss the hermeneutical process as an inappropriate *academic* exercise for the oral task of preaching is a preemptive decision. Preaching entails the pastoral integration of the academic pursuit of Scripture. In utilizing contemporary biblical methods several limitations promote humility:

A.) The interpretation of religious experience disclosed in the text is communicated in language constructs of *other* worldviews wherein the literary form is integrally connected to its meaning.

B.) Any textual interpretation is historically conditioned according to the ability of believers who can never exhaust the reality of the religious experience to which the diversity of insights in Christian tradition bears witness.

C.) Reverence for the text implies that a preacher join others in the struggle to proclaim a life-giving message as contemporary witnesses of the tradition. Solitary preparation for preaching is neither adequate for the task nor the responsibility.

Nonetheless, to equate methodological exercises with the preaching event is to identify exegesis as the heart of proclamation. Similarly, while lecturing on the interpretative history of a text may be a stimulating experience, it is not preaching. Preaching is the public proclamation of the Word which invites the assembly to consider that word in the light of communal and personal worldviews. Preaching involves a hermeneutical process of mediating a personal symbolic world with a textual symbolic world. In a broad dialogical context knowledge and understanding of God, community, self, and text develop via contemporary methods which foster connections. A spiral emerges as a preacher reflects on the textual implications of God, community, and self as part of the struggle to bear and communicate their dynamism. At this point the text often becomes a mirror of a preacher's horizon whose relational images may be challenged, affirmed, or given new dimensions. How a preacher shapes the experience and the insight for proclamation is the final sequence of the process which depends on all the contemplative energy and insight one has to expend.

Appendix

READINGS FOR THE THIRTEENTH SUNDAY OF THE YEAR—C CYCLE

READING I: 1 KINGS 19:16, 19–21

The Lord said to Elijah: "You shall anoint Elisha, son of Shaphat of Abelmeholah, as prophet to succeed you."

Elijah set out, and came upon Elisha, son of Shaphat, as he was plowing with twelve yoke of oxen; he was following the twelfth. Elijah went over to him and threw his cloak over him. Elisha left the oxen, ran after Elijah, and said, "Please, let me kiss my father and mother goodbye, and I will follow you." "Go back!" Elijah answered. "Have I done anything to you?" Elisha left him and, taking the yoke of oxen, slaughtered them; he used the plowing equipment for fuel to boil their flesh, and gave it to his people to eat. Then he left and followed Elijah as his attendant.

READING II: GALATIANS 5:1, 13–18

It was for liberty that Christ freed us. So stand firm, and do not take on yourselves the yoke of slavery a second time!

My brothers, remember that you have been called to live in freedom—but not a freedom that gives free rein to the flesh. Out of love, place yourselves at one another's service. The whole law has found its fulfillment in this one saying: "You shall love your neighbor as yourself." If you go on biting and tearing one another to pieces, take care! You will end up in mutual destruction!

My point is that you should live in accord with the spirit and you will not yield to the cravings of the flesh. The flesh lusts against the spirit and the spirit against the flesh; the two are directly opposed. This is why you do not do what your will intends. If you are guided by the spirit, you are not under the law.

GOSPEL: LUKE 9:51–62

As the time approached when Jesus was to be taken from this world, he firmly resolved to proceed toward Jerusalem, and sent messengers on ahead of him. These entered a Samaritan town to prepare for his passing through, but the Samaritans would not welcome him because he was on his way to Jerusalem. When his disciples James and John saw this, they said, "Lord, would you not have us call down fire from heaven to destroy them?" He turned toward them only to reprimand them. Then they set off for another town.

As they were making their way along, someone said to him, "I will be your follower wherever you go." Jesus said to him, "The foxes have lairs, the birds of the sky have nests, but the Son of Man has nowhere to lay his head." To another he said, "Come after me." The man replied, "Let me bury my father first." Jesus said to him, "Let the dead bury their dead; come away and proclaim the kingdom of God." Yet another said to him, "I will be your follower, Lord, but first let me take leave of my people at home." Jesus answered him, "Whoever puts his hand to the plow but keeps looking back is unfit for the reign of God."

Notes

1. The chapter develops an outline suggested in R. Allen, *Contemporary Biblical Interpretation for Preaching* (Valley Forge: Judson, 1984). Each lectionary reading was chosen according to its suitability in illustrating a particular method.

2. For a historical survey of biblical hermeneutics, see R. Brown and S. Schneiders, "Hermeneutics" *New Jerome Biblical Commentary* (Englewood Cliffs: Prentice-Hall, 1990) 1146–65.; D. Farkasfalvy, "A 'post-critical' Method of Biblical Interpretation" *Communio* 13 (1986): 299–307; E. McKnight, *Post-Modern Use of the Bible: The Emergence of Reader-Oriented Criticism* (Nashville: Abingdon, 1988).

3. Brown, "Hermeneutics," 1155.

4. For a historical survey of textual criticism, see R. Brown et al, "Texts and Versions" *New Jerome Biblical Commentary*, 1083–1112.

5. *Oxford Annotated Bible with the Apocrypha*, RSV, eds. H. May and B. Metzger (New York: Oxford University, 1965). For critical Hebrew and Greek texts, see *Biblia Hebraica Stuttgartensia*, eds. K. Elliger and W. Rudolph (Stuttgart: Deutsche Bibelgesellschaft, 1967–77); *Novum Testamentum Graece*, eds. E. Nestle and K. Aland, 26th ed. (Stuttgart: Deutsche Bibelstiftung, 1979); B. Metzger, *A Textual Commentary on the Greek New Testament* (New York: United Bible Societies, 1971).

6. *Synopsis of the Four Gospels*, ed. K. Aland (New York: United Bible Societies, 1982); *Gospel Parallels: A Synopsis of the First Three Gospels*, ed. B. Throckmorton, 4th ed. (Nashville: Nelson, 1979).

7. For a praxis oriented introduction to structuralism, see D. Patte, *Structural Exegesis for New Testament Critics* (Minneapolis: Fortress, 1990).

8. For sociology of the Bible, see H. Kee, "Sociology of the New Testament" *Harper's Bible Dictionary*, gen. ed. P. Achtemeier (New York: Harper 1985), 961–68; R. Wilson, "Sociology of the Old Testament" *Harper's Bible Dictionary*, 968–73. For social histories of the Bible, see K. Gottwald, *The Tribes of Yahweh: A Sociology of the Religion of Liberated Israel* (New York: Orbis, 1979); G. Theissen, *Sociology of Early Palestinian Christianity*, trans. J. Bowden (Philadelphia: Fortress, 1979). For a review of literature, see C. Osiek, "The New Handmaid: The Bible and the Social Sciences" *Theological Studies* 50 (1989): 260–78.

9. See Allen, 84–94 and a broad perspectus from B. Malina, *Christian Origins and Cultural Anthropology: Practical Models for Biblical Interpretation* (Atlanta: Knox, 1986).

10. Allen, 108, 105–15; see S. Terrien, *The Elusive Presence: Toward a New Biblical Theology* (New York: Harper & Row, 1978).

11. P. Ricoeur, *Interpretation Theory: Discourse and the Surplus of Meaning* (Fort Worth: Texas Christian University, 1976) and L. Dornisch, *Faith and Philosophy in the Writings of Paul Ricoeur* (Lewiston: Mellen, 1990).

12. Allen, 96, 95–104.

13. S. Brown, "Reader Response: Demythologizing the Text" *New Testament Studies* 34 (1988): 235, 232–37.

14. E. Schussler Fiorenza, "Biblical Interpretation and Critical Commitment" *Studia Theologica* 43 (1989): 7, 5–18.

15. Ibid. 6.

16. *Lectionary for Mass* (New York: Catholic Book, 1970), 179–80.

Chapter 3

John's Gospel: A Model of Preaching

THOMAS BRODIE, O.P.

There is a saying that John's Gospel is like a pool in which a child can paddle and an elephant can swim. It corresponds to the preacher's dream: that everyone, regardless of age or education, finds an uplifting message. It also reminds preachers that while John's Gospel may sometimes appear obscure, overall it has unique clarity and power. This gospel is supremely preachable.

The preaching of John has been underlined by recent writers, especially by James L. Heflin in *Southwestern Journal of Theology* (31 [1988] 32–37) and by Raymond E. Brown in *Interpretation* (43 [1989] 58–65).

Focus on Human Life

The essence of John's suitability for preaching consists of its closeness to human life, to the felt reality of day-to-day experience. The Johannine Jesus may be supremely divine, the preexistent timeless Word who is ever united with the Father, but this Word has become flesh and has entered the fray of human time and space. It is John and John alone who suggests what time feels like—a succession of days (1:29,35,43; 2:1) and a succession of years (the three Passovers, 2:13; 6:4; 13:1). (In the other gospels Jesus' ministry could be fitted into just one year). It is John rather than any other evangelist who, by telling of repeated journeys, especially to and from Jerusalem, fills out those years in a way which evokes the journeying of life.

This closeness to human life is found especially in John's Christology. Christology in the fourth gospel is central, but not an end in itself. It is always soteriological, always focused towards human need. The Gospel's opening verses, for instance, give a powerfully poetic picture of the Word as preexisting and creating (1:1-3), but it then goes on to speak of the Word as being increasingly involved in human affairs—as life, as light, and even as a light which contends with the darkness (1:4-5). In subsequent verses the presence of the Word gives way to the more prosaic reality of (human) witness (1:6-8), and finally, as the very form of the text becomes more and more prosaic, it makes way for the most down-to-earth reality of all flesh (1:14, the Word becomes flesh and enables ordinary people to see divine glory).

A similar phenomenon is found, for instance, in the discourse on ongoing creation (5:16-47), a discourse which is like a complex variation on the prologue. Again the initial Christology is high—Jesus is equal to God and is engaged in a delightful process of childlike creation (5:18-20). But again the whole purpose of this divine creativity is to bring life to people, life even to the dead. Jesus' divinity is manifested not to overwhelm but to enlighten, to enable people to see both the problems and the possibilities in their lives.

There are several other indications of this gospel's closeness to plain human reality. First, the language is simple. Furthermore, the Jesus who begins to minister may be divine yet he is an ordinary human. He is not a preacher, as in the other gospels; he is simply someone who walks (1:36). Unlike the other gospels, John tells of Jesus as tired and thirsty (4:6-7), as loving people (11:3,5), as being upset at the death of a friend (11:33-35), and as washing feet (13:1-20).

One of the most fundamental changes wrought by John in adapting the earlier gospel tradition was the replacement of kingdom language with "I am" language. In other words, he changed gospel vocabulary from focusing on something external ("the realm/kingdom of God") to focusing on human existence (the simple reality that "I am"). The "I am," of course, is simultaneously divine and human. It evokes the divine "I am" of the burning bush (Exod 3:14), and thus at the end of chap. 8 it is used climactically to declare an aspect of Jesus' divinity: "Before Abraham was, I am" (*egō eimi*, 8:59). But in the very next episode, at the beginning of the story of the man born blind, it is used in a much simpler form: the man's first words are "I am" (*egō eimi*, 9:9). This may be read as just a self-identification (meaning "I am [he]"), but it is so placed within the story that it is also both a simple statement of human existence and an echo of the divine "I am." In other words, even in making the most elementary self-declaration, the emerging man reflects the divine, evokes the fact that he is in the divine image. This switch by John, from kingdom language to "I am" language, is another form of the Word becoming flesh.

As well as omitting the image of Jesus preaching the kingdom, John leaves out also the parables which compare the kingdom to a feast (Matt 22:1-14; Luke 14:15-24). But he gives something else instead—the wedding feast at Cana (2:1-11). In other words, just at the point when the other gospels (in their opening chapters) are speaking about the kingdom, John introduces a story which illustrates what the kingdom actually feels like: it is like an abundance of wonderful wedding wine, and one comes to know of it by listening to Jesus' words and doing them (the servants knew about the wine, but the steward did not). Thus he gives a wonderfully vivid account, but the focus is on something internal, something close to the heart—a listening process which makes one aware that the world is full of wedding wine.

The Cana incident also accomplishes something else: it introduces the fundamental idea of drinking. For it is not only John's language which is simple; so is most of his imagery—life, light, wind, bread, water, eating, and drinking. He seems, as it were, to respect the Ignatian principle that it is best not to multiply images, but rather to have one unifying focus. And having established the idea of drinking, he weaves it in and out of his subsequent text: at the well (4:1-42); at the end of the bread of life discourse (6:52-58); on the last day of the feast when Jesus promises streams of living water to the thirsty (7:37-39); and on the last day of Jesus' life when he thirsts and when his life pours forth in spirit, blood and water (19:28-30, 34).

In ways which are diverse but complementary, these various scenes suggest that becoming aware of God is as fundamental as drinking, and thus they bring God before the reader/listener with unusual immediacy.

The emphasis on day-to-day human reality is found not only in Jesus but also in other characters. In the accounts concerning Nicodemus (3:1-21) and the woman at the well (4:1-42), for instance, there are paradigmatic illustrations of human situations which tend to shut out the awareness of God. Nicodemus is having a brilliant career; he combines several impressive roles—politician, intellectual, religious leader. And yet there is a sense in which he does not have a clue. The whole world of spirit is quite beyond him. John's portrayal of Jesus meeting him in the dark ("at night") and speaking to him of spirit and of love constitutes a graphic appeal to others who have been taken over by their careers.

Equally graphic is the appeal to those who have been taken over by their erratic love-lives—a situation illustrated by the Samaritan woman. Despite the colorfulness of her history, she is weary; her desire not to have to go on drawing water provides an initial hint that her life is not satisfying. When the discussion switches from her love-life to worship it is not because she wants to change the subject but because the two topics, love and worship, are inherently connected. And after long experience of one form of love, she wants something more; she wants true worship.

John's initial emphasis on the problems which can accompany careers and love-lives illustrates one of his basic concerns, namely to identify those human situations which, even when impressive on the outside, tend to restrict one's deepest development.

Thus many of John's characters are not only colorful; they are also representative. To take another example, the man at the poolside, for instance, is typical of someone who has become so accustomed to a difficult situation that he or she imagines it to be worse than it is. In his view, no one is for him, and someone is always ahead of him—in other words, against him. He no longer really wants to change, to become well (when asked if he wants to be healed, the man cannot say a simple yes).

One of the effects of John's Gospel is that the various characters tend to provide a mirror in which, without being unduly threatened, one may see oneself; one moves in imagination from one character to the next until, in all probability, one character touches a deep chord and there is a deep cry (or sigh) of recognition—"That's me."

A further indication of the emphasis on human experience is the description of faith as a verb, "to believe." It is never as a noun. In other words, faith is not something static or abstract; it is something lived.

The essential point is simple: John is not lost in the mists of history (not even sacred history) nor in doctrinal abstractions. Rather, he has reworked the gospel tradition so as to highlight both its deepest roots in God and its practical implications for human living. He has given a sharp sense of the encounter between the timeless living God (as reflected in Jesus) and Everyperson (as reflected in the Gospel's many representative characters). And it is this encounter between God and Everyperson which makes the Gospel so suitable to preaching.

Preaching through Obscurity

There are times when John's Gospel is quite obscure—so much so that, as an attempt at preaching, it seems to fail. But obscurity can have its purposes. In some of Joseph Conrad's writing, for instance, particularly in *Heart of Darkness*, the style is deliberately obscure. And it is obscure because the content is obscure. Since Conrad was describing the intractable darkness of evil, he used obscurity of style as a way of communicating some sense of that evil. In Francis Coppola's *Apocalypse Now*, which is modeled to a significant degree on *Heart of Darkness*, the film eventually becomes increasingly dark, so much so that even when Marlon Brando fills the screen, it is difficult to see him.

Something similar happens in John. In some of the chapters which speak of disbelief, death, and sin (chaps. 7–8, and to some degree, chap. 5), the obscurity of style seems to be a way of suggesting the difficulty, the mysteriousness, of the content.

In chapter 7, the issue is death. The chapter begins by indicating that for Jesus the threat of death is not just a distant possibility. It is having a practical influence on his decisions about where to go and where not to go (7:1). Furthermore, the feast which is at hand, insofar as it highlights the image of a tent, evokes the tentlike nature of human flesh; like a tent, the flesh (the external body) may collapse easily (cf. John 1:14, "the Word became flesh and tented among us"). And the subsequent discussion (in chap. 7) is largely dominated by allusions both to Jesus' impending death and to the difficulty of recognizing who he really is. Reading this chapter is like watching death approach someone. One sees it coming, and one wonders not only about death itself but also about the person and about their deepest identity and destiny. It is altogether appropriate that such a chapter be written with a certain obscurity.

Chapter 8 emphasizes the ideas of light (8:12) and freedom (8:31-32), but it does so in large part to draw a contrast, to examine the origins of evil and the way in which the heart comes to be driven or generated by a diabolical mixture of murder and lies. The form in which this discussion is cast is that of a conversation with superficial believers ("Jews who believed in him," 8:31). Again, given the nature of the topic, obscurity seems to be appropriate.

At one point, however, in chapter 8, the obscurity is occasioned not by the elusiveness of evil but by the elusiveness of God. When the Jews ask Jesus "Who are you?", his extraordinarily difficult answer ("Why the beginning I speak to you") is a reflection ultimately of God's refusal to give Moses a simple answer concerning God's own self (Exod 3:14). In other words, the difficulty of the answer reflects the difficulty of grasping God; its broken grammar indicates that, in speaking of God, language fails. Thus within the obscurity of chapter 8, the two mysteries of evil and of God are bound together. It is an obscurity, therefore, which is best seen as that not of a bungler but of a master artist.

The prologue is one text which tends to cause a particular problem, not just because it seems difficult and dense but also because it is among the possible readings for Christmas morning. For many preachers its abstract-sounding language seems at odds with the jingle-bells atmosphere of the season. Yet when the prologue is read well it has extraordinary power and solemnity. Its "In the beginning . . ." can capture the heart even more fully than "Once upon a time . . . ." And when it does reach the heart, it speaks more deeply than almost any other story. Through its fundamental images, especially those of light and darkness, of becoming a child of God and of being on the Father's bosom, it addresses the heart's ultimate concerns. Christmas morning is not a time either for sentimentality or moralizing. The sentimentality is unnecessary; it is so much in the air that the preacher does not need to add to it. And the moralizing is out of place; in the words of the old Jewish maxim: "No moralizing on High Holy Days." What people need is a clear, strong statement which will help them to see behind the tinsel and often-confused (family) relationships, a statement which will affirm the fundamental goodness of God and of God's creation, especially of people. That is what the prologue provides. It is a meditation on history, so written that it provides a powerful declaration of realistic optimism. Despite the weight of darkness and rejection, it sees the greater presence of light of grace.

In developing the prologue, it is probably better that the preacher lay the emphasis not on its background but on its foreground, its implication. On Christmas morning, people do not need to hear much of the history of *logos* in Jewish religion and Hellenistic philosophy. But they do need, sometimes terribly, to hear something like the quiet determination of the battered woman who at the end of *Mississippi Burning* decides to stay in her disturbed racist town, because as she says, "There are enough good people here."

Reactions to the Message

Reactions to Jesus are varied. Frequently there is misunderstanding. People have become so accustomed to their restrictions that nothing else makes immediate sense to them. Nicodemus and the Samaritan woman are so preoccupied that when Jesus begins to speak of a further reality their initial reaction is to mock him (3:4; 4:11-12). It takes time before it begins to dawn on them that perhaps there really is more.

The problem in John is that there is always more. Even when one is attentive to the words of Jesus, attentive to the structure and meaning of the text, one cannot master it fully. It has puzzles and complexities which in the end escape one's grasp. It is like a Japanese garden—there is no vantage point from which one can see it all.

This may lead to a certain frustration, to a conviction that this gospel is confused and confusing. But, as already indicated in discussing the obscurity of chapters 7 and 8, the Gospel's difficulty has its purpose. While part of this difficulty may, of course, be due to lack of adequate study, a certain amount of it is due to the fact that the Gospel is meant to constitute a permanent challenge. It not only speaks of God; it is like God—alluring but elusive. With its simple language and vivid scenes it draws one towards it. But one never quite masters it. (At least no one that we know of in the last two thousand years has managed to do it). While study is indispensable, there are moments when one has to let go of the effort to analyze logically and rationally. Like a Zen puzzle or koan which concentrates the mind in order to induce a higher state of awareness, the Gospel challenges the reader to rise above well-worn patterns of thought and to seek concentrated rest at a higher level.

One of the features of the Gospel as a whole is its repetitiveness, a factor which has led people to compare John with the repetitive advance of the waves of the incoming tide. There seem to be at least two purposes to this phenomenon. First, it corresponds in many ways to the felt experience of life's mixture of sameness and change. And further, it has a mantra-like quality which helps to bring the reader to a state of concentration and stillness. This is particularly true of some of the discourses, especially of the last discourse (chaps. 13-17).

The Central Themes

In preaching John's Gospel it is better to avoid peripheral topics concerning the gospel's authorship and background, particularly the hypothesis concerning a distinct Johannine community. Discussion of these questions is extremely inconclusive, and it belongs not to preaching but to historical research.

What is certain on the other hand, and what is vital for the preacher, is the Gospel's central message: human life, however ordinary and difficult, is surrounded by a personal loving presence which bears it along and which seeks to bring it joy. One may reject this presence and thus fill one's life with strife and death. But if one believes—and believing is the key—then one can come to know this personal presence and thereby find peace, even amid strife and death.

It is as though human existence is a fishbowl which is being carried towards the ocean by a mighty river. Everything depends on the river, even the supply of water, but many in the fishbowl are unaware of it. They may live long, travel far, and achieve much, but ultimately their lives are narrow. Some, however, have become aware that outside the fishbowl there is a whole other world with other forms of nourishment and life. And by abandoning the securities of the fishbowl they have managed to establish abiding communication with that wider world.

ABIDING UNION

It is this latter idea—communication or abiding union—which is basic to John. The abiding union which exists within God—where the Word is with God (1:1), and where the only-begotten is on the Father's bosom (1:18)—that union is available to human beings. In fact there is a special character who exemplifies abiding union—the beloved disciple, the one who is introduced as resting on Jesus' bosom (13:23). And there is a special verb, *menō*, "to abide/remain/stay," which is associated with union or with the lack of it. Thus the Spirit "abode" on Jesus (1:33), and the next day the disciples "abode" with him—an abiding which, in the context, is primarily spiritual (1:38-39).

The central idea of this emphasis on union or abiding is that amid all one's life and labors the foundational factor is the presence of God, a presence which can be profoundly life-giving. The God in question is not some distant impersonal force. For while it is indeed true that no one has ever seen God (1:18), yet as the portrayal of Jesus shows, there is a sense in which God has a human face: the picture of Jesus, even in his humanity, is ultimately a picture of God. The gospel's call, therefore, is that one should abide in the presence of the human face of God.

What this implies is that one's life, however busy, has a central quality of rest. There may be much that one still wants to achieve—physically, emotionally, intellectually, spiritually—but even amid serious imperfection and limitedness, one is invited to come to rest before one's God.

Such a quality does not come easily. It has been said, for instance, of modern Germans that even though they have an abundance of leisure time they are never really at rest. To attain a deep quality of rest it may be necessary to exercise discipline—for example, to restrict the use of radio and television, particularly last thing at night and first thing in the morning. Ultimately however the matter is not one of technique but of abandonment to God.

Associated with restful abiding union is the Gospel's emphasis on realized eschatology or the idea that the ultimate divine realities are already present. What this implies in practice is that the gospel hearer is being invited right now to enter into the presence of the divine reality, to come to rest in God by being attentive to the present.

Also associated with restful union is the Gospel's emphasis on sabbaths (5:9-10, 16, 18; 7:22-23; 9:14-16; 19:31; cf. 20:1, 19, *sabbatōn*) and feasts (5:1; 7:2, Tents; 10:22, Dedication; 2:13; 6:4; 11:55, Passover). Sabbath means rest, and within the Gospel sabbaths and feasts are so interwoven that when Jesus takes them both over he is in fact establishing a new order of rest and celebration.

The result of resting in God is that one has a deep peace which sets one free from defining oneself through titles and achievements. Jesus may be the Messiah, but he never needs to declare his messiahship as if it were a self-aggrandizing title. His titles and works are always set in the context of his relationship to God. When, for instance, the Samaritan woman speaks of the coming Messiah, and when Jesus says, "I am he" (4:26), his reply may seem to be a claim for himself, but the phrasing is such (*egō eimi*, literally, "I am") that it recalls the divine presence at the burning bush (Exod 3:14) and thus sets Jesus in a relationship to God. And through this restful freedom, first exemplified so clearly in Jesus, the disciple is able to relish life to the full.

THE SAVING SPIRIT

In seeking to achieve abiding union there are two major obstacles, namely sin and death. Only through the Spirit can these be overcome, and so John's Gospel gives the Spirit a major role. Thus, one of the Gospel's pivotal allusions to sinfulness "Jesus . . . knew what was in the human person," 2:24-25) is followed by the offering of the Spirit (to Nicodemus and the Samaritan woman, 3:5-8; 4:7-24; cf. 3:34). And the increasing allusions to death (especially the death of Jesus, 7:1,19-20, 25, 33-34) are likewise followed by the offering of the Spirit (7:39). In fact Jesus' entire life, from the initial descent of the Spirit (1:32-33), is both fully human and fully Spirit-filled. And it is this Spirit, divine and humanizing (tempered by Jesus' own human experience) which he bestows on the disciples (19:30; 20:22; cf. 14:16, 26; 15:26; 16:7-15).

THE PRIORITY OF SPIRIT (THE BELOVED DISCIPLE) OVER OFFICE (PETER)

As already partly indicated, the Gospel's highlighting of the priority of spiritual union leads it to underline the figure of the beloved disciple, someone who, in his closeness to Jesus (13:23, 25) and in his capacity as a spiritual leader (20:8; 21:7; cf. 19:27) plays a role akin to that of the guiding Spirit (cf. 14:26; 15:26; 16:13).

One of the key dramas of the Gospel is the healthy interplay between the beloved disciple and Peter (13:23-24; 20:1-10; 21:7, 20-23). There is no polemic against Peter and his office, but there is a clear indication that in fulfilling his office Peter is to be guided by the spirit of the beloved, guided ultimately by love (21:15-17). The drama is heightened by the fact that in various ways the character of Peter is associated or shadowed by that of Judas (6:68-71; 13:2, 6; 13:21, 38; 18:23, 10-11; cf. 18:15-16). The Peter who eventually learns from the beloved disciple could also have gone the path of Judas.

BELIEVING LEADS TO COMMUNITY

Just as the Spirit does not militate against office but rather purifies and strengthens it, so interior spiritual union (believing) does not lead to isolation but rather to community, to some form of church. The very first reaction of those who abide with Jesus is to go and tell others (1:35-42, Andrew's believing leads to the introduction of the church-related Peter). And so on through the Gospel: again and again believing opens the way for community. The belief of the man born blind (9:38) opens the way for the image of the sheepfold (chap. 10). The last discourse builds up to an emphasis on unity (including church unity, chap. 17). And the belief of Thomas (20:28) prepares the way for the final multi-faceted picture of the church and of unity (chap. 21). (Chap. 21 is an epilogue, but it is not an afterthought. It is as integral to the Gospel as the prologue).

Conclusion

One of the basic features of John's work is its pervasive unity. Despite the diversity of its characters and the complexity of some of its style, it is profoundly coherent. It's simple central images combine to keep the focus on the fundamental things in life. And ultimately all its themes are inherently connected; they hinge on the foundational insight that amid the difficulties and brokenness of life there is a single unifying Spirit, God's Jesus-like Spirit, and that that Spirit seeks constantly to invite people into union with God and with one another.

Chapter 4

Preaching the Liturgy: A Social Mystagogy

SAMUEL TORVEND, O.P.

1. Introduction

With the publication and pastoral implementation of the *Rite of Christian Initiation of Adults* in the Roman Catholic Church,[1] preachers, catechists, and liturgists find themselves increasingly aware that initiation into the community of believers is not so much a single event whereby one simply declares affiliation with a particular religious body as it is a process of ever-deepening conversion to a way of living with others who share a public mission.[2]

At the same time, pastoral ministers and liturgical theologians, relying on their labors in the RCIA as well as scholarly research on faith development and conversion theory, recognize increasingly that pastoral formation in the Christian faith takes place within a community composed of various groups. i) Some may be interested in joining a Christian community but have little or no articulated experience of the faith (e.g., infants, children, and adult newcomers). ii) Others have made a commitment to formation or re-formation in the faith and are being introduced (or reintroduced) to the liturgical and apostolic expressions of Christian faith (e.g., young people preparing for confirmation/eucharist, catechumens, baptized candidates returning to the church). iii) Finally there are those who have received the sacraments of initiation, gather regularly at the table of the eucharist, and participate in the ongoing life of the Christian community.[3] In other words, the RCIA highlights what in fact are three groups of persons who, in various configurations, exist in many parishes within every Christian communion.

Of course the temptation inherent in such a three-fold grouping is the presumption that baptized Christians (who constitute the largest number of the three) no longer ask the kinds of questions posed by inquirers, nor are they in need of the initial formation offered to catechumens and those returning to the practice of the faith. And yet there remains an acceptable presumption that all the baptized—filled with the charisms of the Spirit, possessing the experience of faith, and participating in the liturgical and apostolic forms of ecclesial life—are capable if not desirous of deepening and expanding their experience and knowledge of that identity and mission which are theirs through sacramental initiation.[4]

For Roman Catholics in particular, as well as for other Christian communions in which the rites of initiation have been reformed, it has become readily apparent that entrance into the church resembles a developmental process that, while beginning with the awakening of faith in a person's life, is unending. This growth includes the process of coming to faith, the initial formation in faith, and ongoing formation throughout the rest of one's life.[5] For the preacher, then, it becomes equally apparent that he or she is preaching in the midst of one assembly constituted of great diversity. Such diversity nonetheless manifests a simple yet profound sacramental and ecumenical truth, namely that the identity which forms all Christians *throughout* their lives is fundamentally baptismal.[6] It is an identity and mission continually manifested, renewed, and challenged in the gathering of the baptized, preeminently in the celebration of the eucharist as well as in other sacramental and liturgical rites.

The question which this chapter addresses is this: how does one preach the liturgical actions which make one Christian (i.e., sacramental initiation) and, by extension, those rites which hold this fundamental identity, this baptismal memory, in ongoing availability for the Christian community? The posing of the question itself is prompted first by the RCIA which incorporates a period of post-baptismal formation for the newly-baptized and the baptized faithful:

> Since the distinctive spirit and power of the period of post baptismal catechesis or mystagogy derive from the new, personal experience of the sacraments and of the community, its main setting is . . . the Sunday Masses of the Easter season. Besides being occasions for the newly baptized to gather with the community and share in the mysteries, these celebrations include particularly suitable readings from the Lectionary.[7]

While the RCIA provides a model for ongoing formation in faith rooted in the experience of the sacramental actions, I would contend that it also proposes a model of preaching. In other words the question can be put this way: how does the preacher evoke, clarify, and enlarge the meaning of sacramental initiation so that all the baptized might experience a more profound conversion to the grace of Christ symbolized in the liturgical actions? Though we will focus primarily on the sacraments of initiation, the question can be raised again in regard to the liturgical celebrations which are extensions and elaborations of this fundamental sacrament of Christian life. How might one preach those graced moments of ongoing conversion symbolized liturgically in such rites as reconciliation, anointing of the sick, or funerals?

Taken together, these questions suggest what may be for some a new form of preaching, that is a sustained reflection on the liturgical actions themselves. This is what the RCIA and the history of preaching know as *mystagogia*, preaching on the "mysteries," on the ensemble of liturgical actions which constitute sacramental celebrations. The contention of this chapter is that mystagogia or mystagogical preaching offers the preacher a method of correlating the life experience of the Christian community, the biblical texts, and the liturgical actions celebrated by the assembly. But at the same time, our line of inquiry will lead us to suggest that mystagogia not only reflects on the meaning of the liturgical actions for the Christian community, but also offers the liturgical actions as paradigms for Christian witness in the world.

To this end the chapter discusses the liturgical context, examines the sources and methods of mystagogical preaching, and suggests the social implications of this form of preaching.

II. The Liturgical Context

There was a time in the not-too-distant past when preachers, catechists, and theologians in the Christian communions could speak of sacraments apart from their liturgical celebration by a community of believers. One need only look at various catechisms or textbooks of the Episcopal, Lutheran, and Roman Catholic Churches[8] to recognize that when the sacraments are treated simply as divine acts or legal requirements for membership they can be readily perceived as discrete though perhaps significant occasions in which one passively receives a particular grace (e.g., forgiveness at baptism) and/or moments in which one enters into a "state" or office (e.g., marriage or the ordained ministry). A narrow concern only for the "correct" dogmatic interpretation (a form of theological reductionism) or the necessary requirements to effect a valid and licit celebration (canonical minimalism) can render homiletical and catechetical reflection on the sacramental actions of the church both ahistorical and individualistic. Such a concern is ahistorical in that the liturgical actions which constitute the sacramental celebration may be understood or experienced as being somehow unaffected by the exigencies of the culture, the time and the place in which they are celebrated. It is individualistic in that the sacramental celebration may be easily interpreted as a moment of solitary encounter with God or Christ, an interpretation which ignores the ecclesial and social dimensions of grace.[9]

Thus, theological or canonical minimalism, ahistoricism and individualism, when they conspire to create the basic parameters of sacramental practice and interpretation, influence the one who preaches. Consider this example: Christian initiation can be celebrated in the privacy of a church parlor or a family's living room during which the minister reads a brief verse or two from the conclusion of Matthew's Gospel (22:18-20, "Go therefore and make disciples"). These verses can be interpreted as 1) the Lord's command, 2) through which sins are forgiven, 3) in order to attain eternal life. A few drops of water are delicately sprinkled on the infant's head while those present coo and cluck over the charm of it all and then depart satisfied. Consequently, no mention is made of baptism until the child is enrolled in preparation classes for penance and/or first eucharist. With such pallid descriptions of entrance into the Christian community, we are all too familiar, for they remain, in so many places, the norm. The question for us is this: how can the preacher, given such a minimalist celebration (though canonically valid and theologically "correct") offer a "maximalist" interpretation of this fundamental sacrament of Christian identity and purpose through the homiletical word? Is it possible that the near-obsessive concern in the Christian West for ritual correctness or scriptural "institution" and theological precision has in fact inexorably reduced our capacity not only to celebrate the rites in their fullness but also to preach their dynamic character?

When one reads the introductions and guidelines which preface the reformed rites of the major Christian communions, and in particular the RCIA, it becomes apparent that the theology of liturgical celebrations of the sacraments has been enriched and is now rooted in three insights gained from the near-Herculean theological labors of the last century, insights which not only affect the liturgy but the one who preaches in the midst of the liturgical assembly.

A. THE SCRIPTURES

First, it has become clear that the liturgical and sacramental acts of the Church are rooted in and spring from the life and history of Israel,

Jesus, and the early Christian community. This history of grace is continually proclaimed in the scriptural readings and enacted in the liturgy. Such labor in biblical research has revealed with incandescent brightness the truth that the salvific purposes of God revealed in the life of Israel, Jesus, and the nascent Christian community are profoundly historical and communal and that apart from history and community, the liturgical and sacramental activity of the Church can be quickly reduced to magic or superstition. Thus, one cannot interpret the biblical readings proclaimed in the midst of the liturgical assembly without recognizing their communal and historical character and the fact that they are now proclaimed in the midst of an historical community.

It is in this context, then, that the preacher is invited to ponder the meaning of the readings proclaimed in the liturgy. But is not possible for the preacher to reflect on the relationship between the scriptural word proclaimed and the liturgical/sacramental act celebrated? One might pose the question this way: *how does this particular reading (or set of readings) interpret the meaning of this particular act?* If, for instance, one is celebrating Christian baptism on the feast of the Baptism of the Lord, one not only asks the meaning of the readings in their own setting and how they interpret the feast but also how they interpret the sacramental actions being celebrated by this particular community. What are the biblical images and stories which cluster around and consequently interpret the liturgical actions being performed by this gathering of Christians? How does the sacramental action continue the historical and salvific purposes of God in the life of this person and community today?[10]

B. THE EARLY CHURCH

The past century of research in patristic studies, using the historical-critical methods pioneered in biblical research, has yielded a rich harvest concerning the festal calendars and celebrations of early Christian communities. From the critical editions and analyses of the ritual texts and homilies of the ancient Church, it has become clearer that the liturgical celebration of the sacraments served as the primary source of theology in early Christianity. If one were to ask an Ephrem, a Chrysostom, or an Ambrose, 'What does it mean to be Christian?' one most likely would *not* be invited to an inquiry class or given a religious tract but taken in hand to the celebration of the Easter Vigil, in effect being told: if you want to know the meaning of Christian life, come and see how Christians are made.[11]

From the analyses of these early Christian liturgical texts and homilies preached on the great days of the Church's festal calendar, it has become clear that the feasts themselves suggest an interpretive key for preaching during the liturgical seasons of the Church. For instance, these early Christian homilies reveal that one preaches the meaning of the incarnation at Christmas, the universal nature of Christianity at Epiphany and Pentecost, the renewal and re-formation of baptismal identity throughout Lent, the paschal mystery at the Vigil, and the trinitarian, that is, the social implications of that mystery during the weeks of Easter. Thus, the homilies of the early Christian preachers offer the contemporary preacher another key to preaching the liturgical actions. They suggest that the feasts and seasons guide and inform the Church's liturgical celebrations and consequently the preacher's reflections on those feasts and rites. According to the pastoral theology of these bishops who preached regularly at the celebration of the sacraments, the Church rightfully celebrates Christian initiation at the Easter Vigil, during the Easter season, at Pentecost, and on the feast of the Baptism of the Lord because the liturgical actions accord with and manifest the meaning of the feast itself. Thus, a certain 'logic' coheres between feast and rite.[12]

Consequently, the contemporary preacher is invited to ponder the relationship between feast or season and the celebration of the liturgical actions which constitute the sacramental celebration. *How does this particular feast or season interpret the meaning of this particular act?* If, for instance, one is celebrating Christian baptism on the Third Sunday of Easter, the preacher must not only ask how the readings interpret the baptismal act, but also how the day and season mark the liturgical actions with their particular 'logic.'

C. SYMBOLIC COMMUNICATION

The third insight revealed in the reformed rites stems from an understanding of symbolic communication as interpreted by the modern liturgical movement. Dissatisfied with simply "streamlining" the liturgical rites and translating them into a vernacular tongue as if one were merely overhauling an older model car, the stated objective of the liturgical renewal in this century begins with this exhortation: "Let the central symbolic actions of the liturgy speak in all the fullness of their natural, ritual, biblical and communal profundity."[13] But such an objective can be extended to include its corollary: "So that the Christian community might be enabled to act corporately as a public, historical promoter of the redemptive work of God within human life and history."[14]

Needless to say, without prescinding from either dogmatic interpretations or canonical regulation, liturgical theologians agree that symbolic, liturgical actions possess layers of meaning. These actions cannot be reduced to a single meaning since by their very nature they always "say" more, reveal more. At the same time, liturgical theologians recognize the historical conditioning of those actions (they are invested with new meanings by ever new communities of faith who live in and respond to changing historical circumstances). In other words, as Christians perform these symbolic, liturgical actions and invest them with meaning, the actions, the rituals possess the power to form them in a particular way.[15] This is to suggest that symbolic, liturgical actions have a pedagogical effect. They can both shape and expand perceptions of identity and behavior.[16]

Perhaps there was a time when preachers could speak in the abstract concerning the sacraments, as if these actions were hermetically sealed capsules of grace offered to isolated individuals apart from the historical context in which they existed. Perhaps there was a time when one could simply ignore the liturgical actions, as if they were mere illustrations of the spoken word. Now the preacher is faced with the truth that these actions mold perceptions and subtly inform purpose and behavior. Thus, *the preacher is invited to ponder the meaning of a particular liturgical action or ensemble of actions in their symbolic power and amplitude.* For instance, what is the symbolic power of plunging a person into the waters of the baptismal pool or simply sprinkling with utter delicacy a few drops of water on a forehead? Which action bears the greater symbolic "weight"? And what is its meaning for the life and death of this particular person and community? What are the meanings of breaking bread and sharing the cup with newly-baptized and those who have returned to the table of the Lord after years of absence? What is revealed in the breaking and giving and eating and sipping: a polite gesture of religious affiliation or the gestures by which one learns to feed the community with one's talents and the hungry with one's substance?

From this brief review of three insights gained from the work of scholars in the past decades, three practical suggestions emerge for the one who is beginning to preach the liturgical actions. One attends to the scriptural readings (what they reveal concerning the action), the feast and season (how this particular time shapes one's interpretation of the action), and the symbolic nature of liturgical actions (what they reveal regarding human activity). From these first insights we now move to a specific discussion of mystagogical preaching.

III. Sources and Method

The *Rite of Christian Initiation of Adults* prefaces its commentary on mystagogy with these words from 1 Peter: "You are a chosen race, a royal priesthood, a holy people; praise God who called you out of darkness and into his marvelous light."[17] As the scriptural introduction to post-baptismal formation in faith, the RCIA suggests that the ensemble of liturgical actions celebrated in baptism have initiated the catechumens and candidates into a chosen, priestly, and holy people who possess, by virtue of baptism, a task: to mediate in the world the "light" received in sacramental initiation. The question remains: how might the preacher evoke, clarify, and expand the meaning of these actions which have made the baptized "missionaries" of Christ? The RCIA responds:

> Mystagogy . . . is a time for the community and the neophytes together to grow in deepening their grasp of the paschal mystery and in making it part of their lives through meditation on the Gospel, sharing in the eucharist, and doing the works of charity. . . . The term 'mystagogy' suggests . . . a fuller and more effective understanding of [the] mysteries through the Gospel message . . . and above all through the experience of the sacraments.[18]

Here, then, the instruction of the RCIA first suggests that the preacher reflects on 1) the scriptural reading (in particular the gospel), 2) the community's experience of the liturgical actions, and 3) the Christian witness which flows from word and sacrament. Furthermore, the commentary suggests that the liturgical assembly is capable of attaining a "fuller and more effective understanding" of the liturgical rites for daily living when word and act intersect in preaching. Is the commentary not suggesting that when the preacher uses the liturgical actions as a "text" for preaching, he or she not only probes the meaning of the liturgy itself but also begins to correlate the liturgical actions of the Church with those actions appropriately exercised by the Church in the public order? Is there a precedent for such a model of preacher?

A. JESUS

Certainly we have the example of Jesus who, in John's Gospel, washes and dries the feet of his disciples, an action which serves as John's *eucha-*

istic narrative.[19] The evangelist writes that during the supper Jesus rose, laid aside his garments and wrapped a towel around himself. He then poured water in a basin and—much to Peter's amazement—washed the feet of his disciples. Only after he had completed this action did he speak of its meaning for his followers:

> If I then, your Lord and Teacher, have washed your feet, you also ought to wash one another's feet. For I have given you an example, that you also should do as I have done to you. Truly, truly, I say to you, a servant is not greater than his master; nor is he who is sent greater than he who sent him. If you know these things, blessed are you if you do them.[20]

Here Jesus first performs the action, then reflects on it. The disciples experience the action first, utterly surprised by the reversal of roles. Not only does Jesus reflect on the action, he offers it to them as the gesture by which they will be known as his followers. They are to continue this gesture of surprising service to each other. The action bears a social significance.[21]

B. PAUL

Likewise, we have the example of Paul who, in his letters to the Roman and Galatian Christians, evokes the experience of their baptism and then comments on the significance of the ritual action. To the Romans, he writes: do you truly understand what happened to you in baptism? Are you fully aware of the implications of the act in which you participated? Do you intend now to pattern your life in accord with the pattern by which you became one with Christ and each other? "We were buried with him" he writes, "by baptism into death, [a liturgical action of the past] so that as Christ was raised from the dead by the glory of the Father, we too might walk [according to that pattern of the past action] in newness of life."[22]

In his letter to the Galatians he again invokes the baptismal actions to enlarge their meaning. One has died to a sinful orientation and has entered into a community in which social distinctions (Jew/Greek, male/female, slave/free) no longer operate as forms of social stratification and division as they do in the larger cultural context. "You have put on Christ," he writes (an allusion to baptismal clothing?), "you are all one in Christ."[23] By reminding his listeners of the liturgical action which they performed, Paul draws out the spiritual significance of the act, but an action bearing social and consequently cultural implications.[24]

C. BISHOPS OF THE EARLY CHURCH

Here we have mentioned two modest examples of "mystagogical catechesis" from the scriptures. While this method of exposing the meanings of "the mysteries" continues and grows in the following two hundred years, it becomes a virtual art by the fourth century. In the mystagogical homilies of the bishops of the fourth and fifth centuries we encounter a rich treasure of preaching on the liturgical actions.[25] Let us examine but two homilies. Gathered at the liturgy in the weeks after Easter, Cyril of Jerusalem writes:

> For some time now, true and beloved children of the church, I have desired to discourse to you on these spiritual and celestial mysteries. But I well knew that visual testimony is more trustworthy than mere hearsay, and therefore awaited this chance of finding you more amenable to my words, so that out of your personal experience I could lead you into the brighter and more fragrant meadows of Paradise on earth.[26]

Perhaps Cyril uses a language which may sound dated to the modern ear. Yet through that language we gain a glimpse of his purpose: to preach on "spiritual and celestial mysteries," to speak on the liturgical actions, the place and the time which constitute Christian initiation. His desire, he says, is to lead the assembly "into the brighter and more fragrant meadow of Paradise on earth." But he notes that this will be more effective after the celebration of the liturgy since "visual testimony is more trustworthy than mere hearsay." Now, *is he not suggesting to the contemporary preacher than one must affirm the experience of those who have participated in the liturgy and also trust their experience (the visual testimony) of the liturgy?* Rather than offering a univocal explanation of the liturgy, one which could readily delimit the imagination if not the interpretive abilities of the participants, he suggests that it is out of their experience of the rites that he intends to draw his reflection. Such an approach simply underscores what was mentioned earlier: the liturgical actions which constitute the sacramental celebration—as symbolic actions—cannot be reduced to a single meaning. They yield a "surplus" though not an "anarchy" of meaning, one which is shaped by the scriptural readings, the feast or season, and the liturgical texts. Cyril continues:

> You were conducted by hand to the holy pool of sacred baptism just as Christ was conveyed from the cross to the sepulchre close at hand. Each person was asked if he or she believed in the name of the Father and of the Son and of the Holy Spirit. You made the confession that brings salvation and

> submerged yourselves three times in the water and emerged: by this symbolic gesture you were secretly reenacting the burial of Christ three days in the tomb. For just as our Savior spent three days and nights in the hollow bosom of the earth, so you upon first emerging were representing Christ's first day in the earth and by your immersion his first night. For at night one can no longer see but during the day one has light; so you saw nothing when immersed as if it were night, but you emerged as if to the light of day. In one and the same action you died and were born; the water of salvation became both tomb and mother for you. What Solomon said is opposite to you. On that occasion he said: "There is a time to be born and a time to die," but the opposite is true in your case: there is a time to die and a time to be born. A single moment achieves both ends and your begetting was simultaneous with your death.[27]

In this section of his homily, Cyril speaks of the liturgical action itself. Note that his preaching seems more poetic than prosaic, more parabolic than literal in order to communicate the depth of meaning in the gestures and words of the ritual. Thus *he recommends to the contemporary preacher the language of imagery and metaphor since they are the vehicles, the tools, the 'lures' through which the imagination of the listener is engaged and enlarged, illuminated and vivified.* Furthermore, he uses a narrative style to rehearse, to tell the enacted story of initiation, a style through which he weaves the biblical stories—not as proof texts—but as images that cluster around a particular liturgical action. Through this method he can speak of the act of physical immersion as a natural drowning, burial in a tomb, resting in the earth's bosom, a form of blindness, the cross of death and the fecund womb from which new life comes forth. Now we might ask, has he gone overboard with too many images? Is the symbolic "surplus" too great? At first it may seem so. Yet Cyril recognizes not only the many meanings, the multi-valency, of the symbolic action but also the varied conditions and experiences of his listeners which will lead them to identify with one or more of the images. Consequently, the various images which are present in the scriptures and biblically-inspired liturgical texts that accompany the action offer the preacher a range of interpretive keys.

At the same time, Cyril has not ignored the place of baptism nor the feast. Concerning the place, he speaks of the candidates being conducted to the "holy pool" as Christ was brought to the tomb after his death. He is able to speak of the baptismal font as a pool because in his time it was spacious enough to hold a number of adults. Indeed, from the descriptions of baptism in the early Church, we know that candidates were stripped naked and lead into the font by deaconesses and deacons. The purpose of this chapter is not to promote the same practice today. It is to suggest, however, that when preachers witness a perfunctory celebration of the liturgy they must inevitably recognize the inherent contradiction between the words proclaimed (e.g., "you have been buried, drowned, immersed in Christ") and any minimalist action performed. Which action better accords with the words proclaimed: a quick sprinkling from a birdbath or copious use of water in a baptismal pool?

Neither does the time of the liturgy escape Cyril's attention. The vigil, celebrated in the darkness of night, becomes a metaphor through which he can speak of the spiritual event taking place: the illumination of the candidates, through the power of grace, in the midst of darkness. You emerged from the dark waters of the pool, he says, as if to the light of day. In this preaching on action, place, and time, *Cyril offers the contemporary preacher a model for drawing on the human senses of sight, sound, smell, touch, and taste in proclaiming the present activity of God mediated through human, symbolic actions.* In this he uses the ordinary actions of the external rite (bathing, anointing, clothing, handlaying, eating and drinking, light and darkness) in order to reveal the deeper structure of spiritual meaning, the action of grace.[28]

IV. The Social Implications of Mystagogical Preaching

While the one who preaches the liturgical actions is, in fact, discerning the movement of grace in the ritual forms of the sacraments, the preacher is also able to speak of these actions as paradigms of grace present in the daily forms of Christian experience.[29] The liturgical actions also have pedagogical effect: the kiss of peace, for instance, does not symbolize the use of violence against our neighbors, rather it "teaches" one the act of forgiveness. The liturgical actions, therefore, can serve as models of Christian activity in the public order. In one of his sermons on baptism, Augustine speaks of this correlation between Christian initiation at the Easter Vigil and Christian witness in the world:

> This day is a symbol of perpetual joy for us, for the life which this day signifies will not pass away as this day is going to pass away. And so I urge and entreat you to direct your entire reason for being Christians and for carrying his name on your forehead and in your heart solely so that life which we are destined to enjoy with the angels, where there is perpetual peace, everlasting happiness, unfailing blessedness, with no anxiety, no sad-

> ness, no death. In the meantime, until we come to that rest, let us work well in this time when we are laboring and are in darkness as long as we see not what we hope for and as long as we are making our way through the desert until we arrive at that heavenly Jerusalem as at the land of promise overflowing with milk and honey. Therefore, since temptations do not cease, let us work well. Let medicine be always at hand, as though kept near to be applied to our daily wounds. Moreover, there is a healing power in good works of mercy. For, if you wish to obtain the mercy of God, be merciful.[30]

First, Augustine speaks of the day (Easter) and one of the ritual actions (anointing the forehead). The liturgical actions orient one, as it were, toward the future, toward that time when anxiety, sadness, and death will have no power over human life. They have a marked eschatological character. But, he says clearly, that time is not present yet. One has not been baptized with the promise of experiencing the fullness of the resurrection on Easter Monday. Rather, the baptized continue their journey through the font and at the table of the Lord—in this world—until that time when they reach the land of promise. And it is while they live in this world that the moral implications of Christian baptism can become visible and effective in their lives. Augustine speaks of the baptismal mandate to "work well in this time," to let "medicine be always at hand," to mediate the healing power of the sacrament in "good works of mercy." Thus he notes the social dimension of the liturgical actions.

Such homiletical reflection, moreover, can be extended to the entire ensemble of liturgical actions, in this case the baptismal liturgy. One has renounced evil and professed faith so that one might continue to resist the forces of evil and practice faith in the world. One has died to sin and been raised to life in the baptismal waters in order to die (following Paul's remarks in Galatians 3) to racism, sexism, and elitism. One has been anointed with the oil of the olive tree so that one might spread the "fragrant odor of Christ" through good works. One has received the kiss of peace in the eucharist in order that one might promote peace through common acts of forgiveness. And one has tasted the "mercy of God" in bread and wine so that one might generously offer such mercy in concrete acts of assistance to the poor and the hungry.

Preaching on the moral and social implications of the liturgical actions invites the contemporary preacher at least to ask the question: *In what ways do the liturgical actions continue to shape and inspire the social mission of the Christian community?* When we recall the examples of Jesus and Paul as mentioned above, it becomes apparent that the followers of Jesus are to confirm with their everyday words and deeds those ritual words and actions which have initiated them into the community of believers. Far from promoting private, individualistic, and minimalist interpretations of the Church's liturgy, mystagogical preaching pushes through the personal and ecclesial meanings to the social and cultural implications and thus provides the baptized with concrete examples of what their baptismal identity and mission might look like in daily life. In this, the mystagogical preacher is attempting to offer a "maximalist" interpretation of the liturgical actions through the readings, the feast, and the contemporary situation of the assembly gathered for worship.

V. Conclusion

We have suggested that the publication and pastoral implementation of the *Rite of Christian Initiation of Adults* has reintroduced into the vocabulary of contemporary preaching the practice of *mystagogia*, a model of preaching which takes as its "text" the experience of the liturgical actions that constitute sacramental celebrations. While much of our discussion has focused on Christian initiation, one can readily use this form of preaching in other liturgical celebrations: the Sunday eucharist, communal anointing of the sick, reconciliation, funerals, morning and evening prayer.

We continued our treatment of mystagogical preaching by suggesting that it is appropriate for preachers and the worshipping assembly to ponder the meaning of the liturgical actions they perform since they are the ritual words and gestures which symbolize the presence of grace in the gathered assembly, grace as a personal, ecclesial, and social presence in human life and history. Furthermore, it was suggested that the readings and the liturgical feasts and seasons offer interpretive keys for the preacher. They shape and inspire the preacher's reflection on "the mysteries" celebrated. For instance, the Sunday readings during Eastertime narrate the appearance of the risen Christ to his followers, a visitation which many times begins with the greeting, "Peace be with you." Would it not be appropriate for the preacher to reflect on the meaning of the exchange of peace within the liturgy, since the liturgical text which introduces the gesture springs from the gospel of the day? Likewise, would it not be appropriate for one to preach the various actions of the eucharistic rite when on four consecutive Sundays during the summer (that time of the ripening of the harvest), the readings from Cycle B are drawn from the "bread of life" discourse in John's Gospel? When taken together, the readings, the season, and the liturgy itself offer a certain cohesiveness which the preacher can employ.

Finally, we suggested that mystagogical preaching is not an exercise in "explaining" the liturgy, as if the liturgical actions have one meaning for all times and places, but a form of preaching on the multi-faceted presence of grace in the life of the individual and the community. This presence is symbolized in the liturgical actions of the assembly and brought to greater consciousness through preaching. Furthermore, we noted that these actions have both pedagogical and social effects. They can teach the assembly Christian patterns of acting and speaking in daily life.

In summary then, let us note some of the factors which may lead preachers to a contemporary practice of mystagogy.

1. Mystagogy presumes the liturgical rites are celebrated in their fullness in a communal setting. Minimalist and perfunctory celebrations yield a narrowed perception of the symbolic power of the rites and consequently diminish the preacher's ability to speak persuasively of their significance.

2. The mystagogical preacher trusts the assembly's experience of the liturgical celebration and draws on this experience of the rites in preaching.

3. The preacher does not rely so much on a systematic and prosaic analysis as the weaving of scriptural imagery, metaphor, and story with the liturgical actions. The preacher's purpose is to evoke rather than define, to illuminate rather than justify.

4. Mystagogical preaching may offer more questions than give answers. Thus the preacher may simply ask the assembly, to what actions in our daily lives is this particular liturgical action inviting us?

5. While baptismal mystagogy takes place primarily within the Easter season, preaching on the liturgical actions may occur whenever the readings, the feast or season, and the needs of the assembly invite such reflection.

6. Since the liturgy is a communal activity, the mystagogical preacher appropriately leads the assembly to recognize the corporate character of its witness in the world, that witness shaped and inspired by the common actions celebrated in the liturgy.

7. The mystagogical preacher remembers that there is, in truth, only one mystagogue: the Spirit. The preacher points, invites, challenges, questions and then steps back because it is the Spirit who is silently moving the assembly through its common work, the liturgy.

To his assembly of believers, John Chrysostom once said, "Imitate Christ . . . and you will be called neophytes (newly-baptized) not only two, three, ten or twenty days, but you will still merit this name after ten, twenty or thirty years, and in fact for all your lives."[31] For the preacher who engages in mystagogia, the genetic configuration of Christian identity is profoundly baptismal. The challenge and delight of such preaching is witnessing to this baptismal memory which is continually proclaimed and enacted through the liturgical rites so that the assembly might bear this paradoxical configuration—the paschal mystery—in the rhythms and movements of its life in the world.

Notes

1. The provisional text of the *Ordo initiationis christianae adultorum* was published in 1974 in the United States as the *Rite of Christian Initiation of Adults* (RCIA). It was received enthusiastically by many parochial and diocesan directors of liturgy and religious education. In 1987, the Roman Congregation for Divine Worship approved the revision and new translation of the RCIA by the International Commission on English in the Liturgy. In 1988, the National Conference of Catholic Bishops mandated the use of the RCIA for all adults or children of catechetical age.

2. See the collection of essays in Robert Duggan, ed., *Conversion and the Catechumenate* (New York: Paulist Press, 1984). On the communal and ecclesiological aspects of the RCIA, see Aidan Kavanagh, *The Shape of Baptism: The Rite of Christian Initiation. Studies in the Reformed Rites of the Catholic Church,* vol. 1 (New York: Pueblo Publishing Company, 1978) 102–149.

3. The RCIA speaks of these various groups as i) "inquirers," (those interested in the faith), ii) "catechumens," "candidates," the "elect," (those being formed or re-formed in the faith), and iii) "neophytes" (the newly-baptized).

4. In this regard, one might speak of all baptized Christians as "catechumens" in the sense that formation in faith is a life-long task. For that matter, one could argue that all the baptized are "neophytes" in that the experience of "enlightenment" is not restricted to those who have only recently received the sacraments of initiation.

5. Regarding ongoing formation in faith from a liturgical perspective, see William Reiser, *Renewing the Baptismal Promises: Their Meaning for Christian Life* (New York: Pueblo Publishing Company, 1988) 1–19.

6. While the major Christian communions have revised their baptismal rites so that one can discern a common pattern among them, no ecumenical theology of Christian initiation based upon these rites has yet emerged. "The need to recover baptismal unity is at the heart of the ecumenical task as it is central for the realization of genuine partnership within the Christian communities," *Baptism, Eucharist and Ministry,* Faith and Order Paper No. 111 (Geneva: World Council of Churches, 1982) 3.

7. *Rite of Christian Initiation of Adults* (=RCIA), Study Edition (Collegeville, The Liturgical Press, 1988) 152.

8. "The sacraments are outward and visible signs of inward and spiritual grace, given by Christ as sure and certain means by which we receive that grace," *The Book of Common Prayer . . . According to the use of The Episcopal Church* (New York: The Church Hymnal Corporation and The Seabury Press, 1977) 857; " 'When the Word is joined to the element

or natural substance, the outcome is a sacrament,' that is, a holy, divine thing and sign," Martin Luther, *The Large Catechism* as quoted in F. Samuel Janzow, *Getting into Luther's Large Catechism* (St. Louis: Concordia Publishing House, 1978) 116; "A sacrament is a sacred sign by which we worship God, his love is revealed to us and his saving work accomplished in us. In the sacraments God shows us what he does and does what he shows us," Herbert McCabe, *The Teaching of the Catholic Church: A New Catechism of Christian Doctrine* (London: Catholic Truth Society, 1985) 15.

9. See Regis Duffy, *Real Presence: Worship, Sacraments, and Commitment* (San Francisco: Harper & Row, 1982) 32–57; Joseph Martos, *The Catholic Sacraments*, vol. 1, *Message of the Sacraments* (Wilmington: Michael Glazier, 1983) 49–85, 183–208; Kenan Osborne, *Sacramental Theology* (New York: Paulist Press, 1988) 86–99, 119–138. Concerning the social dimensions of sacramental celebrations see Christopher Kiesling, "Paradigms of Sacramentality," *Worship* 44:7 (September 1970) 422–432.

10. A liturgical example would be the recitation of the biblical images in the Blessing of the Water: creation, the flood, the Red Sea, the Jordan, the cross, and the dominical mandate to baptize (RCIA 130–131). The image contained within each story offers an interpretation of the salvific activity being accomplished in the contemporary celebration of baptism. "The sacraments carry on in our midst the 'mirabilia,' the great works of God in the Old Testament and the New: for example, the Flood, the Passion and Baptism show us the same divine activity as carried out in three different eras of sacred history," Jean Danielou, *The Bible and the Liturgy* (Notre Dame: University of Notre Dame Press, 1956) 5.

11. On this early Christian perception, Aidan Kavanagh notes that "the liturgy was seen not as a matter of exquisite ecclesiastical ceremonies to occupy clergy and religious but as the way a Christian people live in common. Whatever such a people did as a people was liturgical, an act of corporate worship of God . . . And the whole [act]consummated the Church's mission, a mission perceived above all else to be the corporate living presence of God's tough but graceful pleasure in Jesus Christ for the world," *The Shape of Baptism,* 118. As Cyril of Jerusalem was wont to say, "Seeing is far more persuasive than hearing," *Mystagogical Catechesis* I, 1.

12. See the study by Thomas Talley, *The Origins of the Liturgical Year* (New York: Pueblo Publishing Company, 1986), in which he sets forth in remarkable detail the relationship between the biblical stories as "anchors" for the development of the liturgical year and those rites which enacted the particular biblical stories in ever new Christian communities.

13. See the collection of brief essays in "Central Symbols," *Liturgy* 7:1 (Summer 1987), in particular the article by Gordon Lathrop, "How Symbols Speak: Cosmos, Dream, Word," 9–13.

14. "The Sunday liturgy is not the Church assembled to address itself. The liturgy thus does not cater to the assembly. It summons the assembly to enact itself publicly for the life of the world. . . . The liturgy presumes that the world is always present in the summoned assembly, which although not of 'this world' lives deep in its midst as the corporate agent, under God in Christ, of its salvation," Aidan Kavanagh, *Elements of Rite: A Handbook of Liturgical Style* (New York: Pueblo Publishing Company, 1982) 45–46.

15. "God does not need liturgy; people do, and people have only their own arts and styles of expression with which to celebrate. Like the covenant itself, the liturgical celebrations of the faith community (Church) involve the whole person. They are not purely religious or merely rational or intellectual exercises, but also human experiences calling on all human faculties: body, mind, senses, imagination, emotions, memory," *Environment and Art in Catholic Worship,* Bishops' Committee on the Liturgy, ed. (Washington: United States Catholic Conference, 1978) 8.

16. Robert Browning and Roy Reed, "The Importance of Religious Rites and Sacraments, in the Stages of Human and Faith Development," in their *The Sacraments in Religious Education and Liturgy* (Birmingham: Religious Education Press, 1985) 83–116.
17. RCIA, 152.
18. Ibid.
19. Note the inclusion of the footwashing in the liturgy of Holy Thursday. On footwashing as a 'dominical sacrament' see Browning and Reed, "The Question of New Sacraments and the Sacrament of Footwashing," in *The Sacraments in Religious Education and Liturgy*, 290–300.
20. John 13:14-17.
21. "Not only do the disciples and all Christians share in the fruits of Jesus' lifework, they must also imitate its spirit. . . . It is their duty to practice the humility signified by this act," Bruce Vawter, "The Gospel According to John," in *The Jerome Biblical Commentary*, R. Brown, and J. Fitzmyer, R. Murphy, eds. (Englewood Cliffs: Prentice-Hall, 1968) 451.
22. Romans 6:4.
23. Galatians 3:27.
24. Concerning the social significance of baptism in relationship to social stratification in Pauline communities, see Wayne Meeks, *The First Urban Christians: The Social World of the Apostle Paul* (New Haven: Yale University Press, 1983) 150–157.
25. Ambrose of Milan, *The Mysteries and the Sacraments, Fathers of the Church* 44 (Washington: Catholic University of America Press, 1963); Cyril of Jerusalem, *Procatechesis and Catechesis* and *The Works of Saint Cyril of Jerusalem, Fathers of the Church* 61, and 64 (Washington: Catholic University of America Press, 1963, 1970); John Chrysostom, *Baptismal Instructions, Ancient Christian Writers* 31 (Westminster: Newman Press, 1963); Theodore of Mopsuestia, *Homélies Catéchétiques, Testi et Studi* 145 (Vatican City, 1949).
26. *Mystagogical Catechesis* I, 1.
27. *Mystagogical Catechesis* II, 4.
28. See the comprehensive study of patristic mystagogical preaching at the Easter Vigil by Hugh Riley, *Christian Initiation: A Comparative Study of the Interpretation of the Baptismal Liturgy in the Mystagogical Writings of Cyril of Jerusalem, John Chrysostom, Theodore of Mopsuestia, and Ambrose of Milan* (Washington: Catholic University of America Press, 1974). Likewise note the articles on contemporary mystagogical preaching by Jeffrey Baerwald, "Mystagogy: Structure, Content, Task," *Chicago Catechumenate* 8:4 (May 1986): 4–15; Agnes Cunningham, "Patristic Catechesis for Baptism: A Pedagogy for Christian Living," and Ron Lewinski, "Recovering Christian Mystagogy for Contemporary Churches," in *Before and After Baptism: The Work of Teachers and Catechists*, James Wilde, ed. (Chicago: Liturgy Training Publications, 1988) 15–25, 81–95.
29. The ritual form of the sacrament: eating and drinking the bread and wine of the eucharist—the daily form of Christian experience: the domestic meal, feeding the hungry.
30. Augustine of Hippo, "Baptism," in Adalbert Hamman, *Baptism: Ancient Liturgies and Patristic Texts* (New York: Alba House, 1967) 216.
31. *Baptismal Instruction* V, 20.

Chapter 5

The Spiritual Exegesis of Scripture and Contemporary Preaching: Claiming Sacred History as Our Own

RONALD JOHN ZAWILLA

The history of preaching and the history of biblical exegesis necessarily go hand-in-hand.[1] The Christian imperative to preach contains the challenge to convey the age-old message of the Gospel to people of the present age. The ancient exegetes and homilists show us a way to claim sacred history as our own and to bridge the gap between theory and praxis.

To introduce the topic, a quote from a contemporary exegete's review of the translation of a medieval exegete's commentary on John is helpful:

> As a medieval exegete, Thomas made much of the "spiritual" sense. This spiritual sense—as the *sensus plenior* or "fuller sense"—found a new lease on life some decades back; for a while I viewed it with some favor. It is no longer in vogue—and rightly so. God has spoken in *human* words and we must respect the human conditioning of scripture. Recourse, in our day, to "spiritual" exegesis would be a betrayal of our hard-won understanding of the *message* of the biblical writers.[2]

Referring to the *sensus plenior* and its new lease on life, the author, though he does not specify, probably has in mind a number of works produced in the 40s and 50s.[3] Most notable among these is Henri de Lubac's four-volume *L'exégése médiévale* which meticulously traces the notion of the *sensus plenior* through virtually every Christian writer from antiquity through the Middle Ages. In his preface, de Lubac identifies his aims, desiring, he says, to recapture the unity that once existed between the study of the Bible and spirituality which went their separate ways after the seventeenth century.[4] Prior to the twelfth century, when dialectic was introduced into theological study, theology and spirituality were synonymous with biblical study. The monks, Bernard of Clairvaux at least, were convinced that such study could be done fruitfully only in a monastery.[5] Such was the unity of exegesis, theology, and spirituality.

De Lubac makes two demands of his readers. First, he asks us to banish the notion of the "naiveté" of the Middle Ages; second, he asks us not to view all past approaches in terms of our own. De Lubac's example is the tendency to approach the twelfth century merely as the prelude to the thirteenth.[6] As recent research has shown in the case of eucharistic theology, the assumption that twelfth-century theologians were groping clumsily toward a definition of transubstantiation seriously distorts the issues and terms of the twelfth-century debate.[7] The same, de Lubac, suggests, would be true of medieval and patristic exegetes and preachers. If we make our current values the sole criteria of judgment we shall necessarily conclude that exegetes and preachers of the past were somehow groping in the dark with issues resolved only in our own day by the light of the historical-critical method.

Something of this attitude is revealed in Harrington's review which was quoted at the beginning of this chapter. Toward the end of the review, we read:

> I recall how, repeatedly, throughout my theological studies, especially in Rome, I had been assured that in Aquinas's writings we find the answers to the problems of all time. Even then I could see that there was something odd in the assumption that a thirteenth-century theologian was adequate for the twentieth-century. Had theology stopped short in the Middle Ages? I regret, then, the final sentence of Fr. Weisheipl's Introduction: "For our guide [in the study of John] we can have none better than the Angelic Doctor whom Jesus loved." The *pietas* is, perhaps, understandable. But I, also a brother of Friar Thomas, find many more penetrating insights in the classic commentary of Rudolf Bultmann.[8]

Harrington presents us with a dilemma. While some might share Weisheipl's view, many more would agree with Harrington that neither "thomism," nor any "-ism," has the answer to all our problems. Must we necessarily choose between Thomas Aquinas and Rudolf Bultmann?

Can we, in our preaching of the Gospel today, be true both to contemporary, scientific exegesis and to the insights of the tradition? The issue is a pressing one because, without wishing to be unfair to exegetes, one often perceives a disparagement of everything that precedes modern, scientific exegesis. And to the extent that this is so, there results a sense of alienation. How are we to evaluate patristic and medieval theology much, if not all, of which is based on "faulty" exegesis? How are we to celebrate the liturgy the language of which is filled with typological references? And how are we to preach when typology has dictated the choice of pericopes in the lectionary?[9] It is perhaps too much to be hoped to resolve these questions in the few pages of a chapter, but let us explore briefly the traditional understanding of typology, the four senses, and the theology that underlies them, pointing in the direction of some sort of resolution.

The Spiritual Sense of Scripture

In his *De doctrina christiana* Saint Augustine provided a handbook for the study of scripture and for preaching that was to have profound influence on the medieval West. In this little work he is particularly concerned with the interpretation of difficult passages. According to Augustine:

> [But] the ambiguities of figurative words, which are now to be treated, require no little care and industry. For at the outset you must be very careful lest you take figurative expressions literally. What the Apostle says pertains to this problem: "For the letter killeth, but the spirit quickeneth." That is, when that which is said figuratively is taken as though it were literal, it is understood carnally. Nor can anything more appropriately be called the death of the soul than that condition in which the thing which distinguishes us from the beasts, which is the understanding, is subjected to the flesh in the pursuit of the letter. He who follows the letter takes figurative expressions as though they were literal and does not refer the things signified to anything else. For example, if he hears of the Sabbath, he thinks only of one day out of the seven that are repeated in continuous cycle; if he hears of Sacrifice, his thoughts do not go beyond the customary victims of the flocks and fruits of the earth. There is a miserable servitude of the spirit in this habit of taking signs for things, so that one is not able to raise the eye of the mind above things that are corporal and created to drink in eternal light.[10]

For the purposes of a brief sketch, Augustine's use of 2 Corinthians 3:6 gets to the heart of the matter. Augustine interprets Paul through his own Neo-Platonic worldview according to which things corporeal are taken to be signs of spiritual realities ("things" in the translation cited), which are, in turn, reducible to One, God. Just as body and soul are separate, the soul using the body as an instrument, so the "spirit" uses the "letter" in scripture. Thus, for Augustine, the exegete's task is the discovery of the spiritual message signified in the words of scripture.

There is a lot behind Augustine's statement. First, gentile Christians had some of the same difficulties with the Hebrew scriptures that their pagan contemporaries had with their own mythological writings. Augustine, for example, had great difficulty reconciling the loving God preached by Jesus with the God of the Hebrews, whose recorded actions Augustine sometimes viewed as jealous and vindictive. He wondered how to explain God's apparent toleration of polygamy in the case of David, or incest in the case of Lot, to pagan contemporaries who found such behavior repulsive. Augustine used the same approach as his pagan contemporaries, presuming a deeper, spiritual message.

This implies something that needs to be stated explicitly. Although ancient and medieval writers considered God the author of scripture, and although artists expressed this conviction by showing a dove whispering into the ear of the human writer (both scriptural and ecclesiastical, it should be noted), theirs was not a naive understanding of revelation. They would not have formulated a theology of revelation in the terms used by contemporary fundamentalists, even though they would have accepted the literal truth of creation in seven days, the historicity of Adam and Eve, Job, Daniel, and others we recognize today as mythological or fictitious. Indeed, by the mere fact that they worked from manuscript copies of scripture, they were acutely aware of the fact that God did not "dictate" the literal text, or else they would have had to attribute to God the lacunae, grammatical errors, and impossible syntax which they knew were due to scribal errors, faulty translation, or, in some cases, to the fallibility of the original authors (e.g., some of the New Testament writers for whom Greek may have been at best a second language). And even though many ancient and medieval writers were unfamiliar with, or not well versed in, either Greek or Hebrew (such as Augustine), they were well aware of the discrepancies among various translations and the differing worldviews signified in distinct languages. Augustine, for example, speaks of the importance of knowing the biblical languages (though he himself did not) and of knowing as well the geography, flora and fauna, history and culture of Palestine.

But more important than the difficulties of interpreting the sacred text was Augustine's conviction that the same Spirit who inspired the authors of Scripture also inspires the Church and, indeed, all Christians who read the scriptures in the Church. Moreover, what we today distinguish as biblical studies, dogmatic theology, and spirituality in antiquity and the Middle Ages constituted one discipline that Augustine would simply call wisdom. At once practical and theoretical, this wisdom was simply the quest for God that moved in stages, first approaching faith through the use of human reason, then in the light of faith, exploring the mysteries of faith with human reason, and coming finally to a loving union with God through the contemplation of the mysteries. By reading the scriptures in this way, not as an isolated individual, but in the Church, always mindful of its liturgy and tradition, one arrives at the "spiritual" meaning of scripture. Only with the "scholastics" of the twelfth-century schools was the tendency begun to distinguish, at least hypothetically, the academic study of theology from its practice.

Herein lies part of the problem alluded to at the beginning. For us theory and praxis are two distinct realities; theory, to be scientific, must be as objective as possible, free of the subjective and the personal. The exegesis of patristic and medieval writers often strikes us as both subjective and personal. And it was! But even here there was a theoretical basis.

The Theology of the Word

According to Augustine, there is a simple principle that both leads to and safeguards the integrity of the "spiritual" sense of scripture. It stems from Jesus' summary of the whole law and prophets in the command to love God and neighbor. All of scripture, then, is reducible to this message; if this is not the message you have read when you take up any scripture passage, says Augustine, you have misread the text.[11] This conviction summarizes the rules Augustine gives that, first of all, for the Christian the Old Testament is to be interpreted in light of the New, and, secondly, that obscure passages are to be interpreted with the help of clearer ones. To put it another way, because all scripture is inspired by God through the Logos, every passage of scripture somehow contains the kernel of the gospel.

Behind this lies a theology that sees God equally present to both the inspired writer and the interpreter, as well as in human reason and in nature and history. By one and the same Word, God created and ordered the cosmos, spoke to the patriarchs and prophets, became incarnate in Jesus of Nazareth, and guides the Church through the Holy Spirit. Subjective, personal, and even fanciful, though some patristic and medieval exegesis may at times appear to be, there is still to be noted a striking unanimity on the "spiritual" meaning of scripture that these ancient and medieval writers would account for in terms of this theology of the word (notwithstanding the tendency to repeat the thought of revered predecessors). Moreover, the ancient writers themselves were quick to dismiss, or even label as heretical, more fanciful interpretations such as those of Abbot Joachim of Fiore.[12]

This theology of the word was beautifully formulated in the twelfth century by Hugh of St.-Victor in a little work called *De verbo Dei*. At the very beginning of the treatise, Hugh sets out this theology of the word:

> "God has spoken but once" (Ps 61:12), since God begot one Word through which God made everything. This Word is God's utterance. . . .It must be recognized that God speaks one way through human mouths, another in God's own self. For the scriptures of the Old and New Testaments attest that God does speak to humans through humans. God speaks, therefore, through humans, God speaks through God's own self; many utterances through humans, one sole utterance through God's own self. But whatever God proffered through human mouths, this one [Word] was in them all, and all of them are one in this one [Word], without which none [of the others] could have been uttered in whatever time or place. Let us see, therefore, a great sacrament.[13]

In the divine economy every word of scripture contains, and therefore, speaks of, Christ. The scriptures are an incarnation, as Hugh goes on to elaborate: "The Word of God clothed in human flesh appeared visibly once, and now this very same [Word] comes to us daily under the cover of the human voice."[14] Hugh's language and expressions echo the language and expressions of eucharistic theology. And the echo is quite intentional. Encounter with the word of God was, for medieval theologians, a sacramental encounter rooted in their experience of the liturgy.

This distinction between human words and the word of God, or Augustine's statement that every passage of scripture proclaims the love of God, is the theoretical basis of a "spiritual" sense of scripture. But let us look more closely at the terminology and methodology employed by the patristic and medieval writers. Ecclesiastical writers speak either of two senses, the literal and the spiritual; or of four, the literal, the allegorical, the tropological, and the anagogical. The spiritual sense is a generic term; allegorical, tropological, and anagogical are its subdivisions. Another blanket term for the spiritual sense is typology. Sometimes, too, all three of the spiritual senses are included in the term allegorical.[15]

Something must be said about the relationship between allegory and typology. Allegory is the method used by hellenistic writers for the interpretation of Homer and other mythological literature. Strictly speaking, in allegory, persons and events stand for abstract ideas. By contrast, Christian interpretation of scripture is not, strictly speaking, allegorical but typological, since one concrete event or person is taken for another concrete event or person. That is to say Christians see in scripture a pattern of promise and fulfillment that extends from past to present and present to future. Both ancient and medieval Christian writers tended to use the terms allegory, type, and figure somewhat interchangeably. Moreover, in actual practice allegory and type tend to overlap. But all authors agree that Christian interpretation of scripture must, first of all, be related to the literal meaning of the text, and Thomas Aquinas emphasized that the metaphors, parables, and literary figures found in scripture belong to the literal sense.[16] Christians, after all, accepted the historicity of most, if not all, that the Bible recounts, even when they interpreted its contents in a spiritual sense. Secondly, Christ, or faith in Christ, is the hermeneutic, not philosophical or purely subjective ideas.

Bearing in mind what has been said, let us look briefly at some examples of the three spiritual senses. According to common understanding, the allegorical sense pertains to the faith dimension, the tropological to the moral, and the anagogical to the eschatological. Despite appearances to the contrary, typology is historical in the sense of identifying precedents and patterns in God's activity in history, using these as a basis for future expectation. In lieu of photographic documentation, it should be noted that the themes mentioned here recur again and again in Christian art, from the earliest catacombs through the great medieval cathedrals and later medieval altarpieces and books of hours.

The allegorical sense discovers images or types of Christ and the Church in the text of the Hebrew scriptures. Many of these connections occur already in the text of the New Testament. The figure of the brazen serpent (Nm 21:8), the sign of Jonah three days in the belly of the whale, the sacrificial lamb, the manna in the wilderness, the Temple: all of these are employed already in the Gospels themselves. Paul likens Christ to the desert rock, which gushed water when Moses struck it with his staff (1 Cor 10:4), the paschal lamb (1 Cor 5:7), and sees in Gn 2:24 ("and the two shall become one flesh") the great mystery of Christ and the Church (Eph 5:2). The whole argument of the Letter to the Hebrews rests on the comparison of Christ to Melchisedech, the Gentile priest who offered a sacrifice of bread and wine. Types of the Church include the ark built by Noah, the ark of the covenant, and above all, the city of Jerusalem, which in turn, signifies the Jerusalem that is to come.

The moral sense relates to the Christian life. The sisters Mary and Martha come to mind immediately as examples respectively of the contemplative and active lives. The consummate figure of Christian life is Mary, the Mother of Jesus, who signifies the Church. Medieval writers and preachers in particular liked to use the motherhood of Mary as a figure of the Christian soul in response to the word of God. To cite but one example, the thirteenth-century *Bible moralisée* interprets the story of the nativity in terms of the Christian hearing God's word, conceiving, and bringing forth the Word in Christian love.[17]

Preachers often turned to the Song of Songs, exploring its erotic imagery in terms of the relationship between Christ and the soul. Although such mystical writing began with Origen, the undisputed master is Bernard of Clairvaux. He, along with a number of his twelfth-century Cistercian confrères, excelled in exploring the symbolism of the Virgin and the Song.[18] Medieval illuminators frequently illustrated commentaries on the Song with a man and woman kissing. The man is Christ, the woman, a personification of Church or the individual Christian.

The image of the Deluge, the crossing of the Red Sea, the water-gushing rock, Christ's baptism in the Jordan, the water and blood that flowed from Christ's pierced side, all prefigure Christian initiation. No better example can be found than the homily of John Chrysostom offered in the Roman Breviary for Good Friday, or the anonymous homily of Holy Saturday. Types and figures of the eucharist include the paschal lamb, manna, and the sacrifice of Melchisedech. A very common theme in medieval literature and art, nearly forgotten in modern times, parallels the Virgin nursing the child Jesus and Christ nursing Christians with the blood and water flowing from his pierced heart. It is here that many medieval writers and preachers, especially, although by no means only, female, developed the spirituality of Christ's motherhood.[19]

Frequently the moral and eschatological senses overlap, something which seems particularly apt. Medieval writers and preachers developed a powerful sense of realized eschatology. Mary is perhaps the best example, representing in herself the humanity redeemed by Christ. In this sense, the working out of the doctrines of the immaculate conception and the assumption, reflect the working out of Christian hope for they represent, respectively, the effects of baptism and the hope of resurrection on the last day. At Chartres the north portal of the cathedral recounts the story of the creation and fall, the human ancestors of Christ, the story of Job, and, at the summit of the central portal, the dormition, assumption, and coronation of the Virgin. When medieval Christians contemplated this program, it is hard to imagine that even the most dense did not see in it an expression of their own hope. Preachers frequently drew the parallel between Eve, the mother of all the living, who, with Adam, lost paradise for all her children, and Mary, the new Eve, through whose motherhood paradise is regained for all her children.[20]

One final example is a medieval homiletic device frequently used which is perhaps more metaphoric than typological, but worth mentioning none the less. From the end of the twelfth to the end of the thirteenth century, scholars produced a number of collections of "distinctions" for the use of preachers.[21] These compilations, like dictionaries, listed commonly used scriptural terms, providing an encyclopedic listing of their metaphoric uses. Preachers used them to develop themes for their sermons. From the many examples that could be cited, there is a recently discovered and authenticated sermon of Thomas Aquinas on Luke 14:6 ("A certain man gave a great supper and invited many") for the Second Sunday after Trinity. In this sermon, which is presented in translation at the end of this chapter, Thomas makes use of a "distinction" of several possible meanings of "supper" as the outline of his sermon.[22]

In typical scholastic fashion, which departs from the patristic and monastic homiletic style by being more tightly organized, Thomas divides the text, reserving the second half ("and invited many") for the evening "collatio." To establish the outline for the morning sermon, he divides the text ("A certain man gave a great supper") asking, who is this man, what is the supper he prepared, and why is it called great. The man, of course, is Christ, who is able to provide satisfying spiritual nourishment to humanity because he combines in himself the fullness of humanity and the plenitude of divine grace.

As Thomas sees it, and it is here that he makes use of the distinction, Christ provides humanity with a threefold supper: the sacrament of the eucharist, the refreshment of the intellect, and the complete satisfaction of the heart. In the exploration of these three suppers, Thomas uses a play on words to establish a typological framework. The Vulgate text uses the word *cena*, which was understood to be the principal meal of the day, the evening meal. The *cena* is complemented by the *prandium*—a light meal, or lunch. This distinction enables Thomas to compare and contrast the three *cenae* of Christ with their Old Testament types. If the image that has come down to us of Thomas as a corpulent friar who could enjoy a good meal is true, the culinary imagery in this sermon would argue for its authenticity. In each of the three divisions Thomas explores what constitutes lavish preparation and sensory delight in serving up a satisfying meal and uses these images to convey the spiritual delights of Christ's *cenae*.

For the first, or sacramental supper, Thomas compares and contrasts the Old Testament sacrifice of calves and oxen with the last supper at which Christ gave his flesh and blood for food and drink. The scriptural images Thomas recalls include the manna with which God nourished the Hebrews, texts from Psalms and Wisdom that refer to the sweetness of this "bread from heaven," and, alluding to the real presence, he cites Deuteronomy 4:7: "For what great nation is there that has gods so near to it as our God is to us?" Other images are the table referred to in Psalm 22 and the hearthcake and water God provided for Elias (1 Kgs 19:6): "eating and drinking, he arose and walked, strengthened by this food, forty days and nights to the mountain of God, Horeb."

Christ, who is truth itself, satisfies fully the intellect. This second supper, recapitulated in the divine wisdom of sacred scripture, is contrasted with the wisdom of the Greeks. Philosophy, human reasoning, can lead only so far, but Wisdom, another type of Christ, mixes her wine, sets her table, and beckons, "Come and eat my bread and drink the wine I have mixed for you" (Prv 9:2). The Christian nourished by sacred scripture exclaims with the Psalmist (Ps 118:103): "How sweet are your words to my taste, sweeter than honey to my tongue."

The third supper pertains to the heart, to love, which is evoked with the image of the lover beckoning in the Song of Songs (5:1): "Eat, O friends, and drink, and be inebriated." The state of drunkenness is one frequently used to evoke the overwhelming of the senses by the power of divine love. In this third division Thomas moves not from past to present, but from present to future. The repast of grace in the present, is compared with the wedding feast of the Lamb (Rev 19:9). The embrace of divine love is the ultimate fulfillment of the divine promise: "blessed are the poor in spirit, for they shall see God."

Typology and Contemporary Preaching

To engage the spiritual imagination in reading of the Bible is not an exercise in purely personal and subjective fancy, but is a way to claim biblical history as our own. Spiritual exegesis, properly understood, is historical. But history is more than the establishment of facts and chronology; beyond the objective data there is the question of meaning. For Christians, as for our Jewish brothers and sisters, history is a remembering of God's gracious activity in time on our behalf, which serves to disclose God's activity in the present moment and to provide a basis for hope.

In the liturgy we praise God by remembering God's saving action in the past in order to see the Lord's action in the present, and to express our hope for the future. Preaching, especially in liturgical and sacramental contexts, ought to do the same. In liturgy and in preaching we claim biblical history as our own. The story of Israel, the stories of Jesus, become our story.

Two things safeguard the integrity of the spiritual exegesis from descending to the level of purely personal and subjective speculation or individualistic and saccharine piety. First, spiritual exegesis must be rooted in the literal exegesis of the text. All the patristic and medieval commentators agree on this principle (even if they occasionally violate it in practice!). To establish the literal sense of the text, the intended message of the author, the historical-critical method is an essential and valuable tool. Secondly, spiritual exegesis is a communal exercise. It forms a common stream with the Church's liturgy and spiritual tradition, and it is this communal dimension that preserves a degree of objectivity, or even better, universality. Contemporary knowledge and study of depth psychology, archetypes, and symbol, invite, and even compel us, as preachers to reacquaint ourselves with the great preachers and exegetes of our Christian tradition. The historical-critical method must be there to keep us honest and to provide insights into the text that our forebears never dreamed of. But to paraphrase medieval thinkers, this is merely the prolegomena to a discovery of the meaning of the text for ourselves and those to whom we preach. For it is the preacher, above all, who imitating Christ, prepares and serves up the rich feast of the Lord's supper to those called to the feast.

THOMAS AQUINAS (+1274)
SERMON FOR THE SECOND SUNDAY AFTER TRINITY
"A certain man gave a great supper and invited many" (Lk 14, 16)[1]

There appears to be this difference between spiritual and corporeal delights, that while corporeal delights are obvious to the sensual person and spiritual delights are not, to the spiritual person they are obvious.[2] Hence in Revelation 2:17: "To the one who conquers I will give some of the hidden manna."[3] Since this sermon is about our spiritual refreshment, let us implore the giver of joy to provide me with something praiseworthy to say . . . .

"A certain man once gave a great supper . . . ." Just as the body cannot be sustained without bodily nourishment, so also the soul needs spiritual refreshment for its sustenance. Concerning this spiritual refreshment Psalm (22:2) says : "The Lord leads me over still waters and restores my soul." Significantly it says "over still waters," for just as a loss of natural body heat demands bodily refreshment, so too the soul needs spiritual refreshment on account of the noxious heat of concupiscence that impedes the salvation of our souls. A spiritual water is needed to diminish this heat. Now water cools but does not nourish;[4] spiritual water both nourishes and cools. About this water it is written in John 4:13-14: "the water that I shall give will become a spring of water welling up to eternal life."

In today's gospel the Lord proposes an image of this spiritual refreshment; and two things stand out: first the preparation of this refreshment, in "a certain man gave a great supper"; and, secondly, the notice of this banquet, in "and invited many."[5]

There are three things to consider about the first: Who is this man who gave the supper? Secondly, what is it? And thirdly, how is it great?

Who is this man? He is the Son of God, who is truly human through the truth of his assumed nature, as the Apostle says to the Philippians (2:6-7): "Though he was in the form of God, Jesus did not deem equality with God something to be grasped at, but emptied himself, taking the form of a servant, being born in the likeness of us all." And Jeremiah (cf.17:9): "He is a man and who shall know him?"[6]

The text says "a certain man" as if to say: special things were in him that were not in others, because of which he is a distinguished man, for he possesses the fullness of divinity, the fullness of truth, and the fullness of grace.[7] First, I say, Christ had the fullness of divinity. Others are called gods, but by participation; he is true God.[8] Again, others know something of truth; this man had the fullest knowledge, not only as God but as a human being "in whom are hidden all the treasures of wisdom and knowledge" (Col 2:3). Again, others have certain gifts: some the grace of wisdom, others the grace of eloquence, since graces are divided;[9] Christ had the fullness of grace; hence the Apostle to the Colossians (1:19): "In him all the fullness of God was pleased to dwell." About the fullness of divinity that was in Christ we read in John 1:14: "We have all seen his glory, glory as of the only Son from the Father"; of the fullness of grace and truth: "The Word was made flesh and dwelt among us, full of grace and truth." Thus it appears who this man is.

Next we must see what was the supper he prepared. I say that he prepared a threefold spiritual refreshment: one that pertains to the sacrament, another to the mind, and another to the heart.

First, I say, this man prepared a sacramental supper. What is written in Sirach 29:26 pertains to this sacramental refreshment: "Come here, stranger, prepare the table, and if you have anything at hand, let me have it to eat." Christ was a "stranger" in the world. Although he had made the world, nevertheless, the world did not know him (cf. John 1:10); he came into the world as an outsider. He set a sacramental table and with "what he had at hand," that is with the power the Father had given him, he fed others, namely the faithful. Christ established this refreshment inasmuch as he had the fullness of grace. Now in this refreshment there is a dinner and a supper: the "dinner" is the sacramental nourishment in the Old Testament, the "supper" is in the New.

What the Gospel says (Mat 22:4): "Behold I have made ready my dinner, my oxen and my fat calves are killed," concerns this sacramental "dinner" of the Old Covenant. A dinner is held in the first part of the day; similarly, a banquet of sacramental refreshment took place in the first law when oxen and calves were killed and offered to God.

Because there was a dinner, it was fitting that there should also be a supper. Of this it is said in Matthew 26:26: "Now as they were eating, Jesus took bread, and blessed, and broke it, and gave it to the disciples and said, 'Take, eat, this is my body'." Many outsiders may be invited to dinner, but supper is only for family and servants; Job says (31:31): "had not the men of my tent said: 'Who has not been filled with his meat?' "[10] This is as if to say: only family members are admitted.

See that this supper is great and how it is so. I say that this supper is called great because of its magnificent preparation, the abundance of delight for the taste, and the great power of its effect. All of these were in this repast; therefore it was great.

Should you ask what was provided, you will find a sumptuous provision (cf. Wis 16:20; Ps 77:25): "Bread from heaven he gave them; mortals ate the bread of angels."[11] Those who want to extol food do so doubly: in terms of its origin and in terms of those who partake of it. (It is said:) "This wine came from such-and-such a place; that is, a place where special vines are tended." Or, from the dignity of the partakers, wine may be praised by saying: "This is the wine which the king drinks." For this reason the Psalmist, wanting to tell of the great preparation of this supper, first describes where it came from: "He gave them bread from heaven." Where did it come from? From Heaven. Believe the bread itself speaking (John 6:51): "I am the living bread which came down from heaven";[12] namely, in his divinity, assuming our weakness, while never leaving behind the height of heaven. Again, this food is called precious because of the dignity of those who enjoy it—the angels who are refreshed by the Word of God—for they are the greatest to be refreshed by it. This food is offered to you in this supper. Thus it is that this supper is great because of its greatness of preparation.

But if food that was precious were set before you, but it was not pleasant to eat, the meal would not be considered great. For this reason, too, this supper is called great (secondly) because of its delight to the taste. Hence in the book of Wisdom 16:20: "You have given them bread from heaven, providing every pleasure and suited to every taste."[13] Now delight is caused by three things: memory of the past, hope for the future, and possession in the present. Every delight, however, is in this supper. If you consider the past, what is recalled is delightful. For what could be more delightful than to recall that humankind is saved by the blood of Christ: (Lam 3:19): "Remember my poverty, the wormwood and the gall. . . ." And in the Gospel (Luke 22:19): "Do this in remembrance of me."[14] And the Apostle (1 Cor 11:26): "As often as you eat this bread and drink this cup you proclaim the death of the Lord." In this supper there is also great delight from the hope of future things, since this sacramental meal is a pledge that gives us the hope of future happiness; hence in the Gospel (John 6:54): "Unless you eat the flesh of the Son of Man, you will not have life in you." The greatest delight is in this meal if you reflect on what is present to you there, namely, what is signified and what is both signified and contained. The body of Christ is signified and contained and truly one ought to delight to have within oneself the body of Christ; hence (Deut 4:7): "What great nation is there that has gods so near as our God is to us." Equally delightful is the unity of the Church which is signified only. What is more pleasant than this unity? Psalm (132:1): "Behold, how good and pleasant it is when family members dwell in unity!" Thus this supper gives the greatest delight whether you look to the past, present, or future.

Thirdly, this supper is great because of the great power of its effect, for it unites us to God and makes us dwell in God; hence John 6:56: "They who eat my flesh and drink my blood abide in me and I in them."[15] [They] "abide in me" by faith and love; "and I in them" by grace and the sacrament. If God is within us and we are in God, what is there to fear? Job 17:3: "Set me beside you, Lord, and then let anyone raise a hand against me"; [and] Psalm 22:5: "You have prepared a table before me."[16] Whenever two things are united as one, the lesser goes with the greater. It is necessary, therefore, that the soul united to God goes with God. Thus there is nothing to fear, because God is in us through this sacrament. (1 Kgs 19:6-8): "[Elias] looked up, and behold, above his head was a hearth-cake baked on hot stones and a jar of water . . . and he arose, and ate and drank, and strengthened by that food, he walked forty days and nights to Horeb the mount of God."[17] If we worthily receive this food it will lead us to eternal life. Happy indeed, those who taste this food, but woe to those who taste unworthily, for (1 Cor 11:29) "they eat judgment upon themselves." This, then, is the sacramental repast.

Another is the intellectual refreshment that pertains to the mind that Christ prepares for us insofar as he is full of truth; hence uncreated Wisdom says in Proverbs 9:2: "Wisdom mixes her wine, and prepares her table," then she beckons, saying: "Come, and eat my bread and drink the wine I have mixed for you."[18] Christ is God's wisdom, who mixed wine, namely, the teaching of spiritual wisdom. Because the wine was so strong that none could contain it without its being mixed, he therefore tempered it when he set forth his spiritual teaching. He set his table, that is, the universe of creatures. The dogma of wisdom is called bread and wine: bread that sustains, wine that delights and enflames.

In this refreshment there is a dinner and a supper. The dinner is the teaching of the philosophers, which was signified by Habakkuk (cf. Dan 14:32), where it is said that the reapers were making bread in the field. The reapers are the philosophers, who collect the produce of the field, that is, truth gleaned in creation; hence Romans 1:20: "Ever since the creation of the world God's invisible nature, namely God's eternal power and divinity, has been clearly perceived in the things that have been made."

The supper is the meal of sacred scripture. Hence in Revelation 3:20: "If they hear my voice and open the door, I will come in and sup with them, and they with me." This is the difference between the teaching of sacred scripture and that of philosophy: the philosophical teaching is creaturely; scriptural teaching is inspired.[19] Hence it says: "If they open . . . I will come to them," namely, through the inspiration of the Holy Spirit. Hence in John 16:13: "But the Spirit of Truth will come and teach you all truth." Sacred scripture is called a supper because it is given to the household and servants; hence Proverbs 31:15 says of the woman: "She rises while it is yet night and provides food for her household." This supper is great because it has the three aforementioned characteristics.

It is great, first of all, because of the greatness of its sumptuous preparation, for it deals with the highest things. Hence Wisdom says (Prov 8:6): "Listen, for I will speak of great things." These things are great, because they are beyond every sense. Hence in Sirach 3:25: "Many things above human understanding are shown to you." These things are profitable; hence the Lord says in Is 48:17: "I am the Lord your God; I teach you what is beneficial and lead you in the way you should go." Not all knowledge shows you the way you should go.

Further, this supper is great because of the greatness of its delight to the taste. For there is the greatest sweetness in the words of sacred scripture. Psalm 118:103: "How sweet are your words to my taste, sweeter than honey to my mouth!" Its sweetness is above the sweetness of any other knowledge. Other considerations are called delightful doubly, either because of the thing considered, or because of the consideration itself. A demonstration about a triangle is not delightful because of the thing demonstrated, since no one cares much about a triangle, but it is delightful on account of the consideration itself, which is of the mind. But when something loved is considered, and when the consideration itself is delightful, then it is completely delightful. Thus it is in sacred scripture: not only is there the satisfaction of recognizing truth, but it is also about things loved. Hence Augustine says in the *Confessions*: "Others' pages do not have the expression of the love of God. [They make no mention] of the tears of confession [or of 'the sacrifice you will never disdain, a broken spirit, a heart that is humble and contrite,' nor do they speak of the salvation of your people, 'the city adorned like a bride'], the pledge of your Spirit," and the rest he says there.[20] The refreshment of sacred scripture is great, therefore, because of the great abundance in its preparation and because of its great delight to the taste.

Thirdly it is great in effect. What is its effect? I say that it gives life; hence Blessed Peter (John 6:69): "Lord, to whom shall we go? You have the words of eternal life." Words lead people to the faith by which they live, and to charity, through which they are enflamed. Hence in Sirach 15:3: "She will feed him with the bread of life and understanding," etc.[21]

In the third place, Christ has prepared for us a refreshment of love, whence in Song of Songs (5:1): "Eat, O friends, and drink,"—in this life through grace—"and be inebriated, my dearly beloved"[22]—and in the future through glory. Christ gives us this refreshment insofar as he has the fullness of divinity. Psalm 83:12: "For God loves mercy and truth; the Lord will give grace and glory."

In this meal there is the dinner of grace, namely in the present. To this dinner the Lord calls in John 21:12: "Come and dine." The supper of this refreshment we await in the future, in glory. Hence in Revelation 19:9: "Happy are those called to the marriage supper of the Lamb." This is the supper to which no one is called except those who are worthy, of the family, and the household servants, hence in Isaiah 65:13: "Behold my servants shall eat and you shall be hungry."

This supper is greater than the others because of the same three previously mentioned conditions. The greatness of its sumptuous preparation is that one should sit at the table of God. Whoever sits at the king's table enjoys a lavish preparation, and as it is said in Luke 22:29-30: "I assign to you . . . a dominion; that you might eat and drink at my table." Does God have a physical table? Surely not; for the God's refreshment is joy. But in what does Christ rejoice? Surely over himself, for unless his joy were in himself, he would not be happy. And there they will see him in essence, and thus they will rejoice in him.[23] Job 22:26: "Then you will abound in delights from the Almighty." What more precious food is there than God? Surely none.

Should you ask about the greatness of delight in taste, it would be superfluous. For whatever is delectable, is delectable insofar as it is good, or insofar as it has the likeness of good.[24] But if lesser goods, or things that participate in goodness, are delectable, how much delight does that food give which is infinite goodness. Psalm 15:11: "At your right hand are delights forever." Again, Psalm 30:20: "O how great is the abundance of your sweetness, Lord!"

Thirdly, this supper is great because of the greatness of love's power, for in it is perpetuity of life. The saints will lack nothing. Psalm 21:27: "The poor will eat and have their fill." The poor will eat—but which poor? Surely the poor in spirit, hence Matthew 5:3: "Happy are the poor in spirit." Or else the poor, that is, the humble, or the voluntarily poor, those who have riches but despise them.[25] These will arrive at the supper, but those who have spirits encumbered by temporal things will not come. Hence in the Gospel (Matt 5:6): "Happy are they who hunger and thirst for justice, for they shall have their fill"; and (Ps 21:27): "Those who seek the Lord will praise God"; and Augustine: "We shall see, we shall love, we shall praise."[26] "Their hearts will live forever and ever" (Ps

21:27), not only with a bodily life, but with the life of a soul joined to God. May [Christ] deign to vouch for us, who with the Father, etc.

Notes

1. A good deal has been written on the history of exegesis; see especially: G. R. Evans, *The Language and Logic of the Bible: I. The Earlier Middle Ages*, and, *II. The Road to the Reformation* (Cambridge: Cambridge University Press, 1984–1985); Henri de Lubac, *L'exégèse médiévale: les quatre sens de l'écriture*, 2 vols. in 4 (Paris: Aubier, 1959–1964); *Le Moyen Age et la Bible*, eds. Pierre Riché and Guy Lobrichon, vol. 4 of *Bible de tous les temps* (Paris: Beauchesne, 1984); Beryl Smalley, *The Study of the Bible in the Middle Ages*, 3rd edition (Oxford: Basil Blackwell, 1983); *The Gospels in the Schools, ca. 1100–1280* (London: The Hambledon Press, 1985); and, *Studies in Medieval Thought and Learning from Abelard to Wyclif* (London: The Hambledon Press, 1981). For the history of preaching see Jean Longère, *La prédication médiévale* (Paris: Etudes augustiniennes, 1983).

2. Wilfrid Harrington, rev. of *Commentary on the Gospel of John, Part I*, by Saint Thomas Aquinas, trans. J. A. Weisheipl, and F. R. Larcher, *The Thomist* 47 (1983): 152–153.

3. In addition to De Lubac and Smalley cited above, Harrington may have in mind several more popular works such as John L. MacKenzie, *The Two-edged Sword: An Interpretation of the Old Testament* (Milwaukee: Bruce, 1956); and Thomas Merton's *Bread in the Wilderness* (New York: James Laughlin, 1953). For preachers M. F. Toal edited and translated *The Sunday Sermons of the Great Fathers: A Manual of Preaching, Spiritual Reading, and Meditation*, 4 vols. (Chicago: Regnery, 1955–1963).

4. De Lubac, 1.1, 11–14.

5. See Bernard's sermon *On Conversion*, in *Bernard of Clairvaux: Selected Works*, trans. G. R. Evans, *Classics of Western Spirituality* (New York: Paulist Press, 1987), 65–99, preached in 1140 to the scholars of Paris. According to the accounts more than 20 of them quit the schools and followed back to Clairvaux. For a masterful treatment of spiritual exegesis see the Introduction written by Jean Leclercq.

6. De Lubac, 1.1, 15–16.

7. See Gary Macy, *The Theologies of the Eucharist in the Early Scholastic Period: A Study of the Salvific Function of the Sacrament according to the Theologians, c. 1080–c1220* (Oxford: Clarendon Press, 1984). What Macy's study concludes is that theologians were not concerned with the transformation of the elements *per se*, but with how the sacrament brings about a saving communion with Christ.

8. *The Thomist* 47 (1983): 154–155.

9. Many contemporary authors are asking similar questions, sensing that biblical scholars should also move beyond criticism to do theology. For a survey of the history of historical criticism and some of the newer methods see Edgar V. McKnight, *Post-Modern Use of the Bible: The Emergence of Reader-Oriented Criticism* (Nashville: Abingdon, 1988). See also Paul Ricoeur, *"Biblical Hermeneutics," Semeia* 4 (1975): 29–148, and *The Philosophy of Paul Ricoeur: An Anthology of his Work*, eds. E. Reagan and D. Stewart (Boston: Beacon Press, 1978). Sandra M. Schneiders makes use of Ricoeur in her work; see, for example: "Paschal Imagination: Objectivity and Subjectivity in New Testament Interpretation," *Theological Studies* 43 (1982): 52–68; "Faith, Hermeneutics and the Literal Sense of Scripture," *Theological Studies* 39 (1978): 719–36; "From Exegesis to Hermeneutics: The Problem of

the Contemporary Meaning of Scripture," *Horizons* 8 (1981): 23–39; and "Feminist Ideology, Criticism, and Biblical Hermeneutics," *Biblical Theology Bulletin* 19 (1989): 3–10.

10. *De doctrina christiana* 3.5, trans. D. W. Robertson, Jr. (Indianapolis: Bobbs-Merrill, 1958) 83–84.

11. *De doctrina christiana* 1.35–36 (Robertson, 30–31).

12. Abbot Joachim (c. 1132–1202) upheld a trinitarian division of history such that the period before Christ is that of the Father, the present dispensation is that of the Son, and that of a coming age would be that of the Spirit, when there would be no need of the Church. Needless to say the Church did not agree and Joachim's works were condemned at the Fourth Lateran Council of 1215, although Joachim's sanctity of life was never in question.

13. *De verbo Dei* 1.1. Translation my own; cf. Hugues de Saint-Victor, *Six opuscules spirituels*, ed. and trans. Roger Baron, *Sources chrétiennes* 155 (Paris: Editions du Cerf, 1969) 60.

14. *De verbo Dei* 1.2 (*Sources chrétiennes* 155) 60–61.

15. Thus Thomas Aquinas defines the four senses and their relationship in the *Summa theologiae* 1.1.10: "The author of scripture is God in whose power it is to signify meaning not only by words, as human beings do, but also by things themselves. So, whereas in every other science things are signified by words, in this science what is signified by words also has signification. Therefore that first signification whereby words signify things belongs to the first sense, the historical or literal. That signification by which the things signified by the words also themselves have a signification is called the spiritual sense. . . . In the New Law, whatever our Head has done is a type of what we are to do. Therefore, so far as things of the Old Law signify the things of the New Law, there is the allegorical sense; so far as the things done in Christ, or so far as the things which signify Christ, are types of what we ought to do, there is the moral sense. But so far as they signify what relates to eternal glory, there is the anagogical sense."

16. In his reply to argument 3 (that the parabolic does not belong to one of the four senses) Thomas maintains that when the sacred text uses metaphoric language that language belongs to the literal sense: "The parabolic sense is contained in the literal, for by words things are signified properly and figuratively. Nor is the figure itself, but what is figured, the literal sense. When Scripture speaks of God's arm, the literal sense is not that God has such a member, but only what is signified by this member, namely, operative power."

17. Several of these large picture bibles were produced in the 13th century. One, which belonged to Louis IX, is in the treasury of the Cathedral of Toledo (Spain); others are to be found in the great manuscript collections of Oxford, London, Paris, and Vienna. The *bible moralisée* is the ancestor of the *biblia pauperum* of the later Middle Ages. For an appreciation of the iconography of these bibles see Gail Ramshaw, "Type as Biblical Symbol," in *Worship: Searching for Language* (Washington: The Pastoral Press, 1988) 49–65.

18. Origen, *Commentary on the Song of Songs*, trans. R. P. Lawson, *Ancient Christian Writers* 26 (Westminster: Newman Press, 1957); Bernard of Clairvaux, *On the Song of Songs*, trans. Killian Walsh, 4 vols., *Cistercian Fathers* 4, 7, 31, and 40 (Kalamazoo: Cistercian Publications, 1971).

19. See Caroline Bynum Walker, *Jesus as Mother: Studies in the Spirituality of the High Middle Ages* (Berkeley: University of California Press, 1982), and *Holy Feast, Holy Fast: The Religious Significance of Food to Medieval Women* (Berkeley: University of California Press, 1987); for a discussion of this theme in art see Barbara G. Lane, *The Altar and the Altarpiece: Sacramental Themes in Early Netherlandish Painting* (New York: Harper and Row, 1984).

20. See, for example, Bernard of Clairvaux, *Magnificat: Homilies in Praise of the Virgin Mary*, trans. Marie-Bernard Saïd and Grace Perigo, *Cistercian Fathers* 82 (Kalamazoo: Cistercian Publications, 1985).

21. On this medieval literary genre see Richard and Mary Rouse, "Biblical Distinctions in the Thirteenth Century," *Archives d'histoire doctrinale et littéraire du moyen âge* (1975) 27–37; and, *Preachers, Florilegia, and Sermons: Studies on the 'Manipulus florum' of Thomas of Ireland. Texts and Studies* 47 (Toronto: Pontifical Institute of Mediaeval Studies, 1979).

22. According to Louis-Jacques Bataillon, "Le sermon inédit de saint Thomas d'Aquin 'homo quidam fecit cenam magnam'," *Revue des sciences philosophiques et théologiques* 67 (1983): 353–70, this sermon is in the form of a *reportatio*, i.e., a transcription made as Thomas preached; for a discussion of Thomas's authentic sermons and an overview of his themes see Jean-Pierre Torrell, "La pratique pastorale d'un théologien du xiiie siècle: Thomas d'Aquin," *Revue thomiste* 82 (1982): 213–45.

Sermon Text Notes

1. The text given here is the author's translation of Bataillon's Latin edition, *Revue des sciences philosophiques et théologiques* 67 (1983): 360–65. The editor's notes have been included and expanded.

2. Gregory the Great, *Homily 36* (*PL* 76.1266A), used as the seventh lesson at Matins for the Second Sunday after Trinity; cf. *Catena aurea in Lc 14.10.*

3. Many of the biblical texts cited by Thomas in this sermon were also used as antiphons or responses in the Office of Corpus Christi, according to the primitive form of the liturgy as represented by the thirteenth-century MS Paris, Bibliothèque Nationale lat. 1143. On Thomas and Corpus Christi, see Pierre-Marie Gy, "L'office du Corpus Christi et saint Thomas D'Aquin. Etat d'une recherche," *Revue des sciences philosophiques et théologiques* 64 (1980) 491-507. Rev 2:17 is antiphon 5 of Lauds.

4. Cf. *In IV Sent* 8.1.4.2.ad 2.

5. In scholastic fashion, Thomas divides the text in two parts; the first will serve as the morning sermon, the second as the evening collation. Only the morning sermon is translated here.

6. Gregory the Great cites this text in the homily mentioned above (PL 76.1266D). It is interesting to note here that when Thomas wrote he did not always have an open Bible at hand, for here and elsewhere he sometimes gives a faulty attribution, paraphrases texts, or conflates them.

7. Cf. Col 2:9; John 1:19.

8. Cf. John 10:34-36 and Thomas' *Super evangelium s. Johannis lectura* 10.6.4 (Turin: Marietti, 1952) 272.

9. Cf. 1 Cor 12:8,4.

10. Matt 26:26 and Job 31:31: Corpus Christi, Response 5 at Matins. The notion that the evening meal is an intimate occasion is an important aspect of Thomas's eucharistic thought. See *Summa theologiae* 3.73.5.

11. Wis 16:20: Corpus Christi, versicle at the *Magnificat*; Ps 77:25: Response at Terce.

12. Corpus Christi, *Benedictus* antiphon.

13. Cf. *Summa theologiae* 3.73.4.

14. Luke 22:19 (+Lam 3:19): Corpus Christi, Response 6 at Matins.

15. John 6:56 and Deut 4:7 together make up Response 7 at Matins for Corpus Christi.

16. Ps 23:5: Corpus Christi, Antiphon 5 at Matins.

17. 3 Kgs 19:6-8 (+Jn 6:52): Corpus Christi, Response 3 at Matins. This type of the eucharist sums up for Thomas his conviction that in the eucharist we already possess eternal life. See *Summa theologiae* 3.79.2: whether the attainment of glory is an effect of this sacrament.

18. Corpus Christi, Antiphon 1 at Lauds; Response at Vespers.

19. Cf. *Summa theologiae* 1.1.1.

20. The text has been expanded to include "the rest that he [Augustine] says there." See *Confessions* 7.21 (Trans. R. S. Pine-Coffin, Harmondsworth, England: Penguin, 1961) 155.

21. Corpus Christi, Response 8 at Matins.

22. Corpus Christi, Versicle/Response at Matins.

23. Cf. Thomas, *Super I ad Timotheum* 6.3 in *Super epistolas s. Pauli lectura,* 2 vols. (Turin: Marietti, 1953) 262.

24. Cf. Thomas *Sententia libri Ethicorum* 9.22 (1255b 17).

25. Cf. Thomas *Super evangelium s. Matthaei lectura* 5.2 (Turin: Marietti, 1951) 66–67.

26. *City of God* 22.30 (Trans. Gerald G. Walsh, et al., New York: Doubleday, 1958) 544.

Section II

Systematic Theology

Chapter 6

Religious Language and Preaching

BENJAMIN J. RUSSELL, O.P.

Many writers in the fields of philosophy and theology, especially in recent decades, have addressed what is called "The Problem of Religious Language." However, preachers have paid little attention to the implications of this discussion. This chapter is an attempt to introduce two specific language problems into the context of homiletics, first by presenting an overview of the problems and then by considering the implications of these problems for preaching. This latter part of the chapter also includes some general suggestions for approaching these problems in preaching.

Part I: Two Problems with Religious Language

Among the many complex activities in which we human beings engage, the use of religious language is one of the most complex. This complexity is aptly manifested in the two problems which I address. The first is the problem of the validity of religious language: whether religious words and sentences have any valid meaning; the second is the problem of the creative force of language, specifically for our discussion, the creative force of religious language.

The problem of the validity of religious language is a very real one, and is not simply a matter of word games. Because we are used to religious words and encounter them in the framework of our daily lives we are prone to assume meanings for them. But if we step back and erase our assumptions about the meaning of religious words, we can see that they are problematic. The statement that "there is one God in three Divine Persons" is an incomprehensible statement; it describes nothing in our experience. In fact, we cannot even get an image of the Trinity; theologians tell us that this is a mystery—something beyond our understanding or even our *ability* to understand. What, then, in our experience could these words possibly refer to except to themselves? And yet we blithely use the word "Trinity" and the words that make up its definition, as well as other religious terms, as though there were no problem at all, as when a newspaper announces that "Mary Immaculate trounces Holy Trinity."

The validity of "God talk," or any other kind of religious expression, has been challenged and questioned throughout the known history of humanity. Believers say that, while there is a God, we cannot know fully what God is because of the limitation of human intellect and experience. However, if we cannot know what God is, then how can there be any valid referent to the word "God"? We can know what rain is, or what a fire hydrant is; when we use those words we have every right to expect that our hearers will attach the same concept to the words as the concepts we have. But we cannot have such sure expectations when we use religious language. For example, when I say, "God is providential," what I am thinking, and seeing in my imagination, may be quite different from what another is thinking or seeing; and my experience of God's providence will necessarily be different from others', because I will not have experienced God acting in my life in exactly the same way as someone else. (One might note here that there is the deeper theological question of what it means even to say that "God acts" in any sense. However, to investigate this problem here would lead us far beyond the intent of this chapter.) The only way that we could come to know the similarities and differences in what we are thinking and imagining would be for each of us to describe clearly and completely what the words mean to us. And this would involve describing our experiences of God's providence. The fact that the referents of religious words are abstract and beyond our earthly experience, while at the same time our religious experience remains intensely intimate and personal, makes our use of words with religious connotations subject to misunderstanding and ambiguity.

In recent decades, there have been those who have questioned whether "God-talk" and religious language in general has any valid meaning at all, i.e., whether such language can refer to any reality for humans. There have even been those of one such school who have declared that "God is dead," claiming that the word "God" has absolutely no valid meaning, since we cannot know what God might be. These discussions have arisen out of the schools of linguistic analysis, recently dominant in western philosophy, schools descended from Logical Positivism and occasioned by Ludwig Wittgenstein with the publication of his *Tractatus Logico-philosophicus* in 1921.

Wittgenstein saw a close, formal relationship among language, thought, and the world. Language and thought work like a picture of the real world, and to understand any sentence one must grasp the reference of its constitutive elements, both to each other and to the real. For Wittgenstein, language can indicate an area beyond itself: unsayable things (non-demonstrable things) do exist; but some who have come after him have denied that words which refer to non-demonstrable things have any validity. In 1953 Wittgenstein published his *Philosophical Investigations* in which he presented language as a *response* to, as well as a *reproduction* of, the real.

In other words, the insight which Wittgenstein had is that language is linked to reality, not only as signs by which we try to communicate our experiences of reality and our thoughts about reality to one another, but also—and more importantly—language is linked to reality as, in a sense, *creating* reality. The language we hear, learn, and use and the *connotations* we learn to attach to words shape our perspective of the world to an extent which has the effect of creating a world for us, or at least of creating a prism through which we view and experience the world. We find an excellent example of this creative force of language in our current awareness of, and concern about, inclusive language in the liturgy. What has been the impact of centuries of exclusively male language in our liturgy? It has created a religious world which is dominantly male. God, of course is male; Jesus, of course, came to save all men. This is a reality in which Christians live.

Thus, the problems of religious language which I am addressing are two: 1) Can religious words have any real content, i.e., can they refer to any real actualities beyond our own concepts, images, or imagination? How can we speak of any reality that is beyond sense experience or empirical verification? 2) What kind of creative force does our religious language shape? What kind of world does our religious language create?

THE VALID CONTENT OF RELIGIOUS LANGUAGE

In approaching the first problem—the validity of religious language—I would like to begin with a quotation from the astrophysicist Carl Sagan. In Chapter 23 of *Broca's Brain*, entitled "A Sunday Sermon," he says:

> The most common questions asked (me—after a lecture) are on unidentified flying objects and ancient astronauts—what I believe are thinly disguised religious queries. Almost as common—particularly after a lecture in which I discuss the evolution of life or intelligence—is: "Do you believe in God?"

> Because the word "God" means many things to many people, I frequently reply by asking what the questioner means by "God." To my surprise, this response is often considered puzzling or unexpected: "Oh, you know, God. Everyone knows who God is." Or "Well, kind of a force that is stronger than we are and that exists everywhere in the universe." There are a number of such forces. One of them is called gravity, but it is not often identified with God. And not everyone does know what is meant by "God." The concept covers a wide range of ideas. Some people think of God as an outsized, light-skinned male with a long white beard, sitting on a throne somewhere up there in the sky, busily tallying the fall of every sparrow. Others—for example, Baruch Spinoza and Albert Einstein—considered God to be essentially the sum total of the physical laws which describe the universe. I do not know of any compelling evidence for anthropomorphic patriarchs controlling human destiny from some hidden celestial vantage point, but it would be madness to deny the existence of physical laws. Whether we believe in God depends very much on what we mean by God. (New York: Ballantine; 1979, 330.)

The traditional resolution which Roman Catholic theologians usually offer to this first problem is that developed by St. Thomas Aquinas in considering the names of God (ST I, 13) and by others after Thomas, notably John of St. Thomas in his treatise *On Signs*. This response is that religious language is valid and does refer to realities beyond human ideation because it is analogous language.

The explanation of analogy is based upon the ways in which we use words to signify what we mean. There are three basic kinds of word usage: a word may be used univocally, when used to refer to one and only one reality. The best example of univocal speech is a proper name: "President George Bush" can refer to only one reality.

A second kind of usage is equivocation, whereby one word refers simultaneously to two distinct referents; this kind of usage is the pun, e.g., Why is Sunday the strongest day? Because all the others are weekdays. (Puns usually work only when spoken.)

The third kind of usage is analogous usage. This kind of usage involves comparison. An analogy is a comparison made between, or among, things which have something in common, although they are also different. We may make an explicit comparison between two things, in which case we have a simile: "My love is like a red, red rose." Or we may make an implicit comparison, in which case we have the figure of speech known as metaphor: "Jesus is the Lamb of God"; "the mighty ship of state."

Another kind of implicit comparison, one of which we are not always aware, is the analogy of proportionality. While we can say that a rock has being, a rose bush has being, a cat has being, a human has being, we can see that we do not mean the same thing in each case. There is a big difference between the being of a rock and the being of a human. Each has being in proportion to its nature; each "is" according to a proportion of participation in being. In the same way, then, we can say that God is being (the pure act of being, or the dynamic act of Being) even though we cannot comprehend the being of God. We can make an analogy between our being and God's being, and the use of the word "being" is valid in all cases, because it is based on our experience of being and our awareness that our being is proportionately infinitely different from God's being. A key point to remember about analogy is that the difference is always much greater than the similarity: analogous things are more unlike than alike.

The proposal of analogy as the solution to the problems of religious language is not a facile response to a made up problem. The very analysis of analogy is itself fraught with difficulties. Can we validly say that analogy exists in things, or are just the words analogous? Does an analogy have root in extra-mental reality, or is it just a use of words?

To illustrate further: reflect on the familiar words of the beginning of the Nicene Creed: "We believe in one God, the Father, the almighty; maker of . . . all that is . . . unseen." What do these words mean? To what in our experience could they possibly refer?

While the idea of analogy is usually applied in philosophy and theology specifically to God language, other elements of religious language also have analogical overtones to the extent that the primary referent is often far removed, at least, from sensory experience. Some additional examples may amplify the point. Consider what the following words mean to you: covenant, conversion, grace, salvation, redemption, law, sin, revelation. The list is somewhat long for an example, but the purpose of the list is to indicate that what is being exemplified applies to the vast majority of words used in theological and homiletic discourse. All of these words have a wide range of possible meanings, both outside and within the context of religion; but even when they are used within a religious context a variety of possible meanings remain. Even such words as "good," "truth," "love," and "unity," words which may refer only to terrestrial experiences, can evoke quite diverse concepts in different people because of their abstract nature. The only route to grasping them is analogy.

THE CREATIVE FORCE OF RELIGIOUS LANGUAGE

Bearing this in mind, let us now turn to the second question about language: How is it possible that language can create reality? Many people balk at this idea. Our assumption about the world is that we enter it, discover it, and then talk about what we have found: a reality already present and given to us. We perhaps may find it difficult to accept the fact that we, in at least some sense, create reality, because then we might have to take responsibility for what we have created.

Language creates reality through the psychological processes of imagination: words are associated with images in our imaginations; these associated images are stored in our memories. This process is a creating of reality because reality is not confined to the extra-mental. The "real" is not only what is outside our minds. What is mental is also real. Our concepts have real existence as concepts, as do the images of our imagination and memory. They are real, albeit in our minds. Mental reality is reality, although it is a reality distinct from extra-mental reality. When we hear a word we see an image; past associations are evoked and inserted into the present, thus making the present be what the word evokes from the past. For example, among certain tribes and ethnic groups, reality is inhabited by elves, sprites, leprechauns, and the like. The meanings and connotations of words we learned in childhood shape our world view; and our world view *is* what constitutes reality for us. Some might express this idea by saying that there is no uninterpreted human experience; we bring a framework of perception to all our experience, filtering experience, combining experiences, etc.

Are Mickey Mouse, Scarlett O'Hara, Bambi, and Superman real? Yes, they are real imaginary beings. So, too, are the images and thoughts of our own minds real, as products of our minds and imagination. They are mental realities. And in terms of impact on our lives, what goes on in our heads has far greater force than what we encounter outside ourselves.

Joseph Campbell, the famous authority on mythology, in an interview with Eugene Kennedy in *The New York Sunday Times Magazine,* April 22, 1979, provides an example of language's creation of reality in the religious sphere. He refers to

> an outmoded understanding of the universe, that we will be delivered by some benign visitation, by forces from other planets. It is the idea of the Kingdom's coming from a source other than from within ourselves. The Kingdom of God is within us, but we have this idea that the gods act from "out there."

He later points out that, in Christian belief, salvation has, in fact, come from within the human race in the person of Jesus of Nazareth. Nevertheless, we persist in viewing salvation as coming from outside this world, and our religious, as well as our non-religious language, continues to create this erroneous version of the reality of salvation as we continue to utilize the language of religious myth on our ordinary speech. Even though Christ the Savior has already come among us, for many Christians the expectation of his return from somewhere else has greater impact than his previous appearance. For them what is yet to be is more real than what has already happened.

Despite the fact that we know that the earth goes around the sun, we continue to speak of the sun rising and setting; thus, in the reality of our everyday world, the sun goes around the earth.

Despite the fact that we have seen pictures of earth from the moon, and therefore know that there is no "up" or "down" from the earth, but only "out," we still talk about heaven as being "up" and hell as being "down" (so for us, Australia is hell; an idea that Australians may be uncomfortable with, until they stop to think that for them, we are in hell). These words are not just figures of speech; they actually constitute reality for a large number of people who never think of praying to the God within them but must always look upward when in a crisis. The expressions: "Jesus ascended into heaven" and "Jesus descended into hell," may well be apt and meaningful symbolic phrases; however, without explanation the words create a real heaven that is above the earth and a real hell that is below the earth.

The answer to the old Catholic Baltimore Catechism question, "Why did God make you," provides another example: "God made me to know him, to love him, and to serve him in this world and to be happy with him forever in the next." Leaving aside the reality of a male God that the answer evokes, I submit that this answer created a world for Catholics that 1) placed them at the center of the universe: to save *my* soul became the goal of life, which idea was easily translated into taking care of myself without having to have any real concern for others who were different from me. And 2) the answer made this world secondary to "the next" (where one will be happy forever) to such an extent that this world didn't count for much—real salvation is in the next world, not in this world. I do not wish to place undue responsibility on this answer alone for the kind of world Catholics inhabited (and which some continue to inhabit) into the 1960s. Such phrases as "the one true religion" and others like it also played a role.

Part II: The Implications of the Problems of Religious Language for Preaching

Both of the questions discussed above (What validity does religious language have? What reality does religious language create?) are obviously questions of paramount importance to the preacher. If religious language has no meaning or validity, then all preaching is nonsense. In addition, the preacher, being in a position of authority toward the listeners, is constantly creating a reality for the listeners, or is at least reinforcing or destroying an already existing reality.

These issues imply two general suggestions to the preacher: 1) be aware of what the words you use mean to *you* and take pains to make your meaning clear; 2) be a theologian so that as you play a role in creating a worldview for your hearers you will assist them in developing reality in accord with the general theological tradition of the Church rather than in accord with misleading piety or mere adaptation to modern culture or religious fads.

PREACHING AND THE IMPLICATIONS OF ANALOGY

As to the first of these suggestions, we have seen that the first issue concerning religious language—its validity—leads us to an awareness that religious language can be valid only as analogous language. Hence, preachers need to remember always that they are speaking at best in analogies.

If the words of the preacher are simply univocal, i.e., have but one and only one meaning for the preacher, in other words if the preacher is close-minded and locked into a set worldview, then the preaching will not move the audience to conversion (which is the purpose of preaching: conversion primarily of the hearers, but also of the preacher); it will be a harangue at best and the only movement of the audience will most likely be a movement to unfruitful fear. Univocal preaching was the kind of preaching brought to this hemisphere by the European colonizers of both Roman Catholic and Protestant persuasions. Today we are painfully aware of, and reaping the harvest from, the effects of that kind of preaching as we see "Christian" morality equated almost exclusively with sexual morality, individual advancement promoted among "Christians" over social concern, racism justified by "Christian" people, etc. I assume that we have learned some lessons from that experience and would not be eager to repeat that approach today.

I would also assume that equivocal preaching would be totally ineffective, although a sermon composed of puns might be highly entertaining to people of a certain bent of mind.

Thus I focus on analogy in preaching. In this context the effective preacher must have an awareness of several things: that the language he or she is using is analogous; that each religious word uttered contains vast depths of meaning; that each time a religious word is used it refers to realities that are more dissimilar from our experiences than similar to our experiences (a point that cannot be too much emphasized); and that the religious word can mean vastly different things to different people.

In cultivating this awareness, preachers must first begin with an analysis of their own understanding of the religious words they use in preaching. We must realize, for example, that "God" is not a univocal word, because we don't know the inner reality that we intend to point to with the word. "God" can be an analogous word only. Hence, while I may and should share what the word "God" means to me as I preach, I must try to do so in ways that might resonate with the meaning of the word for my hearers, and I must be open to the meanings which that word may have for them. I may not assume that my idea of God is the only one, nor may I assume that my hearers share my concept of God in all its details, even when my hearers, are of the same religious denomination as I.

Since they are analogous words, religious words can easily give rise to misunderstandings about, and confused interpretations of, what preachers may mean. Preaching devoid of examples and clarifying stories, of images and metaphors, can easily cause misunderstanding and confusion precisely because the concepts which we attach to religious words arise out of our lived experience, even more than out of educational learning. Experience shapes religions and religiosity perhaps more than any other sphere of our lives. It is our experience of life and of others in our lives that gives meaning to religious words far more than can any catechism. Hence, in our preaching we must give flesh to our words by exemplifying what we mean by them, by sharing the experiences which have given meaning to the words for us.

Here we can see, from a different perspective than that simply of effective techniques in preaching, how important is the role of examples, similes, and story-telling in the homily. In giving flesh to a word by using these forms of explicit analogy the preacher can make her/his meaning of religious words clear to the hearers and can invite the hearers to expand their own concepts and connotations, their own images and memories associated with those words. The listeners can share vicariously in your experiences and your understanding, and thus their reality can begin to expand and open up to new possibilities. They can be challenged to reflect upon their own stories and experiences, to rectify erroneous understandings arising from hurtful experiences and to dig deeper into their good experiences to find God in their lives.

As an example, let me ask: How does a child who was abused by its father understand God as Father? The prime analogate for us (the known object or experience on which we base an analogy) of "father" is the biological father; we understand God the Father as proportionate to, or analogous to, our biological fathers. It is possible to enable the person who was abused as a child to develop a healthy relationship to God as Father if God is described as the kind of father that the person might wish to have had. But if the preacher merely says, "We should love God because God is our Father," then the person might well find that difficult indeed.

Out of necessity we preach from our own experience and our own understanding of the words we use; and we are heard within the experience of our listeners. If we assume that we all have the same or similar experiences and fail to spell out what we mean by the words we use, through explanatory devices, then the door is wide open for misunderstanding by, or even perhaps damage to, a listener.

It is also necessary for preachers to have grappled with their own life experiences, to have obtained an understanding of themselves in order to make their words clear and insure that they are preaching the Gospel and the tradition of the Church rather than preaching themselves. Mary's witness that "God has cast down the mighty from their thrones and has exalted the lowly" would result in very different sermons on the text from preachers such as Martin Luther King, Jr., and Jim and Tammy Bakker; or such as Archbishop Tutu and Jerry Falwell; or from you or me. What is important is that you know you and that I know myself so that we might be aware of what we are saying when we preach.

It is a good example for us to note that St. Paul did not hesitate to use his own conversion experience as an explanation of such religious words as "conversion," "mission," "Divine power," "God's love." He referred to his life experiences regularly: his chains, imprisonment, shipwrecks, journeys, tent-making, even his own weaknesses. If we wish to say what we mean when we preach in religious language, then we ought to do likewise.

THE CREATIVE POWER OF PREACHING

Even more important, however, and more challenging for the preacher is the second issue that emerges from this consideration of the problems of religious language: the realization that the language which the preacher uses creates reality for the audience. For it is precisely in the exercise of this aspect of language that the prophetic role of the preacher—calling God's People to an awareness of the divine, the mysterious, the spiritual—emerges. While this realization may seem to pose an awesome burden for the preacher, it is also a wonderful challenge and opportunity; it is the heart of the mission to preach.

To exemplify the implication of this dimension of language: consider what reality might be created for a congregation in Praetoria by the preacher's words "Jesus Christ came to save all men," if the enfleshment of that proposition were such as to include the black citizens of South Africa as well as the white, women as well as men; if "salvation" were a word applied to human rights and decency in this world as well as being forever with God in the next. What a difference such preaching could make in that country compared with preaching which equates the words "all men" with whites and primarily white males, at that. Consider further that the entire course of the history of the United States would have been quite different if the word "man" had encompassed blacks and native Americans in the world of the explorers, the missionaries, and the conquistadors; but that was *not* reality for those people. Debates raged over the question of whether the natives were "men"; and even a papal pronouncement declaring them to be men could not eradicate the world which decades of using the word "man" to mean white, primarily European, males had created. Indeed, Bartolome de las Casas, who came to be known as a champion of the humanity and rights of Native Americans, had to undergo a religious conversion experience before that reality could change for him.

As shapers of reality for their hearers, preachers bear a great responsibility. They must explicate symbols and create a world within which conversion is made possible. This is why I said at the beginning of the section that our consideration implies the suggestion that preachers should be theologians. The world which the Christian preacher creates in the minds, hearts, and intellects of the hearers must be in accord with the best available understanding of the Scriptures and with the general theological tradition of the Church. Otherwise, the hearers can be led not just into error but into a reality which deviates from the very reality that is Jesus Christ.

The reality which the Christian preacher should be intent on creating is one which will enable the hearer to grasp more clearly the meaning of the Christ event and the continuation of that event into our own time. By coming to know and understand the Lord Jesus more fully and more accurately, the hearer will be converted to a deeper love of Jesus and to a deeper commitment to the values, teachings, and meaning of Jesus. But preachers can do this only if they make certain that their preaching is rooted in sound theology and biblical exegesis.

The examples which I have used throughout this presentation have tended to be examples from what may be called the "dogmatic" sphere of theology and Christian life. However, the same points may be made in reference to the moral sphere as well. What does the statement "Do good and avoid evil" mean? What is "good"; what is "evil"? Both of these are analogous terms. Consider the injunction to "love God with your whole heart, strength, will and . . . love your neighbor as yourself." The variety of possibilities of what those words might mean to any given person is tremendous, which is undoubtedly the reason why so many Christians constantly have questions about the implications of these admonitions. Preachers should take the same approaches to these moral issues as to biblical and doctrinal teachings, that is they should have a clear awareness of what the words mean to them, must preach those meanings clearly through examples, similes, and stories, and must reflect upon the reality that the preaching will create for the hearers, while at the same time insuring that this word is in accord with the Gospels and church tradition.

Hence, the principle that the preacher should know the congregation is broader than simply having an awareness of the age, educational level, or socio-economic status of the congregation. In addition to these things, the preacher should have some understanding of the psychological state of the hearers as well as the religious life-experiences which the congregation may be bringing to the preaching event. An exhortation to works of mercy will register differently in the ears of a mother or father with two children under the age of five than in the ears of the local middle-aged banker or of the young single person looking for meaning in life. Often they are all in the same congregation; the words of the preacher should be crafted in such a way as to touch them all.

And so the things we have probably already heard about constructing good homilies and/or sermons, things such as: know what we are talking about, use examples and stories, be clear and well-ordered in our presentation and have one clear, central point, are not just clever techniques for rendering an audience overawed at the greatness of our preaching. They are necessities for preaching, arising out of the nature of the religious language we use, necessities that will communicate with some exactness and will not harm people.

Conclusion

The preacher does not speak to a universal audience, but always to a limited, definable, and describable group of people. So the preacher cannot speak in generalities or in universal terms (as does the Church when addressing a universal audience, or in the symbols of liturgy). Indeed, it is precisely the task of the preacher to give specificity to the universal message of the Gospel and the tradition of the Church. But this can never be done if the preacher hears the universal language of Jesus or of the Church as univocal language. It is only by plumbing the depths of the analogies of religious language that the preacher can make that language meaningful and real for the individual hearer.

The message does not belong to you or to me, nor is it to be heard only by you or by me; the message is for all peoples of all times. It is our responsibility to grasp the message within our own time and place, within our own experiences; to clothe it with our own stories and examples and to offer it to our own people as clearly and as accurately as the analogies and our reality will allow. To recognize the singular implications of the nature of the religious language in which we preach is the beginning of the task.

Chapter 7

The Role of Theological Communication in the Act of Preaching

CARLA MAE STREETER, O.P.

Introduction

How is preaching distinct from theological teaching? The fact that these two forms of theological communication are often not distinguished prompts this chapter. One form of theological communication is preaching. Because there are other forms such as teaching and writing (and the precise skills called into play with audio and video) we will focus here on the specific role theological communication plays in the preaching act.

Is such a clarification a mere exercise in semantics? Will this make a difference? Preaching is distinct from teaching, although preaching incorporates sound teaching. Classroom teaching does differ from liturgical preaching, although at times a good teacher can move people as profoundly as a good preacher. Our purpose here is to distinguish as well as relate preaching and teaching. Although it is clear that preaching implies theology, we need to understand how theology flows from religion.

I. Theological Communication

A. THEOLOGY AND RELIGION—A DISTINCTION

It is important to note that theology and religion are related yet distinct. Theology is a reflection and articulation on religion as that religion arises out of a specific culture. If theology is a specific type of reflection and articulation, it clearly makes use of human intelligence to do that reflecting and articulating. For this reason we need to understand how the mind processes data. Because religion deals with ultimate Mystery and with the worship that is human response to mystery, religion is theology's concern.

Religion has both an inner and an outer dimension. The inner aspect deals with the human heart grasped by divine Mystery, and the outer aspect addresses the manifestation of that encounter in human history. Together these two dimensions form the content of a specific faith "tradition": the encounter itself, the creedal beliefs, cultic symbols, worship practices, and codes of moral conduct particular to that group.

The outer aspect of religion is an attempt to respond to the religious experience of the divine personally taking hold of the human heart. This response will be more or less authentic, as conversion deepens the ongoing transformation of the human life. Religious response varies, ranging from lifestyles that attempt to make permanent the withdrawal that mystical experience always entails, to lifestyles that choose to emphasize the sacramental engagement that contact with the divine demands. Common to all, however, are the beliefs, worship, and mores honoring the Holy One who has inrupted into human consciousness.

As a reflection and articulation on both the inner and outer aspects of religion, catholic theology recognizes in them a Trinitarian dimension. The interior grasping of the human heart by the divine comes by way of the gift of God's love poured out into our hearts through the Holy Spirit (Rom 5:5). This activity of the Spirit moves toward a continual manifestation of the Word. We recognize here the implicit missions of the Spirit and the Word active in human cultures throughout history.

Authentic religion demands expression that is grounded in the Spirit and manifests itself ever more fully in truthful integrity. It flows from the human heart not merely from ritual, for ritual itself is an outer aspect of religion, an expression of religion in spirit and in truth. Human hearts and minds are enfleshed in human persons with histories, geographies, names, and faces. Authentically religious persons deeply influence the progress or decline of the human cultures where they find themselves. They affect the substance of the culture though they may be unaware of it, because cultures are woven of the distinct meanings and values of a people.

North American culture upholds distinct meanings and values, for good or for ill. The United States includes several ethnic groups, and multiple sub-cultures, from Harlem to Houston. Religion identifies the ultimate meanings and values in a culture, those that refer to the divine, however it is encountered, worshipped, communicated, or privatized. A culture may be content with symbolic expression. It may refrain from theological reflection as we know it. When theology is used, however, it is a critical reflection on religion in a specific culture, if it is authentic theologizing. This explains in part the phenomena of black theology, liberation theologies, and feminist theologies, of Orthodox, Protestant, and Catholic theologies that vary even within a specific faith tradition.

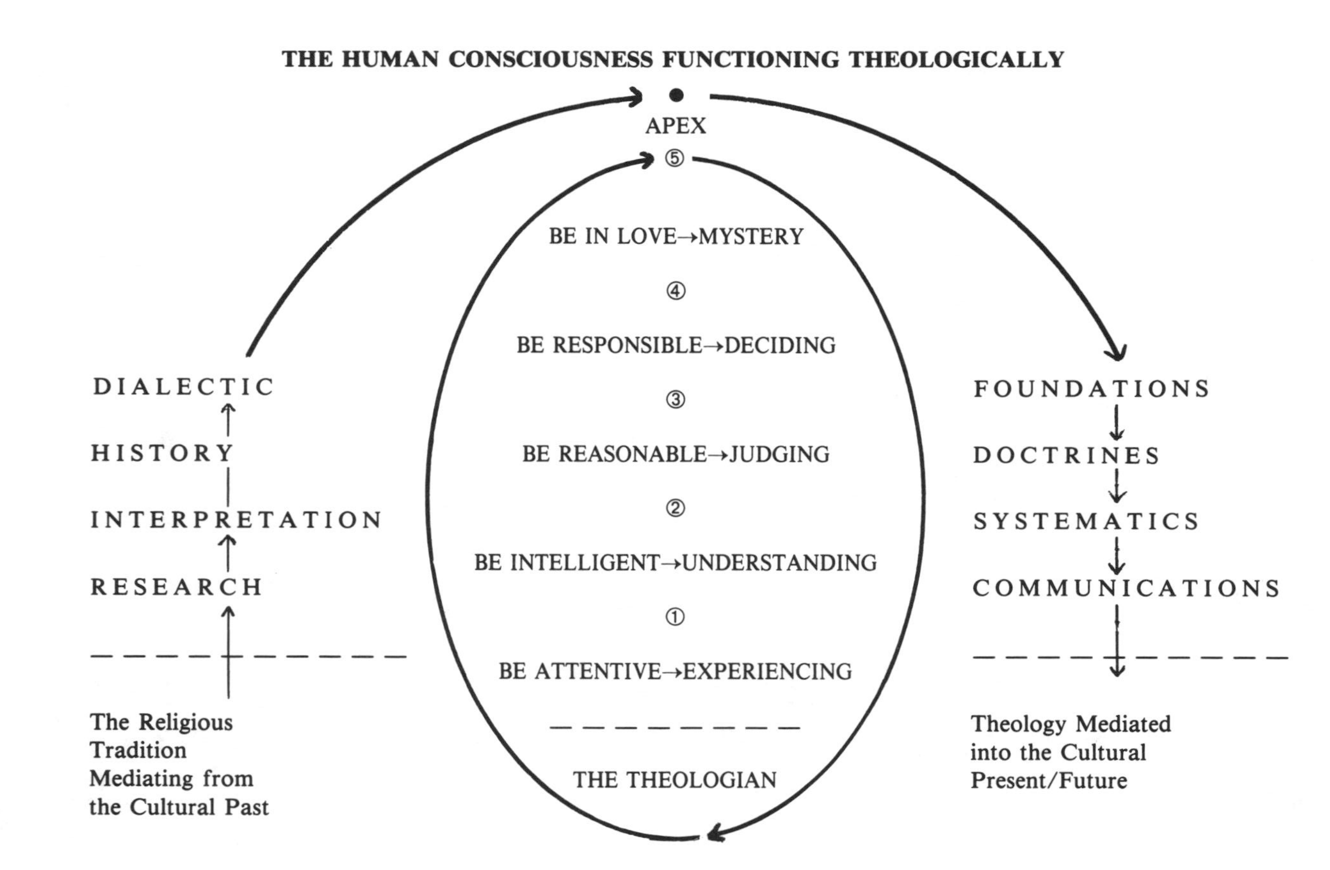
THE HUMAN CONSCIOUSNESS FUNCTIONING THEOLOGICALLY
APEX
⑤
BE IN LOVE→MYSTERY
④
BE RESPONSIBLE→DECIDING
③
BE REASONABLE→JUDGING
②
BE INTELLIGENT→UNDERSTANDING
①
BE ATTENTIVE→EXPERIENCING
THE THEOLOGIAN
DIALECTIC
HISTORY
INTERPRETATION
RESEARCH
The Religious
Tradition
Mediating from
the Cultural Past
FOUNDATIONS
DOCTRINES
SYSTEMATICS
COMMUNICATIONS
Theology Mediated
into the Cultural
Present/Future
Revised: 1988
Carla Mae Streeter, O.P.

Theological reflection, wherever it is done, is a process. It begins with sources, proceeds with pertinent questions, and reaches firm or probable conclusions. Conclusions prompt decisions and actions, and what is acted upon reveals what is valued.

This process is sketched in the diagram on page 104. It moves from sources to convictions, and from convictions to commitment and communication. This dynamic prompts us to identify theology as a discipline that *mediates* between religion and its cultural base (Lonergan, MT, xi). This mediating role has two phases: the phase mediating religious meaning *from* the culture by means of the texts and traditions already there, and the phase mediating religious truth, interpreted anew in light of contemporary questions and concerns, *back into* the culture. This provides a dynamic tradition, one in touch with both past and present. What is mediated is revelational data which faith holds to be ultimately valuable, even though it must struggle to understand and explain it. Theology also critiques the human religious response preserved in the heritage of the culture.

In the first phase, theology mediating from the culture, the mind attends to the writings, art, and symbols the culture has provided, seeking the truth intended. The first step is therefore *research*, a seeking out of the sources, texts, artifacts, etc. which reveal the religious meanings and values of a people. Next comes the *interpretation* of those sources as close as possible to the intention of the mind that authored or created them. A third step appears as the mind works. Threads of meaning are uncovered, meanings that move forward and develop. This is Lonergan's understanding of *history* as a function. A final step is the direct opposition of various meanings and the need to rank the value of each for that culture. This is known as *dialectic*. It should be noted that thus far, these tasks can be done by believer and non-believer alike, for they deal with religion as a phenomenon of history.

Not so with phase two. The data dealt with so far springs from the culture. Scholarship deals with it. To enter phase two, however, one must pass through the heart and deal with what is found there. The *inner* aspect of religion presents itself, not to be swept under the academic carpet. If the scholar continues into phase two, he or she becomes a theologian, one who reflects upon and seeks to articulate the religious experience of a community from within that community. To do this, one must address the inner aspect of religion, the specific encounter of that community with the Mystery of the divine. At this point, the *outer* aspects of religion, the texts, beliefs, worship, and mores of that tradition become the actual data worked on in phase one.

As the diagram indicates, the movement in phase two is from above downwards. The first area to be thematized is called *foundations.* It refers to the objectifying of the conversions brought about by personal encounter with the divine. It becomes evident at this point that spirituality must again be restored to its place at the heart of the theological enterprise as something essential not peripheral, for it deals with the inner aspect of religion. From this articulation, and in light of all that is known of the past tradition through phase one, the theologian carves out fresh language regarding *doctrines*, language speaking meaning to this age as well as conversing with the past. Next, these doctrinal articulations are interrelated. They become a coherent *systematics*. Finally, theological *communications* emerges as a specific function. The theologian enters the classroom or stands before a congregation to attempt the unique task we are addressing here: the act of preaching.

Truth must now be communicated anew to *this* culture to challenge it to the transformation that makes it evermore distinctly human. Religion itself is not exempt from this challenge, for it too may have degenerated into empty pietism. As a cultural phenomenon, each religious tradition must remain open to this same challenge of transformation, of conversion.

For Christians, this double dynamic of an inner encounter moving toward an outer historicized manifestation also suggests an incarnational pattern. The Spirit, encountering human willingness in the Jewish woman Mary, brings forth the Word in the historical, Jewish Jesus. This incarnational paradigm is reflected in every authentic theological effort: through the Spirit, a new word is again enfleshed in and through the historical human language of that time and place.

B. THEOLOGICAL COMMUNICATIONS AS A SPECIFIC FUNCTION

This return *to* culture, the right side of the diagram, is critical. The word that has emerged theologically must now be mediated *back* to the present culture. If this return is not done well, people might hear only the precise and very specific language of theology. They may understand little or nothing of this. The specific function called theological communications deals with transposing theological meaning into the commonsense language of the women and men in the marketplace. These hearers have little or no access to theological jargon. Its distinctions and clarifications, essential for the precision of the theological discipline, have little or no meaning for the butcher, the baker, or the Buick sales manager.

Theological communications is a functional specialty that is concerned with theology in its external relations. It is concerned with theology's relations to its "public" (Lonergan, MT, 132). To be effective, theological communications must be concerned with three types of external relations: those that are interdisciplinary, those calling for general transposition from the realm of theory to the realm of common sense, and those needing to be adaptive to the various media used in the culture.

As in no time before in history, theology needs to be ready to communicate with other disciplines. Because each of these disciplines has a specific theoretical language of its own, theology will do well to recognize that fact in its dealings with the arts, with languages, with literature, other religions, the sciences both natural and human, and with philosophy, history, and psychology.

Theology also needs to be "transposed" for the common man and woman on the street. This means the development of transpositional language, expressions rich with imagery, metaphor, and analogy, that carry theological meaning without bogging down the hearer in theological jargon. Transposition done well provides the hearer with a bridge—a bridge moving from the special precise theological language of study back into the commonsense language of everyday human existence. Commonsense language is rich in imagery and description. It lacks the clarity and explanation needed for precise theoretical study. But make no mistake. Commonsense language carries theological impact. It is the transposition back into this mode that enables study to bear fruit by impacting life precisely where people are living.

In addition, theology needs to be adaptive to today's media forms. This calls for media awareness and sensitivity. A whole range of skills is called into play here: audio, visual, and dramatic. Effective theological communication is the epitome, the mature fruit of the theological task. Without it theology can be sterile, or at best, be confined to talking only to itself.

II. Preaching

The art of preaching is the mature fruit of theological communication. As such, it is the crown of theological reflection and articulation. It is not merely another form of theological expression such as teaching or writing. Preaching differs from the ordered presentation of theological information that is teaching. Preaching is communication that is aimed at the transformation that means *conversion*. It informs, as does teaching, but that is not its primary purpose. How does the preaching act move its hearers toward conversion?

Preaching means or intends something beyond information. It unashamedly displays the conviction and personal commitment of the preacher. It stops at nothing short of calling forth the same kind of commitment in the hearers. Preaching mediates between the word of God and the word the culture seeks to instill in us. It may directly challenge the values of the culture. It may also refine the meaning and impact of the word of God regarding this situation in this culture at this time.

Finally, preaching is the primary act of the self-constituting process that we call "church." The community called church is actually formed by this word. It is brought more and more into being every time that word is preached. More, the community enters into this formation by its choice to engage the word. The word is God's word, but the word is also ours seeded with our surrender, watered with human tears, baked in the oven of human grief, and served at the table of our gathering together. Because preaching means or intends something beyond mere information, it is *formational*.

Preaching intends something incarnational. Nothing is to be left unaffected. It deliberately sets out to capture our imaginative minds. The fact that it grasps us cognitively, however, does not make it identical to teaching. The human being is not just intellect. Preaching pushes for renewed motivation, and motives are affectively charged, leading to choice. Preaching seeks effectiveness. Its aim is to trigger human consciousness into an effective *response*. Informed free human response actually constitutes the substance of true value in a culture. If so, then sound preaching triggers this powerful human dynamic.

While teaching focuses on the orderly presentation of data, and, in the person of a dynamic teacher, seeds are often planted for the transformation of the world, it is preaching that motivates hearers to begin that transformation NOW. Preaching actually midwifes a new creation in and through the human TODAY. Although it uses sound teaching, its goal is more radical: it communicates with an eye toward transforming intersubjective relations, artistic sensitivity, symbolic imagery, linguistic impact, and incarnate inculturation. It is after the transformation of the entire person as a communal member of a specific culture.

By its very nature, preaching is a mediating activity. The preacher mediates between the word of God and the congregation. The mediation is mutual. The congregation often effects the conversion of the preacher. The first, however, to be impacted by the mediation is the preacher. Caught, as it were, between the word and the hearers, the preacher is called to conversion. In turn, the word coming through the preacher lures the hearers toward conversion.

The trinitarian and incarnational dimensions of the preaching act reveal themselves in this dynamic of grace and the human. Preaching is itself a human act. The source of what is preached is divine mystery. The word is proclaimed through the power of the Spirit. Just as the divine procession of the word and the spiration of the Spirit within the Godhead itself is God's self-expression in wisdom and love, so the double mission of word and Spirit in our world completes that divine self-expression in creation.

III. The Relationship of Theological Communications and Preaching

The mere expression of theological truth need not be preaching as we have noted. Theological communication takes on a nuanced meaning when we refer, as does Lonergan, to communications as a *functional* specialty. Operationally, this means the final theological task is transposition from the realm of theory to the world of common sense.

In reality, this implies three transpositions when applied to the act of preaching. The first transposition is the preacher's encounter with the scriptural word. The preacher's concrete common sense images and concepts become, for a time, mute before the common sense imagery and concepts of the word. The preacher's first task is to hear the word in the language of its time and writing.

It is Advent. The setting is a priestless parish in southern Texas. The married deacon, José, who administers the parish with his wife, Maria, sits down to be with the word of God for a while in preparation for the communion service he and Maria will conduct on Sunday. The text is Luke's annunciation narrative.

If he is wise, Jose will temporarily put aside preparing a homily. Instead he will simply bring himself before the word of God and listen, letting it first prepare him. This is a vulnerable moment for the preacher.

It leaves one with a terrifying emptiness, and time pressure will often suggest that this first transposition be skipped. Allowing oneself to be engulfed by the emptiness is a critical moment. The stillness speaks volumes. It bespeaks the radical need of the preacher and identifies the preacher with the poverty of the people who will be gathering. The need creates a hunger—a hunger for meaning and insight. One cannot give what one does not have. It is here that the preacher becomes radically mendicant, a beggar in search of bread. The cry of the poor one will not go unheard. Like a reed hollowed out and pierced, the preacher is readied for the shepherd's breath. There is room because of the emptiness.

Was this woman Mary like this? Was she so empty of egoism that there was room for the breath to move? The messenger tells her that being like this is blessed; being empty, needy; being creature. God is looking for welcome space, like a bird seeking a nesting place. A woman's womb? Tissue? Blood and bone? Hands, feet, and hair? This is too much. God should know better than to get mixed up in all this. This can *hurt*.

The second transposition takes place when the preacher transposes from the scriptural word back into the personal word of his or her reality. It is here that the scriptural word now enters the personal filter of the preacher's imagery and concepts. If there is little or no theological depth in the preacher, or more harmful, if the theological formation that is there arises from a fundamentalist mindset, then the word will be affected by this personal factor. Yet this is only half the story. In this second transposition the theology of the preacher is also called into question by the recurring encounter with the word. In light of the contemplative silence before the word, it is often the preacher's former images and favorite concepts that undergo change. This can be detected in honest earthy questions. It is in this second moment that the personal theological convictions of the preacher are refined in light of the scriptural word. It is here also that the rich but ambiguous depths of scriptural language pass into a focused interpretation afforded by sound theological discipline that the community recognizes as its own.

José and Maria have two children with a third on the way. The memory of the joy and mutual surrender of their lovemaking intrudes itself into his thoughts, and he is almost embarrassed. Yet it fits—he can't deny it: their "yes" with this woman Mary's yes, their fruitfulness and hers. Is that how it is with us? Is that how close this God wants to come? José thinks of the old ones in his congregation, of the widows, of the single and the divorced. He remembers the children and the teens. What of them?

What of their hungers? Will this holy One find welcome? What will these incarnations look like?

Finally, from this mutual encounter, theology in light of scriptural word and word focused on humanness, on incarnation, the third transposition can be made. Using all the skills of the preaching art, the scriptural word now focused in theological insight must now once again be clothed in the rich language of imagery and analogy, metaphor and story, to impact a congregation today, where it lives, here and now. José has to break bread for his elderly and widows, his teens and children. *How* this will take place is not the preacher's concern. *That* it take place focuses all the preacher's energy. Preaching is utterly concrete and existential. It is utterly practical. Should all else fail, it will transform at least the preacher who engages in it, for the inner word has already deeply moved José. The preaching act is the culmination of all other forms of theological communication. José is not merely going to teach his people; he is going to preach to them.

The word itself has provided him with a structure. It is familiar to all his hearers. There is a lot of space in Texas. But some hearts may not have any. Can we be needy before God? Can we admit that we don't have it all together, that we long for a lot of things, some of them selfishly? Can we empty ourselves enough of some of the rubble at least to let God breathe love in us? If we say yes, then the incarnations will start, the space will come alive. It will be filled with words to be said or left unsaid; the walking in someone else's skin; the telephone call; noticing the look on someone's face. Why doesn't God just leave us alone. To come to meet us in skin, in hair, in blood and bone and tissue and tears is just a little too much. Or is that what is being "announced" to us today, something not just for Mary but for all of us. Is God asking us to give our little worlds a good word, a word-made-flesh? In *our* flesh—yours and mine?

Conclusion

Theology is a reflection on and articulation of the role of religion in a culture. In its external relations theology functions finally as communications, the skillful transposition out of its own special precise language to the commonsense language of daily affairs.

The most powerful and effective form of theological communication is the act of preaching. Aimed at conversion, it moves beyond teaching to activate the self-constituting human process that we call "church." It informs and forms the assembly into the very community of those committed publicly and explicitly to discipleship in Christ Jesus. In this sense preaching is intensely Eucharistic, for it is the bread of the Word broken; it nourishes the community into becoming what it is to be. Properly leavened, this community becomes a sign of what God in the Spirit intends through the Word. It becomes an incarnate word for the world.

Theological study is indispensable to sound preaching. It is related to the preaching act through a series of transpositions subtly enacted within the preacher. The preacher enters into the scriptural word only to be faced with his or her own personally worded reality. This reality will be attuned theologically through the understanding the preacher has, be it adequate or not. The final transposition is effected when the scriptural word, refracted through the human prism of the preacher, shines its various hues into the commonsense world of the hearers. Like a lampstand holding a welcome light on a hilltop, the preacher helps traveling companions find home.

Work Cited

Bernard Lonergan, *Method in Theology* (Dartman, Longman and Todd, 1972).

Chapter 8

Revelation and Proclamation: Shifting Paradigms

MARY CATHERINE HILKERT, O.P.

At a recent international meeting of the *Societas Homiletica* on "The Formation of Preachers in Church and University," David Buttrick, professor of homiletics at Vanderbilt Divinity School, observed that "we grope not only for methodology, but for some new theoretical basis for homiletics in philosophical theology, which itself seems to be searching renewal."[1] He noted that the field of homiletics is being affected profoundly not only by a paradigm shift in biblical criticism, but also by a similar shift of paradigms in systematic theology. Contemporary scholars, he remarked, are "not only challenging methodological conventions, but proposing structures of thought that are clearly breaking with the ruling neo-orthodoxy that has been with us for half a century."[2] In addition to the rise of hermeneutics and critical theory, Buttrick identified the field of fundamental theology, in particular the theology of revelation, as one of the areas of dramatic change within systematic theology.

The true "shaking of the foundations"[3] that has been occurring in both Catholic and Protestant traditions in the theology of revelation in the twentieth century has crucial importance for our understanding of what is going on in the preaching event. The Reformation traditions, which have well developed theologies of preaching, have traditionally highlighted the power of the proclamation of the Word to convert sinful humanity. In the Catholic tradition where sacraments were emphasized as the locus of the encounter with God, preaching was often omitted from sacramental celebrations prior to the liturgical renewal of Vatican II. Further the phrase "theology of preaching" remains relatively new to Catholics even now. Yet in the context of the biblical and liturgical renewal of the past 25 years, theological resources for a theology of preaching drawn from the Catholic "sacramental imagination" have begun to emerge, especially in the thought of Karl Rahner, Edward Schillebeeckx, and liberation theologians. Tracing the contrast of the "dialectical imagination" as found in Karl

Barth, Rudolph Bultmann, and the new hermeneutic theologians with the "sacramental imagination" of Karl Rahner, Edward Schillebeeckx, and Latin American liberation theologians provides insight into the contributions each has to make to the contemporary ecumenical search for a theology of preaching.[4] Paul Tillich's recognition of the strengths of each tradition provides a helpful bridge between the two.

Dialectical Imagination: The Proclaimed Word Effects Grace

KARL BARTH

The neo-orthodoxy that Buttrick describes as ruling (Protestant) theology for half a century is identified largely with the Swiss theologian Karl Barth. His 1922 commentary on the Epistle to the Romans has been described as "a bombshell" that divided the German theological world into "advocates and bitter detractors."[5] Barth's criticism of anthropocentric liberal theology[6] was directly related to his responsibility to preach the Gospel in the pastoral ministry of the Swiss Reformed Church. His experience in ministry led Barth to reject the liberal view that located revelation within religious experience and history, a perspective in which he himself had been formed during his years of theological study at Berlin, Tübingen, and Marburg. As David Jenkins described Barth's fundamental critique of Protestant liberal preaching: "When preachers spoke about God it sounded as though they were doing little more than speaking about humanity in a loud voice."[7] From Barth's perspective, the liberal failure to take seriously the extent to which sin has destroyed the image of God in humanity resulted in a fundamental misreading of the tragedy, terror, and despair of human existence and a related blindness that failed to perceive the radical "good news" of the "strange new world of the Bible" where God—not human beings—is at the center of reality:

> The Bible tells us not how we should talk with God but what he says to us; not how we find the way to him, but how he has sought and found the way to us. . . . We have found in the Bible a new world, God, God's sovereignty, God's glory, God's incomprehensible love.[8]

Turning to the Protestant Reformers' touchstone, the Epistle to the Romans, Barth rediscovered the wholly-other, living God and the infinite qualitative difference between God and human beings. There can be no continuity between revelation and creation since creation destroyed by sin reveals only God's "No." The hidden God (*Deus Absconditus*) of Christian revelation can never be discovered directly in human history or experience, both of which are deeply scarred by sin. (*Finitum non capax infiniti*).

Nevertheless, "while we were still sinners" God chose to be revealed in the paradox of the humanity of Jesus and the scandal of the cross. While there is no way from humanity to God, the way from God to humanity has been revealed in Jesus Christ who came to deliver self-contradictory human beings from their slavery to sin. Yet God's self-revelation in Jesus remains indirect and veiled. In a world where sin continues to rule, the paradox of revelation remains always "in spite of." Barth writes:

> That the promises of the faithfulness of God have been fulfilled in Jesus the Christ is not, and never will be, self-evident truth, since in Him it appears in its final hiddenness and its most profound secrecy. . . . In Jesus the communication of God begins with a rebuff, with the exposure of a vast chasm, with the clear revelation of a great stumbling-block.[9]

God's "triumph of grace" in freely turning toward humanity in reconciliation in and through Jesus Christ is the specific focus of Barth's later theological writings. In spite of the incarnational emphasis of this phase of Barth's writings, it remains clear that revelation is not to be sought or discovered directly within humanity or creation. Rather, "the conception of an indirect revelation in nature, in history, and in our self-consciousness is destroyed by the recognition of grace, by the recognition of Jesus Christ as the eternal Word who was made flesh."[10]

For Barth, the "Word of God" refers strictly speaking to Jesus Christ, the incarnate word, the sheer grace of God's reconciliation with us. Scripture, the written Word of God, witnesses to the incarnate word, since it is the record of salvation history that culminates in Jesus Christ. Granted that the Bible is the word of human beings and historically-culturally conditioned, Barth proclaims that by the miracle of grace it is both human word and Word of God when the Holy Spirit reveals the true meaning of a passage by showing its meaning in terms of Jesus Christ. Barth cautioned against the claim that the Bible *is* God's Word; he preferred to emphasize that we have heard God's Word and we hope to hear it again. Specifically the Bible becomes God's Word when it is proclaimed and heard in the Church in the power of the Spirit. When the Word is the commission, theme, and judgment in preaching in such a way that the Holy Spirit seizes the heart of the believer and summons the decision of conversion, the words of the preacher become God's Word as well.

The implications of this dialectical or neo-orthodox theology (also known as "theology of the Word of God") for a theology of proclamation are clearly drawn out by Barth in his classic *The Preaching of the Gospel* as well as in a number of essays including "The Need and Promise of Christian Preaching."[11] In contrast to the liberal model, Barth is quite clear in his conviction that the proclamation of the Gospel is not a matter of interpreting human experience (whether the preacher's or the congregation's) or human history religiously. Rather, the preacher's task is to announce what God has made known to us in Jesus Christ. As Barth insists: "Not general reflections on man and the cosmos, but Revelation is the only legitimate ground for preaching."[12] Revelation is totally God's action; the preacher is not to be seen even as mediator:

> It is not the function of the preacher to reveal God or to act as his intermediary. When the gospel is preached, God speaks: there is no question of the preacher revealing anything or of a revelation being conveyed through him. . . . Revelation is a closed system in which God is the subject, the object, and the middle term.[13]

The preacher is the herald who bears witness to God's sovereign power and grace in Jesus Christ. When the proclamation of the Word is true to revelation, the Spirit of God effects reconciliation and calls for the human response of obedience to the Word. Barth reminds us, however, that the relationship between humanity and God is "effected from on high by a divine miracle. [We are] not naturally disposed to hear the Word of God: we are children of wrath" (Eph 2:3).[14]

RUDOLPH BULTMANN

Although his emphasis is significantly more anthropological than Barth's christological approach, Rudolph Bultmann is often grouped with Karl Barth and Emil Brunner in the paradigm of "dialectical theology" or "crisis theology" because of their common emphasis on divine transcendence and human sinfulness. Like Barth, Bultmann viewed revelation as the salvific encounter with the living God in the reconciling event of the cross and resurrection of Jesus Christ as made available to believers in and through the proclamation of the Word of God. Through the preaching of the Gospel in the power of the Spirit, hearers of the Word are revealed to themselves as sinners and called to the conversion of authentic self-understanding (radical obedience, freedom, and trust) through faith. Bultmann preferred to talk of *Heilsereignis* or *Heilsgeschehen* (salvation event) rather than what he perceived to be the mythological language of *Heilsgeschichte* (salvation history) in order to emphasize the event character of God's revelatory action in proclamation. Underlining that revelation occurs precisely in and through the Word, he remarked that "God encounters us at all times and in all places, but he cannot be seen everywhere unless his Word comes as well and makes the moment of revelation intelligible to us in its own light."[15]

Influenced by Martin Heidegger's existential philosophy, Bultmann disagreed with Barth, however, on the crucial question of whether there is a "point of contact" in human experience for the preaching of the Gospel. Convinced that there is no presuppositionless exegesis, Bultmann argued that the ultimate existential questions of human existence constitute the preunderstanding necessary for hearing and interpreting the Gospel as a call to authentic existence. Nevertheless, he remained convinced that the proclamation of the cross and resurrection of Jesus provides the only ultimate answer to the questions of human existence. Thus the biblical texts continue to "call us up short" and challenge, expand, and even dismantle our limited human pre-understandings.

Bultmann's well-known concern for the demythologization of the biblical text (and remythologization in the categories of existential philosophy) was ultimately a concern for the effective proclamation of the Gospel. He feared that mythological language would become a false stumbling block preventing twentieth-century secular thinkers from attending to the true challenge of the "Word of the cross" calling hearers to authentic existence. The revelatory event of preaching is intended to confront the hearer with a crisis not of understanding, but of decision.

NEW HERMENEUTIC THEOLOGIANS

The insights of dialectical theologians Karl Barth and Rudolph Bultmann with their profound appreciation of the power of the Word were taken a step further by the group of theologians identified as post-Bultmannians or "the new hermeneutic theologians," notably Ernst Fuchs and Gerhard Ebeling. While Bultmann admitted that the Word of God challenged and dismantled all human presuppositions, the new hermeneutic theologians stressed that *the Word of God interprets and judges us* in delivering us from the grip of inauthenticity "like a flash of lightning that strikes."[16] Building on dialectical theology's emphasis on the character of revelation as event, the new hermeneutic theologians developed a more philosophical approach to language, meaning, and the functioning of words.

Emphasizing the linguisticality of human existence, the post-Bultmannians focused on the language of a text and viewed the proclamation of the Word not only as a salvation-event, but precisely as a language-event. Jesus, the Word made flesh, was described as the language-event (Fuchs) or Word-event (Ebeling) that creates new possibilities of what it means to be human. The shift to the singular "hermeneutic" rather than the traditional "hermeneutics" was intended to signal their conviction that human interpreters do not use hermeneutical method to "figure out" a biblical text, rather "The Word interprets us." Rather than our "questioning of the text," the Word of God calls our understanding of existence into question through the medium of the biblical text.

Influenced by Heidegger's later writings and the work of Hans-Georg Gadamer, the new hermeneutic theologians opposed philosophical efforts to explain Being or ultimate reality. In contrast to the modern attempts to grasp, manipulate, and ultimately to master reality, Heidegger and Gadamer encouraged a more contemplative stance of trusting that Being reveals itself through language (translated by the new hermeneutic theologians into the conviction that God expresses self through Word). Highlighting the dimension of revelation as gift (the unveiling of mystery), the new hermeneutic theologians described the hermeneutical task as that of "dwelling in the Word," "letting truth happen," "letting the Word emerge," "waiting in trusting silence for a word that will be given." The role of the interpreter of the Word (and hence the preacher) is openness and submission to the self-disclosure of the Word and obedience to its demands. Playing on the German expression for response or answer (*Antwort*) to the Word (*Wort*), Fuchs emphasizes that faith's response to the Word is the result of the Word having come to birth in us, making us responsible, creating us as witnesses.[17]

The Word-event theology of the new hermeneutic theologians offers a strong linguistic foundation for proclamatory preaching in which the text becomes a Word-event once again in and through the power of the Spirit. The christological focus on the power of the Word to convert the human hearers of the Gospel is the strength of this approach. On the other hand, the implicit anthropology in this perspective raises questions concerning the role of the preacher (We do not interpret the Word; the Word interprets us) and makes clear that grace is not to be viewed as a radical transformation of the human person or society. Robert Funk underlines the dialectical approach to grace, sin, and anthropology that undergirds the new hermeneutical stance (as well as more classic neo-orthodox theology) by contrasting the way the Pharisee and the publican (who realizes that he/she is a sinner) respond to parables of grace. Sinners, says Funk, hear and understand parables of grace—grace interprets the sinner. Pharisees, however, insist on interpreting the Word of grace rather than letting themselves be interpreted by the word. Two of Funk's five theses regarding the deeds and parables of grace reveal clearly the classic Reformation foundation of the new hermeneutic approach: 1) "Grace always wounds from behind—where we feel most vulnerable," and 2) "Grace is not something man can have at all."[18] P. J. Burns has summarized the relationship between grace and preaching in the new hermeneutic approach, highlighting the classic Reformation view of the human person as *simul justus et peccator*:

> Salvation comes to man—existing in his distorted relationship to a guilty past and a threatening future not as a liberated witness but as a crumpled-up question mark—through the concrete proclamation of the Word of God summoning him to faith. Faith is thus authentic human existence, healed linguisticality grounded in God. . . .[19]

The theology of preaching that emerges from the Reformation traditions is classically described as a law-gospel hermeneutic. The preacher first diagnoses the human situation under the burden of God's law which we have not the power on our own to observe. The "first word" to be said about the human condition, Richard Lischer reminds us, is the "bad news" of our failure to live in fidelity to God's covenant, resulting in the condition of enmity with God. We are "children of wrath."[20] The primary task of the preacher, however, is to announce the good news that in and through the death and resurrection of Jesus Christ we are no longer "under the law"; rather we live in the freedom of the children of God. The dialectic of both judgment and grace (*simul justus et peccator*) remains the fundamental truth of the human situation. The final victory of God's grace over the sin of the world in the life, death, and resurrection of Jesus Christ, however, gives the final word to grace: "We preach life and death—with the advantage to life."[21]

PAUL TILLICH

A BRIDGE BETWEEN THE DIALECTICAL AND SACRAMENTAL IMAGINATIONS

Before contrasting the Catholic tradition's sacramental heritage with the dialectical Protestant emphasis on the Word, one important Protestant theologian and preacher who drew from the resources of both traditions deserves mention: Paul Tillich. Tillich shared the neo-orthodox critique of what he called "the bourgeois synthesis of liberal theology"[22] and emphasized the power of sin in his description of humanity's radical existential estrangement from our essential being. His theological method of correlation, however, was developed in explicit rejection of the Barthian kerygmatic approach that denied a point of contact in the human situation for the hearing of the Gospel. As Tillich critically assessed this approach: "The message must be thrown at those in the situation—thrown like a stone."[23]

By way of contrast, Tillich's apologetic theology took seriously the need for theology to be in dialogue with its historical and cultural situation and urged that mediation between religion and culture need not involve uncritical adaptation. Convinced that religion is the depth dimension that reveals what is truly of "ultimate concern" or gives unconditional meaning to human life, Tillich asserted that both theology and preaching should begin with an analysis of the human situation. While human beings are estranged from God in our concrete existential situation, the divine and the human can never be separated since God is the very ground of being. Existential analysis of the human situation, Tillich suggested, reveals structures of anxiety, conflict, doubt, and guilt and discloses the ultimate human question to which the Gospel responds: "the question of a reality in which the self-estrangement of our existence is overcome, a reality of reconciliation and reunion, of creativity and meaning and hope."[24] Yet while philosophical and or psychological analysis can bring to light ultimate human questions and the fundamental human need for grace, only the power of the New Being in Jesus the Christ can reconcile the fundamental estrangement and alienation in human existence.

Tillich's apologetic method of communicating the Christian message, whether in theology or preaching, begins with an analysis of the predicament of human beings that highlights both the estrangement from our own deepest truth ("the old eon") and the potential latent in the present crisis which Tillich describes in one of his sermons as openness for "the creative moment which may appear in the midst of what seemed to be waste."[25] The "eternal now" of God's reconciling grace, the healing of our fundamental alienation, is offered paradoxically, Tillich reminds us, in the present moment of existence "while we are still sinners." Thus an existential crisis is also a moment of grace in which the challenge to radical courage in the face of doubt, despair, death, or even non-being is extended to believers in and through the symbols of Christian faith.

If the good news of salvation is to be heard today, however, contemporary reinterpretation of those symbols in a way that highlights their revelatory possibility to evoke an awareness of God's offer of courage and hope in the present moment is crucial. Like Bultmann, Tillich was convinced that the crisis of faith for many contemporary believers was rather a crisis of culture and language. Thus he argued:

> Many of those who reject the Word of God reject it because the way we say it is utterly meaningless to them. They know the dimension of the eternal but they cannot accept our names for it. If we cling to their words, we may doubt whether they have received a word from the Lord. If we meet them as persons, we know they have."[26]

The task as the preacher or theologian (or any minister of the Word) is therefore first to help people to recognize their human situation in its depth dimensions—to "open up an empty space in the soul"[27]—and then to interpret the biblical symbols and Christian message in a way that reveals the religious response to that empty space, the real power of New Being available in and through Jesus the Christ.[28] Revelation occurs when the dialogical relationship between the preacher and listeners evokes an awareness of God's presence for those who embrace the challenge of "the courage to be."[29] Tillich concurred with Bultmann's judgment that the categories of existential psychology were the most productive for creative contemporary reappropriation of the biblical message. Thus in his preaching he consistently reinterpreted the central Christian symbols of sin and grace in terms of separation/estrangement/sickness and reunion/reconciliation/and health.

In his emphasis on the negative moment within any description of the relationship between the divine and the human, his insistence on the paradox of "the abounding of sin and the greater abounding of grace" as "the two all-determining facts of life"[30] as well as his underscoring of the ambiguous, estranged, and broken dimensions of human existence, Tillich remains rooted in the dialectical imagination. Yet in identifying the possibility of the gracious presence of God being disclosed within the created and the human[31] and in his method of apologetic theology and preaching that searches for a point of contact in the human situation for the revelation of God, Tillich reveals dimensions of the sacramental imagination more frequently associated with the Catholic theologians to whom we now turn.

The Sacramental Imagination: Grace Come to Word and Action

It is in terms of anthropology that the dialectical and sacramental imaginations diverge most dramatically. Even the 1983 ecumenical breakthrough statement from the U.S. Lutheran-Roman Catholic dialogue on "Justification by Faith" highlights the theological differences in this area:

> The Lutheran hermeneutical understanding of justification by faith in some ways heightens the tension with Catholic positions. It does so by excluding from the gospel proclamation all reference to the freedom and goodness of fallen human beings on the ground that this would undermine the unconditionality of God's promises in Christ. . . . Theological disagreement about the structure of thought in relation to proclamation of the gospel, though serious, need not be church-dividing.[32]

While different emphases in theological anthropology need not be church-dividing, disputes about the relationship between sacraments and preaching as well as Scripture and tradition were central to differences between the Reformers and the Roman Catholic Church at the time of the Reformation. The belief that God and not the human interpreter was the source of grace in the preaching event had been accepted throughout the Christian tradition. In scholastic language Thomas Aquinas described God as the principal cause of preaching while the apostles and preachers were the instrumental cause through which God preaches.[33] In the polemical context of the Reformation, however, in order to defend the validity and necessity of the sacraments against the Reformers who emphasized the power of the preached Word, most scholastic theologians began to make a new distinction: the principal cause of preaching is a human cause, while the principal cause in the sacraments is God; therefore, only the sacraments can be said to "confer grace." Disputes about the efficacy of the proclaimed Word and the relationship between sacraments and preaching dominated Catholic theological writings about preaching well into the twentieth century. Various authors proposed that preaching brings about faith, but not sanctifying grace, and argued that preaching cannot be considered an eighth sacrament.

Further, the Catholic emphasis on tradition (usually understood as church teaching) resulted in an implicit propositional and doctrinal understanding of revelation. From the time of the Catechism of the Council of Trent a systematic presentation of Catholic doctrine was presumed to provide the best guide to preaching. While bishops and priests (who were the only official preachers) were encouraged to explain the Church's doctrines in a pastoral way that would draw believers more deeply into the whole mystery of faith, by 1936 preaching had become merely "the vulgarization of theological tracts" in the estimation of Josef Jungmann.[34] The major Catholic theologian to rethink the theology of revelation and specifically the relationship between Word and sacrament in the twentieth century was Karl Rahner.

KARL RAHNER

Rahner's influence on the Second Vatican Council's dogmatic constitution on revelation was considerable. Entitled *Dei Verbum* (The word of God), that document shifted Catholic theology beyond a post-Tridentine and Vatican I propositional approach to revelation (as a body of truths beyond the grasp of reason to be accepted on the authority of the one revealing them) toward a relational, incarnational, sacramental, and trinitarian perspective rooted in the biblical conviction that "God is love." If God *is* in God's very being self-communicating love, and if God has freely chosen to extend to humanity the relationship of friendship then, Rahner suggests, humanity must be structured as openness or desire to receive that offer of love. The explicit social, historical mediation of that love (grace) is necessary precisely because we as human beings are constituted as body-spirit (spirit-in-the-world), and we can experience an invitation at the spiritual depth dimension of our existence (transcendental pole) only insofar as it is mediated or made known to us in and through the social, tangible, and concrete manifestations of our bodies, our histories, our world. Like all free personal self-communication, grace (God's offer of self-communication or friendship), requires the Word to re-veal (un-veil) definitively the offer of relationship. Thus Rahner argues that God's self-offer which has remained anonymous or ambiguous throughout human history and creation, came to the explicitness of word in the Hebrew prophets and to the definitive and irrevocable pledge of God's love for humanity in the Word-made-flesh, Jesus.

Using the incarnation as the key from which to interpret all of reality, Rahner proposes that all reality is structured symbolically—signs of grace (or as Augustine said the "footprints of the Trinity") are to be found everywhere if "we have eyes to see." Here Rahner opposes the emphasis of a Word-event theology by insisting that the Word of proclamation or the sacramental Word is not an event breaking into our "guilty past and the threatening future," but rather "grace is *here*. It is present wherever we are. It can always indeed be seen by the eye of faith and be expressed by the word of the message."[35]

In his approach to the once-neglected theology of the Word in the Catholic tradition, Karl Rahner drew on the resources of the later Heidegger as did the new hermeneutic theologians, but from an anthropological foundation that views creation and human existence as fundamentally graced. Granting that sin has profoundly altered God's original vision for human life, Rahner nonetheless remains convinced with St. Paul that "where sin abounds, grace abounds still more" (Rom. 5:20). The significance of this very different anthropological foundation for Rahner's approach to the Word as symbol and the event character of "grace come to word" is underscored in his essay "Priest and Poet" where he writes:

> Only a Protestant and a theologian of the most extreme dialectical obscurity could maintain that the divine grace, redemption, and our new freedom, light and the love of God remain so much in the beyond that one can experience nothing at all of them in this world; that on the contrary all human discourse witnesses to the word and to the reality of God only by its character of absolute paradox.[36]

In contrast, Rahner speaking from a sacramental perspective emphasizes the continuity between creation and redemption, and the openness of humanity for the divine. We are structured from creation as "hearers of the Word"; while sin has affected, it has not destroyed, the image of God within humanity. Thus Rahner can make the claim that contrasts sharply with the dialectical perspective: "Preaching is the awakening and making explicit of what is already there in the depths of [the person], not by nature but by grace."[37] Ultimately Rahner's theology of revelation and his theological anthropology are inseparable and both contribute to his conviction that the Word announces the grace that is already there in the depths of the person and in the midst of human history and creation.

The close connection between anthropology and grace in Rahner's thought allows him to locate the Word of God within the primordial words that emerge from the depth of the human heart. Reflecting on the connections between the vocation of the poet and that of the priest (and by extension, the preacher), Rahner contrasts the use of human words that simply convey information (technical or utility words) from "depth words" that he calls "living words" or "gifts of God." "They bring light to *us*, not we to them," Rahner remarks.[38] While citing explicitly the influence of the later Heidegger here, Rahner parts company with the Word-event theology of the new hermeneutic theologians in claiming that these primordial words "spring up out of our hearts" precisely because of the call to grace located at the depths of the human heart from the first moment of existence (Rahner's supernatural existential). With that understanding of the human as graced, Rahner can assert that "the primordial words of human beings transmuted by the Spirit of God are allowed to become words of God."[39] Human words have the potential to become sacraments of divine love.

Human words spoken from the center of ourselves, words like "I love you," "I have a dream," or "Here I stand; I can do no other," are in a profound sense revelatory—they allow a deeper dimension of reality to emerge. These kind of "depth words" are not merely signs which point to a reality that exists independently of the naming. Rather, in a public, conscious, historical way, the word "embodies" the deeper spiritual reality from which it emerges. Primordial words become sacraments—they function as symbols which allow a deeper mystery (the offer of grace) to become more concretely present and available to humanity.

Rahner's understanding of the roles of scripture and explicit preaching as words of the Church's faith and identity becomes clear only within the larger context of his treatment of the Church as sacrament in his vast schema of "a world of grace."[40] To return to the heart of Rahner's sacramental vision, grace, the self-communication of God in love, has an intrinsically incarnational structure—it is oriented toward the fullness of its expression in embodied Word. God has spoken throughout creation and history "in varied and fragmentary ways" as the Letter to the Hebrews states, but only in Jesus, the word of God incarnate, has God spoken God's own self-expression. Jesus, the Word made flesh, becomes the primordial sacrament of God in the midst of human history. As the ongoing body of Christ in the world, the Church participates in the abiding sacrament of Christ to the extent that the Church embodies, speaks, and acts upon the grace and truth of Jesus Christ. Preaching and the sacraments, preeminently the eucharist, function as the Church's self-expression naming, proclaiming, and celebrating the mystery of God's saving self-offering of love in the life, death, and resurrection of Jesus.[41]

While he never worked out a fully developed theology of preaching, it is clear that for Rahner, the preaching of the gospel must necessarily connect people's ordinary experience with the experience of grace that has been revealed both throughout the history of salvation culminating in Christ (as recorded in the scriptures) and within the depths of the human heart (in and through the power of the Spirit). Thus the role of the preacher is to bring to Word the depth dimension of the mystery of human existence as God's self-offer of love through interpreting that experience in light of the Scriptures, the liturgy, and the whole of the Christian tradition and thus draw hearers of the Word into a deeper relationship with God which is at the same time a deeper experience of their everyday human life and relationships as graced.[42]

EDWARD SCHILLEBEECKX

Edward Schillebeeckx, who shares Rahner's profound concern for the credibility of the Christian faith and the proclamation of the Gospel in the contemporary world has, like Rahner, located revelation within human experience. In pointing to experience as the locus of revelation, however, Schillebeeckx does not locate revelation in the transcendental depths of the human person, but rather in history. *Human* history, he notes, always involves interpreted experience. The very structure of human experience might be described as revelatory according to Schillebeeckx, since human beings learn by a process of discovery. We are born into a world of language and culture that provides us with frameworks for interpreting our experience, and yet new experiences can and do challenge, expand, even break down our previous frameworks for perceiving the world. New experience frequently challenges the former horizons of our world and adds new dimensions to our living tradition of experience.

Expanding on this idea, Schillebeeckx observes that experience has a narrative structure. Here he stresses that experience is shared; meaning is communicated through words and stories. Traditions, formed from collective experience, become the social framework for understanding. We are born into multiple traditions of shared meaning—our family and ethnic and racial traditions, the values and stories of our religions (or the "religion" of secular humanism), the myths, symbols, and values of our nation, etc. Further, when we want to share an experience of great significance, we ordinarily "tell the story" of what happened to us. Through narrative, one is able to offer others the possibility of a new experience—or of interpreting their past history in such a radically new way that they truly experience themselves and their lives differently.

In the midst of our ordinary daily lives certain events or experiences provide a kind of "gestalt shift" in the way in which we live and understand ourselves and the world. Whether suddenly or gradually, something unexpected happens in which, upon reflection, we recognize deeper dimensions of ourselves and reality. We reach the boundaries and limits of human experience in moments of love or joy or insight that seem so profound that secular language is no longer adequate to express the "surplus of meaning" we have experienced. We also reach the limits of human language and understanding in the negative experiences of human suffering, injustice, and death when we know the "pain of contrast" with our hopes for "salvation" or the "fullness of life." Instead, human life appears ultimately absurd or cruel, and reality itself random, if not malicious.

Forged consciously in the face of immense global suffering, Schillebeeckx's conviction that revelation occurs within, yet transcends, human experience focuses particularly on those negative experiences of injustice or apparent meaninglessness, raising the question of God's presence in apparent absence or even in the midst of evil. Here Schillebeeckx argues that God is to be encountered not directly (in unmediated presence or as willing or even permitting evil), but rather "on the underside" or "in contrast." God is present to the majority of the world's population in the way God was present to Jesus in the crucifixion—as source of endurance and hope in the darkness and apparent abandonment and as promise to be the faithful "God of the Living" (realized in the resurrection's final defeat of the forces of evil and "undoing of death").

While Schillebeeckx has not developed his own contemporary theology of preaching, implications for proclamation flow directly from both his theology of revelation and his christological writings which insist that in our day christology needs to adopt a narrative-practical approach (a retelling of the story of Jesus that moves its hearers to "go and do likewise").[43] In speaking the Word of faith of the community, even or perhaps especially in the midst of suffering, persecution, or the experienced absence of God, the preacher names the creative presence of God to be found in "fragments of salvation" and in "hidden revelation." The "fragments" which the preacher identifies as salvation experiences are to be found in the hope that emerges in the most hopeless of situations, the protest that rebels in the name of all that is human, and the persevering trust that clings to God even when God seems distant or absent. The community's hope proclaimed by the preacher is grounded in the resurrection of Jesus in which Jesus' own trust in God in the face of the ultimate rejection of the crucifixion was confirmed and vindicated as God brought life and a new future even out of death. Living in the spirit of the risen Jesus, the Christian community proclaims the hope of new possibilities even in the most hopeless of human situations and lives in trust. In continuity with the biblical experience, the preacher announces that "in our human experiences we can *experience* something that transcends our experience and proclaims itself in that experience as unexpected grace."[44] The proclamation of the Christian community names that "unexpected grace," that transcendent dimension within the depths of ordinary human history. The preacher speaks the Word of God in speaking the word of faith of the community.

In a unique blending of the sacramental imagination's insight that grace *is* to be discovered in human history and experience with the dialectical caution that sin and suffering abound and God remains a "hidden God," Schillebeeckx returns to the shared conviction that only "the eyes of faith" enable us to see God's presence in a world that often stands "in contrast" to the promise that God is "God of the Living" and "Compassion is at the heart of reality." The conviction that, despite all the evidence to the contrary, the love of God is at the center of reality is ultimately an experience of reality available only within the language of faith.[45] Thus Schillebeeckx rejects as a false dichotomy the question of whether "faith comes from hearing" (Rom 10:17) or faith begins with experience. The Christian story that is now recorded in the scriptures, he notes, began with an (interpreted) experience—the experience of salvation from God in Jesus. Further, that story can be passed on to others only if it remains the living experience of a community of believers who continue to hand on the story in a vital way that addresses the experience of others. As Schillebeeckx reminds us:

> Christianity is not a message which has to be believed but an experience of faith which becomes a message. Then, as an explicit message, it seeks to offer a new possibility of life experience to others who hear it within their own experience of life.[46]

Again this would suggest for preachers that "announcing the good news of salvation" means proclaiming not only "God's wonderful deeds" in the past history of salvation, but also the prophetic task of pointing to the continued workings of the Spirit of God in our present day. The preacher is called to tell the Christian story in such a way that people can recognize the experience of grace—God's presence—in their everyday lives. Another way of approaching the role of preaching then is that the preacher interprets the human story in light of the story of Jesus and the story of Israel.[47]

As Schillebeeckx's *Jesus* book makes clear, however, the preaching of the gospel can never be told only in words. Jesus announced the reign of God not only in his teaching and preaching but also by inviting sinners and outcasts to the shared intimacy of table. He proclaimed mercy and healing in touching lepers and entering the homes and the lives of the sick and grieving. He spoke of justice and a God's revisioning of the social order in his relationships with women and Samaritans and the poor. The story of hope in human history is a narrative that must be told ultimately with human lives if it is to be heard as credible. Precisely because the Christian message is a living tradition of grace—the mystery of God-among-us—it must be handed on through the lived experience of the community as well as through Word. Proclamation interprets the life of discipleship, but the community's shared discipleship embodies the proclamation. In fact, Schillebeeckx argues that

> Christians should have the right to use the word God only where they find their identity through their identification with life which is still unreconciled and in their actual attempts at reconciliation. What is promised to us in the story which the church tells us about Jesus is disclosed precisely in this praxis in conformity to the message of Jesus.[48]

Further, precisely because we claim the Gospel is universal salvation—good news for every time and culture—the Gospel must be proclaimed authentically in the uniqueness of every time and culture. New dimensions of the story (what Schillebeeckx calls "new memories of Jesus") emerge as the proclamation of the Gospel is heard in the voices of women and children, from the context of South Africa and Asia, in the life stories of African-American, Native-American, and Hispanic communities, in the struggles of refugees and communities that offer sanctuary and resistance. In every new situation Christian communities are called to proclaim the "fifth gospel" with their lives.

LATIN AMERICAN LIBERATION THEOLOGIANS

Schillebeeckx's emphasis on the role of praxis and the community in handing on the Christian tradition and on enculturation as the major hermeneutical challenge for those who would announce the Gospel in the twentieth century reflects the way his own theological perspective has been affected by the voices emerging from the third world and particularly from liberation theologians. In the Catholic context, liberation theology emerged in the late 1960s in Latin America. In 1968, the year Gustavo Gutierrez published his first article using the term "liberation theology," the Latin American Bishops conference met in Medellin, Colombia, and issued a prophetic message that affirmed the core of any theology of liberation. They called for "an understanding of the good news of Jesus Christ as a call for consistent commitment to the poor, the hungry, and the oppressed, who constitute the nameless majority of the Latin American population." The Medellin documents go on to describe the institutional violence and the exploitative relations of dependency in the Latin American social situation and to point to the need for cultural and economic liberation. Five years later, Gutierrez's now classic book *A Theology of Liberation* appeared in which he described the project of liberation theology as:

> an attempt at reflection, based on the gospel and the experiences of men and women committed to the process of liberation in the oppressed and exploited land of Latin America. It is a theological reflection born of the experience of shared efforts to abolish the current unjust situation and to build a different society, freer and more human.[49]

Given that context, Latin American liberation theologians underline the 1971 Synod of Bishops' statement that "action on behalf of justice and participation in the transformation of the world fully appear to us as a constitutive part of preaching the Gospel."[50] Liberating praxis, rather than existential questions, becomes the preunderstanding necessary in order for both the hearing and the proclaiming of the Gospel. The liberating Word of the Gospel cannot be separated from liberating praxis; rather, it is precisely commitment to and involvement in action on behalf of justice and peace that enables one to hear the good news in all its power and truth.

This new hearing of the Gospel from the experience of the powerless[51] makes clear that identification with Jesus' preaching of the reign of God, his respect for the dignity of every human person, and his particular compassion for the marginalized of his society, has very real political and social consequences for those who would preach the "good news of salvation" in our day. Catechists and other ministers of the word of God who foster base communities centered on the Word of God in politically repressive situations are profoundly aware of the connection of Jesus' death with his prophetic preaching and liberating lifestyle. The Scriptures cannot be faithfully proclaimed if conversion of heart is separated from commitment to transformation of the concrete political and social structures that continue to impoverish, oppress, or marginalize God's people in our cultures and churches. Just as Jesus' preaching caused conflict and met rejection so will the preaching of a church that is faithful to the vision of the reign of God that he preached. Yet as Oscar Romero, the archbishop from El Salvador who was assassinated by government soldiers during the celebration of the Eucharist, once preached:

> A church that doesn't provoke any crisis, a gospel that doesn't unsettle, a word of God that doesn't get under anyone's skin, a word of God that doesn't touch the real sin of the society in which it is being proclaimed, what gospel is that? Very nice, pious considerations that don't bother anyone, that is the way many would like preaching to be. Those preachers who avoid every thorny matter so as not to be harassed, so as not to have conflicts and difficulties, do not light up the world they live in. . . . The gospel is courageous; it's the good news of him who came to take away the world's sins.[52]

Highlighting this prophetic dimension of preaching and the transformative power of grace from a liberation perspective, Leonardo Boff remarks that

> In its prophecy the Church is judge, in the light of the revealed word, of the socio-historical reality into which it is inserted. The Church proclaims God's design, and denounces anything that opposes that design. In its pastoral ministry the Church animates the Christian life, coordinates the various tasks incumbent on the Christian, creates the vital synthesis between gospel and life, and joyfully celebrates the presence of the grace that sets men and women free.[53]

While many liberation theologians describe the liberating Word as transformative of sinful social structures, that perspective can overlook the complexity that comes with the classic Catholic claim that God's Word can also be discovered in human experience and culture. More representative of that claim is Brazilian Carlos Mesters' suggestion that it is impossible to separate the Bible, the life of the community, and the socio-political realities of the surrounding world. In a brief article entitled "Life is the Word—Brazilian Poor Interpret Life," he shifts the focus of locating the word of God only or primarily within the scriptures by citing as the central conviction of basic Christian communities that "the word of God is within reality and it can be discovered there with the help of the Bible."[54] Precisely because of the conviction that God's word is spoken also in the experience of people's lives, liberation theologians remark that preaching is most effective when members of the community are encouraged to tell their own stories. The focus is on the Word of God heard in the community reflection on daily life and political struggle in light of the Scriptures, rather than on the proclamation of an individual preacher or priest.

A further difficulty with the focus on the Scriptures as the liberating Word of God comes from third world women doing theology, who note that while "the poor find that the word reaffirms in a clear and direct way that God is with them in their fight for life, . . . women find clear, explicit cases of the marginalization or segregation of women in . . . both Old and New Testaments."[55] As the Word of God in human words, the Scriptures contain sinful human perspectives as well as the revelatory Word of God, and all too frequently the two have been identified. In the Catholic tradition and beyond, women liberation theologians are calling for an expansion of the fundamentally critical perspective of liberation theology: the "good news of salvation" can be heard and proclaimed only by communities actively committed to overcoming all forms of sin that block the reign of God—including patriarchy.

Liberation theologies are not to be limited, of course, to either Latin America or the Catholic tradition.[56] In fact, the emphasis on the sinful social situation and the transforming Word of God is more characteristic of the dialectical imagination than the sacramental perspective. However, characteristic threads of the Catholic perspective that have implications for a theology of preaching are evident in liberation theology's stress on grace operative in and through the human and the corresponding role of human praxis as cooperation in God's transformation of the world, in the emphasis on hearing the Word of God in community, and in the location of God's word of revelation in the life struggles of the community as well as in the Scriptures.

Conclusion

As the field of homiletics gropes for a renewed theological foundation in an age of ecumenical dialogue, both the dialectical imagination of the classic Reformation traditions and the sacramental imagination of the Catholic traditions have distinct contributions to make. Precisely because an understanding of what is going on in the event of the preaching of the Gospel is rooted in presuppositions about the possibility of encounter between God and human beings, we are dealing with mystery and ambiguity. No one theological perspective can adequately explore the mystery of how God is made known to humanity (revelation) or how the mystery of the human person and community is to be understood (anthropology).

The dialectical imagination of the classic Reformation traditions highlights the utter transcendence of the wholly-other God and the brokenness (sin) and unfinished (eschatological) dimensions of the human person and human history. In that theological context, after the truth, limits, and needs of the human situation are clearly named and faced, the good news of salvation is discovered in the proclamation of the event of Christ Jesus. Preaching becomes the announcing of the Word of salvation that creates an utterly new human possibility. The stress here is on God's "nevertheless" in Christ Jesus. Through the power of the Spirit, the Word of God creates a new context—it does not require human openness to hear. Even if some degree of openness to the Gospel proclamation is admitted (Bultmann's preunderstanding located in existential questions), the emphasis is on the discontinuity that the Word of God effects in totally transforming all human horizons and expectations.

The sacramental perspective, on the other hand, emphasizes a mysterious connection between the divine and the created: the "footsteps of the Trinity" are to be found throughout creation. In this incarnational vision, all of creation was designed in and for the word, Christ Jesus. From the beginning, human beings were structured in the image of God—hearers of the Word. Sin has profoundly disordered, but not totally destroyed, this original plan of God, yet in the redeeming grace of Jesus Christ, humanity has been transformed and empowered to share responsibility for the transformation of the world. The emphasis here is on God's immanent presence and power—the Spirit dwelling within creation and human history "renewing the face of the earth." Precisely because as human beings we are body-spirit, however, the reconciling grace or presence of God among us is necessarily enfleshed—first in Jesus, the very self-expression of God, and then in the Church, called to be tangible sign and herald of the good news of salvation. In terms of preaching, Karl Rahner captures the sacramental imagination in his reminder that "the Holy Spirit runs ahead of the preacher." Preaching in this theological framework becomes a matter of discovery and announcement of the presence of God (grace) hidden within all human life as illuminated by the scriptures. Rather than the Gospel creating a totally new context, one might speak of "grace come to Word."

A fully Christian theology of preaching will incorporate the truth of both perspectives. The mystery of the Trinitarian God has been made known through both Word and Spirit. The wholly other God who remains hidden and absent in contemporary culture is at the same time the mystery of love revealed in Jesus and the Spirit. Contemporary attempts to retrieve pneumatology suggest that the role of the Spirit "running ahead of the preacher" and the role of grace in ordinary human life need to be incorporated into a theology of preaching that still recognizes and accounts for the radical conversion that the proclamation of the Gospel can and does effect in human life.

In terms of the human community, the ambiguity in the human experience of both hearers and proclaimers of the Gospel can never be dismissed or forgotten. We are both images of the divine conformed to the word and "children of wrath" affected profoundly by the sin of the world and of history. Yet as St. Paul reminds us "where sin abounds, grace abounds still more." We are called to be ministers of the Gospel and servants of the reign of God, but it is always *God's power* at work within us. The transformation that grace effects is real, yet "all creation groans" for all that is unfinished in our world. In the face of the global suffering and the sinful structures of our time, proclamation of the Christian gospel requires both words and deeds of justice and mercy. Both the dialectical imagination's focus on the power of the proclaimed word to bring about conversion and the sacramental imagination's stress on the presence of God's grace throughout our lives have a contribution to make in the contemporary ecumenical search for a more adequate theological understanding of the mystery of the preaching event.

Notes

1. David Buttrick, "On Doing Homiletics Today," unpublished paper delivered at conference of the *Societes Homiletica*, Deland, Florida, August 21, 1990, 1. Note also Buttrick's comment in *Homiletic* (Philadelphia: Fortress, 1987): "Both Catholic and Protestant literature on the theology of preaching has dwindled since the sixties. We seem to be waiting for some new beginning in systematic theology" (486).

2. Ibid. 5. Buttrick points to American scholars Edward Farley, Francis Schüssler Fiorenza, and David Tracy as representative of this shift. See Tracy's *Blessed Rage for Order* (New York: Seabury, 1975), Part I for the notion of paradigm shift. Cf. Hans Küng and David Tracy, eds., *Paradigm Change in Theology* (New York: Crossroad, 1989).

3. The expression, a reference to Isaiah 24:18, is borrowed from Paul Tillich's first collection of sermons, *The Shaking of the Foundations* (New York: Charles Scribner's Sons, 1948).

4. For foundational discussion of the "dialectical imagination" and the "analogical imagination" (referred to in this article as the "sacramental imagination") as "classic theological languages," see David Tracy's *The Analogical Imagination* (New York: Crossroad, 1981) esp. 405–445.

5. James C. Livingston, *Modern Christian Thought From the Enlightenment to Vatican II* (New York: Macmillan Publishing Co., 1971) 325. Livingston provides a helpful overview of Barth's theology including the christological shift in his later writings (324–44).

6. Whether associated with the German theologians that Barth was responding to including Friedrich Schleiermacher, Albrecht Ritschl, Wilhelm Hermann, and Adolph von Harnack, or the American tradition of theological liberalism as represented by such figures as William Adams Brown, Horace Bushnell, and Walter Rauschenbusch, the goal of the liberal tradition was, in the words of the famous American preacher Harry Emerson Fosdick, to make it possible to be both "an intelligent modern and a serious Christian." (*The Living of These Days* [New York: Harper and Brothers, 1956], vii.) The major historical and cultural shifts of the 19th century had resulted in religious alienation and a real inability to hear the proclamation of the Gospel in the terms of either traditional Protestant Orthodoxy or pietism/revivalism. From Schleiermacher's *Speeches on Religion to Its Cultured Despisers* to Ralph Waldo Emerson's Harvard Divinity School Address in 1838 or the preaching of Harry Emerson Fosdick at Riverside Church a century later, the concern of the liberal tradition of preachers was to find a point of contact in contemporary human experience and culture for the hearing of the Christian Gospel.

While diverse and complex, the liberal theological tradition of the late nineteenth and early twentieth centuries in both European and American contexts was characterized in general by an emphasis on the immanence of God, the location of revelation in human experience and history rather than in inspired scriptures or dogma, recognition of the historical and cultural conditioning of the Bible and all forms of tradition, stress on the human and historical Jesus and an ethical interpretation of his preaching of the Kingdom of God, a social and ethical conception of salvation, and an optimistic view of human nature, destiny, and evolutionary progress with a corresponding underemphasis on original sin and its corruption of humanity.

For a basic overview of Protestant Liberal Theology in its European context, see Livingston, *Modern Christian Thought: From the Enlightenment to Vatican II*, 96–114, 245–70. For the American context, see Kenneth Cauthen, *The Impact of American Religious Liberalism* (New York: Harper, 1962), and Sydney Ahlstrom, *Theology in America: The Major Protestant Voices from Puritanism to Neo-Orthodoxy* (Indianapolis: Bobbs-Merrill, 1967).

7. David Jenkins, "Karl Barth," in *A Handbook of Christian Theologians*, ed. Martin E. Marty and Dean G. Peerman (Nashville: Abingdon, 1984) 398.

8. Karl Barth, *The Word of God and the Word of Man*, trans. Douglas Horton (New York: Harper and Brothers Publishers, 1957) 43, 45.

9. Karl Barth, *The Epistle to the Romans*, trans. Edwyn C. Hoskyns (New York: Oxford University Press, 1968) 98.

10. Karl Barth, *Revelation* (London: Faber and Faber, 1937) 51.

11. Karl Barth, *The Preaching of the Gospel*, trans. B. E. Hooke (Philadelphia: Westminster, 1963) and "The Need and Promise of Christian Preaching," in *The Word of God and the Word of Man*, 97–135.

12. Barth, *The Preaching of the Gospel*, 22.

13. Ibid. 12.

14. Ibid. 80.

15. Rudolph Bultmann, *Kerygma and Myth*, ed. Hans Werner Bartsch (New York: Harper and Row Publishers, 1961) 206–07.

16. The reference is from Fuchs' essay on "Translation and Preaching," as cited in James M. Robinson's "Hermeneutic Since Barth," in *The New Hermeneutic*, ed. James M. Robinson and John R. Cobb, Jr. (New York: Harper and Row, Publishers, 1964) 63. See also the discussion of the new hermeneutic in Robert W. Funk, *Language, Hermeneutic, and the Word of God* (New York: Harper and Row Publishers, 1966) 47–71. For a political, rather than an existential, development of dialectical theology in the service of the preaching of the Gospel, see Jürgen Moltmann, "Toward a Political Hermeneutic of the Gospel," in

Religion, Revolution, and the Future, trans. M. Douglas Meeks (New York: Charles Scribner's Sons, 1969) 83–107.

17. See Avery Dulles, "Hermeneutical Theology," *Communio*, Summer (1979) 23.

18. Robert W. Funk, *Language, Hermeneutic, and the Word of God,* 10–18. Cf. Richard Lischer, *A Theology of Preaching* (Nashville: Abingdon, 1981) 54–55: "even in our redeemed state . . . grace remains an unnatural and often surprising intrusion." See Part Two of Funk's book for one approach to the relationship between dialectical theology, the new hermeneutic, and the extensive literature on parable, metaphor, and the "shock of conversion" that is frequently alluded to in homiletic texts. For further development and additional bibliography on parable and metaphor, see Sallie McFague, *Speaking in Parables* (Philadelphia: Fortress, 1975), and *Metaphorical Theology* (Philadelphia: Fortress, 1982).

19. P. J. Burns, "Hermeneutics (Contemporary)," *New Catholic Encyclopedia*, vol. 16, 206.

20. Lischer, *A Theology of Preaching*, 50.

21. Lischer, 65. Cf. Herman G. Stuempfle, Jr., *Preaching Law and Gospel* (Philadelphia: Fortress, 1978).

22. Paul Tillich, *Systematic Theology*, Vol. I (Chicago: University of Chicago, 1951) 5.

23. Tillich, *Systematic Theology*, I:7.

24. Tillich, *Systematic Theology*, I:49.

25. Paul Tillich, "Holy Waste," in *The New Being* (New York: Charles Scribner's Sons, 1955) 48.

26. Tillich, "Is There Any Word from the Lord?" in *The New Being*, 121.

27. Ibid. 124.

28. See Paul Tillich, "Communicating the Christian Message: A Question to Christian Ministers and Teachers," in *Theology of Culture* (New York: Oxford University Press, 1959) 201–213; cf. *Systematic Theology*, I:3–28.

29. See *Systematic Theology* I:159. cf. *The Courage to Be* (New Haven: Yale University Press, 1952), and "The Eternal Now" in *The Eternal Now* (New York: Charles Scribner's Sons, 1956) 122–32.

30. See "You Are Accepted," in *The Shaking of the Foundations* (New York: Charles Scribner's Sons, 1948) 153–63.

31. Tillich argued that Christianity requires both "Catholic substance" (the concrete embodiment of Spiritual Presence) and the "Protestant principle" (of critique of the demonic and profane within all such embodiments). See Thomas Franklin O'Meara, "Tillich and the Catholic Substance," in *The Thought of Paul Tillich*, ed. James Luther Adams, Wilhelm Pauck, and Roger L. Shinn (New York: Harper and Row, 1985) 290–306.

32. "Justification by Faith," U.S. Lutheran-Roman Catholic Dialogue Statement, *Origins* 13 (October 6, 1983) #154.

33. In Ep. I ad. Thess., c.2, lect.2.

34. See Domenico Grasso, *Proclaiming God's Message: A Study in the Theology of Preaching* (Notre Dame: University of Notre Dame Press, 1965) xxvi–xxviii.

35. Karl Rahner, "Priest and Poet," *Theological Investigations* Vol. III, trans. Karl -H. and Boniface Kruger (Baltimore: Helicon, 1967) 313.

36. Ibid.

37. Rahner, "Nature and Grace," *Nature and Grace* (New York: Sheed and Ward, 1963) 134.

38. Rahner, "Priest and Poet," 296.

39. Ibid. 317.

40. See Leo O'Donovan (ed.), *A World of Grace* (New York: Seabury, 1980) for an excellent one-volume introduction to Rahner's thought that parallels his own synthesis, *Foundations of Christian Faith* (New York: Seabury, 1978).

41. For Rahner's own treatment of these themes see especially "The Word and Eucharist," *Theological Investigations* IV: 253-285; "What is Sacrament?" *Theological Investigations* XIV: 135-148; "Priest and Poet," *Theological Investigations* III: 294-317; "Poetry and the Christian," *Theological Investigations* IV: 357-367; and "Considerations on the Active Role of the Person in the Sacramental Event," *Theological Investigations* XIV: 161-184.

42. For a development of a theology of preaching based on Rahner's theology see Eileen McKeown, *A Theology of Preaching Based on Karl Rahner's Theology of the Word* (Ph.D. dissertation, Fordham University, 1989). See also Avery Dulles' article "Revelation and Discovery," in *Theology and Discovery*, ed. William J. Kelly (Milwaukee: Marquette, 1980) 1-29, for clarification on how conversion and real discontinuity and surprise are involved in the explicit discovery of what was already implicitly present.

43. See Schillebeeckx's *Christ: The Experience of Jesus as Lord*, trans. John Bowden (New York: Crossroad, 1981) 29-79 and *Church: The Human Story of God*, trans. John Bowden (New York: Crossroad, 1990) 15-45 for his theology of revelation located in human experience. For an overview of Schillebeeckx's theology of revelation, see Mary Catherine Hilkert, "Discovery of the Living God: Revelation and Experience" in *The Praxis of Christian Experience: An Introduction to the Theology of Edward Schillebeeckx*, ed. Robert J. Schreiter and Mary Catherine Hilkert (New York: Harper and Row, 1989) 35-51. For a theology of proclamation based on Schillebeeckx's contemporary theology of revelation see Mary Catherine Hilkert, *Towards A Theology of Proclamation: Edward Schillebeeckx's Hermeneutics of Tradition as a Foundation for a Theology of Proclamation* (Ph.D. dissertation, Catholic University of America, 1984).

44. Schillebeeckx, *Christ*, 78.

45. Note Schillebeeckx's definition of revelation in the *Christ* book: "God's saving action in history as *experienced* by believers and *interpreted* in religious language and therefore *expressed* in human terms, in the dimension of our utterly human history" (78).

46. Schillebeeckx, "Can Christology be an Experiment?" *Proceedings of the Catholic Theological Society of America* 35 (1980) 2.

47. Note a similar approach in the United States Bishops' Pastoral *Fulfilled in Your Hearing: The Homily in the Sunday Assembly* (Washington: United States Catholic Conference, 1982): "The preacher does not so much attempt to explain the Scriptures as to interpret the human situation through the Scriptures" (20).

48. Schillebeeckx, "God as a Loud Cry," in *God Among Us: The Gospel Proclaimed*, trans. John Bowden (New York: Crossroad, 1983) 76-77.

49. Gustavo Gutierrez, *A Theology of Liberation*, trans. and ed. by Sister Caridad Inda and John Eagleston (Maryknoll: Orbis, 1973) ix.

50. *Justice in the World* (Washington: United States Catholic Conference, 1971) 34.

51. Leonardo Boff describes this stance and its implications: "To adopt the place of the poor is our first deed of solidarity with them. This act is accomplished by making an effort to view reality from their perspective. And when we view reality from their perspective, that reality simply must be transformed. Reality is exceedingly unjust for the majority of men and women in Latin America. It impoverishes them and pushes them out on the margins of society. To adopt the place of the poor means to assign priority to the questions the poor raise, and then honestly to face up to these problems." *When Theology Listens to the Poor* (New York: Harper and Row, 1988) ix.

52. Oscar Romero, *The Violence of Love: The Pastoral Wisdom of Archbishop Oscar Romero*, trans. and compiled by James R. Brockman (New York: Harper and Row, 1988) 54.

53. Boff, *When Theology Listens to the Poor*, 32.

54. Carlos Mesters, "Life is the Word—Brazilian poor interpret life," in *SEDOS Bulletin* (Rome), No. 13, September 1985, as quoted in *Ministries and Communities* (publication of *Pro Mundi Vita*) 47 (1986) 4.

55. Elsa Tamez, "Women's Rereading of the Bible," *With Passion and Compassion*, ed. Virginia Fabella and Mercy Amba Oduyoye (Maryknoll: Orbis, 1988) 174.

56. See, for example, the helpful homiletic resource, *Liberation Preaching: The Pulpit and the Oppressed,* by Justo Luis Gonzales (an ordained minister in the United Methodist Church) and Catherine Gunsalus Gonzales (an ordained minister in the Presbyterian Church) [Nashville: Abingdon, 1980]. For a feminist reconstruction of a theology of proclamation as "the creation of discourses of emancipatory transformation"see Rebecca S. Chopp, *The Power to Speak* (New York: Crossroad, 1989).

Section III

Pastoral and Spiritual Theology

Chapter 9

The Living Word: An Overshadowing of the Spirit

JOAN DELAPLANE, O.P.

> In the beginning God created the heavens and the earth. The earth was without form and void, and darkness was upon the face of the deep; and the Spirit of God was moving over the face of the waters (Gen 1:1-2).[1]

From the opening lines of the Hebrew testament, accounting for the source of all life and creation, to the revelation of a new heavens and a new earth in the final pages of the Christian testament, the overshadowing of God's Spirit is seen as the dynamic or creative power of God at work. "What gives life is the Spirit" (John 6:63).

The intensified theological pursuit of christology and ecclesiology these past few decades has focused on pneumatology only indirectly. Until recently, in fact, the whole area of pneumatology seemed to be rather consistently by-passed. Now, however, with the charismatic movement, and a Vatican II experience within the Church as a stirring of the waters, there is a renewed interest in the work of the Holy Spirit.

In the whole area of the preaching enterprise as well, the consciousness of the role of the Holy Spirit is crucial. It is the conviction of this writer that without consciousness of the place of God's Spirit, the whole preaching endeavor for some individuals may easily become overwhelming and discouraging; for others, simply an ego-trip. One might assume that all preachers realize that the Spirit of God is the understood principle of each facet of preaching preparation, the preaching act, and the preaching response. Until recently, however, many books on preaching gave little or no articulation to the place of the Spirit. Volumes could be written—have been written—about each of these facets from a theological, scriptural, and pastoral point of view. The focus of this writing, however, will be solely from a preacher's perspective in relation to the critical role of the Holy Spirit. It is this awareness that can reinforce for the preacher, and the Church as a whole, the awesome realization that . . .

"we are ambassadors for Christ, God making appeal through us" (2 Cor 5:19-20).

Spirit Overshadows the Formulation and Transmission of the Word

Of all the human struggles to say something of our finite experience of the infinite, two expressions often surface: source of life; source of love. It is the nature of love to need to communicate with the beloved. Through faith, Christians believe that God has spoken and is speaking a word of self revelation, a word of truth, and a word of love to God's people. The Hebrew peoples, from Abraham and Sarah through Joseph, Joshua, Moses and Miriam, experienced God in their midst. Through a sense of call, dreams, burning bushes, mountain tops, and crumbling walls, the Hebrews experienced a God who was involved in their lives. They experienced a liberating God, a God whose Spirit hovered over them in their faith journey as sure as a cloud by day and pillar of fire by night. Through the gift of the Spirit, the people named their experience as God at work in word and deed. Through the gift of faith, they could see beyond a natural parting of waters and the appearance of manna to the presence and the power of a liberating God. They could hear a word of saving love and covenantal promise. The word heard by Moses on Sinai resonated with a word of truth in the chosen people's hearts. Moved by the gift of faith, people gave expression to their experience of the word and deed of the Infinite.

Such human wording, of course, would always be restricted by the finite conditions, always limited, always falling short. The gift of the Spirit, however, enabled them to recognize the Spirit of truth within, among, and beyond them. Truth resonated with truth, saying "Ah, yes!" The people of God came to know their identity in relationship to that God, and, as a result, to understand their relationship to one another. The story and the tradition were passed on from generation to generation first orally and then in written form. The truth of the experience was believed in faith and evidenced in the changed lives. Eventually the people of God, moved by the Holy Spirit, affirmed certain texts as canon.

Then, in the fullness of time, the Spirit of God overshadowed a Jewish maiden, and God's truth and love was spoken preeminently in the word made flesh, Jesus. The story and tradition of a people's faith experience of Jesus was again passed on from generation to generation, first orally, then in written form. Once again, the truth of the experience believed in faith and evidenced in the changed lives, was all the work of the same

Spirit. The Church, eventually, by the power of that Spirit, affirmed certain texts as canon. This canon remains a living word in our midst; thus calling for assiduous study on the part of the preacher.

Just as people struggled with the mystery of human and divine in Jesus, so, too, humans continue to struggle with the reality of the mystery of the human and divine in the word of God. There are some who find the presence of sexism, violence, historical and scientific inaccuracies just too much to call the text the Word of God. Their focus is on the all-too-human word and its limitations. On the other hand, there are those who find it difficult to deal with ambiguity and mystery, and they long for the security of clear black and white answers to life's dilemmas. These individuals need to approach the text with the focus only on the divine, the "of God-ness." The tedious task of study for what the text meant to particular writers, editors, people in the past, and application of varied hermeneutical tools for what the text means for a particular people today is abandoned by both groups. According to Raymond Brown, however, " 'The mystery of the word of God' is appreciated only when we take both sides of that expression seriously."[2] We are confronted in faith with "the seeming contradiction of a divine self-revelation in human terms."[3]

"All scripture is inspired of God and is useful for teaching, for reproof, correction, and training in holiness" (2 Tim 2:16). Almost all Christians would agree that the Bible is inspired; but what "inspired" means is the basis for continued discussion and dialogue. It is beyond the scope of this chapter to deal with all the varied understandings. According to Paul Achtemeier, however, inspiration of the scriptures is "to be understood, namely, as the continuing presence of the Spirit with the community of faith as it preserved and renewed its traditions in response to the new situations into which God led it."[4] The realization that the Divine and the human are both involved in the mystery of this communication is essential. One cannot underestimate either the role of God or the human role.

This Word of God in human words can never be fully grasped or understood, but multiple biblical hermeneutics can assist the ongoing human search for "faith seeking understanding." Besides the historical-critical method of approaching a text, biblical scholars, in the past few years especially, have enabled believers to adjust the lens and perceive the truth within a text from varied angles, a truth never fully exhausted: reader-response; canonical criticism; structuralism; sociological, feminist, or liberation perspectives. Each method of interpreting a text has some insight to offer; no particular hermeneutical approach is definitive. Again, one must depend on the work of the Holy Spirit. As Fred Craddock has put it: "Inspiration has more to do with getting the word off the page than on it."[5]

The study of sacred scripture alone might indeed be formidable were it not for Jesus' assurance: "But the Counselor, the Holy Spirit, whom the Father will send in my name, he will teach you all things, and bring to your remembrance all that I have said to you" (John 14:26). God's Spirit was present inspiring authors to write the word on the page; enabling scholars to unveil the truth there; guiding exegetes; and God's Spirit will continue to be present to deliver the living word accurately from the page for God's people.

If the Spirit of truth is at work and cannot contradict the Spirit of truth in the word, how does one account for such varied understandings of the word? The Spirit is at work, but in very limited human beings. Even when there seems to be much discrepancy and disagreement as to meaning, faith-full disciples hold fast to the belief that "Thy word is a lamp to my feet and a light to my path" (Ps 119:105). Through dialogue in the community of believers, openness to discover truth, and disciplined study, there is the trust that truth will be found. Again, we are speaking from a faith perspective, a "stumbling block" and/or "folly" to unbelievers to whom such a stance may well appear naive and unsophisticated.

To pass on the tradition and the living word faithfully demands great discipline and serious study. Besides the varied hermeneutical approaches to the text, the preacher must likewise integrate knowledge from many other fields as well: i.e., theology, sociology, psychology, the arts, communications, pastoral skills. The Church and modern society have come to appreciate more and more the complexity, the necessity, and the interrelatedness of each of those fields. It is the unifying Spirit of God that can enable the preacher to integrate and then articulate the truth therein.

Spirit Overshadows the Preacher of the Word

From the Hebrew testament to the Christian testament to our present times, the commission, the courage, and the challenge to speak God's word is accomplished in the power of the Spirit. The ministry of the prophets is described as the work of the Spirit (Zech 7:12; Neh 9:30). Micah is "filled with power, with the Spirit of the Lord, and with justice and might" (3:8). It is God's Spirit that rests upon Ezekiel (2:2-7), and puts words in the mouth of Isaiah (59:21). And in the Christian testament Peter on Pentecost sees the fulfillment of the word from the prophet Joel that God will "pour out my Spirit upon all flesh, and your sons and your daughters shall prophesy, and your young shall see visions, and your old shall dream dreams" (Acts 2:17).

The Book of Acts constantly refers to the Holy Spirit's guiding the missionary activity of individuals and the Church. Baptized into the life, death, and resurrection of Jesus, and, therefore, into his mission to preach the Good News, there is the assurance: "You shall receive power when the Holy Spirit has come upon you; and you shall be my witnesses in Jerusalem and in all Judea and Samaria and to the ends of the earth" (1:8).

The focus, of course, for a minister of the word is always the preacher par excellence, Jesus. Jesus is revealed as conceived by the power of the Holy Spirit, full of the Holy Spirit at baptism, led by the Spirit into the desert, and in the power of the Spirit came into Galilee to begin his ministry. He presented himself in the Synagogue as one anointed by the Spirit. "Not only, then," says Donald Gelpi, "does the Divine Breath abide with Jesus; She dwells in Him as in inexhaustible source of life. And She abides as the source of His testimony concerning God."[6]

So, too, the preacher must be sensitively aware that, like the Hebrew prophets, like their model Jesus, like the early Christian preachers of the Good News, the same Spirit of God is present, assuring that God's word "shall not return to me empty, but it shall accomplish that which I purpose, and prosper in the thing for which I sent it" (Isa 55:11).

Accenting the place of the Spirit, therefore, emphasizes that there is no room for paralyzing fear or cowardliness in the preacher. Protesting that Aaron was a better speaker was of no avail to Moses; Jeremiah's youth proved no impediment to the work of the Spirit. With Paul we hear:

> I was with you in weakness and much fear and trembling; and my speech and my message were not in plausible words of wisdom, but in demonstration of the Spirit and of power, that your faith might not rest in human wisdom, but in the power of God (1 Cor 2:3-5).

Paul puts the preaching event and all ministry in clear perspective when he reminds the believer:

> Not that we are competent of ourselves to claim anything as coming from us; our competence is from God, who has made us competent to be ministers of a new covenant, not in a written code but in the Spirit; for the written code kills, but the Spirit gives life" (2 Cor 3:5-6).

There is no place either for preachers to be envious of others' gifts. Each person is a unique syllable of the word, and God's Spirit is at work with the diversity of gifts and talents. God's Spirit will choose as God wills: from a shepherd Amos to a judge Deborah, from an eager Samaritan woman to a courageous Mary of Magdala; from an articulate John Chrysostom to a stammering John Vianney; from a charismatic Martin Luther King to a humble minister of the word in the barrios. Again, how impoverished the Church would be if there were recorded only one evangelist's experience of Jesus. No, the Church needs its Fulton J. Sheens and Walter Burghardts; and the Church needs the deep faith conviction of the shy and retiring. The Church needs the word of God spoken from the faith perspective and experience of women and of men, of the poor and the wealthy, of the African-American, Hispanic, and Asian people of God.

In speaking of the Spirit and the individual gift of preaching, one must address the topic of authority to preach. All Christians are called to preach by virtue of their baptism; there is a unique call to some, however, to preach publicly and officially in the name of the Church and within worship. How is this call discerned? By whom? What criteria are used in the discernment process? These are some of the questions with which individuals and the Church are wrestling today.

The Church bears the responsibility of safeguarding and passing on faithfully the saving word. Openness to the Spirit abiding within enables the Church to call forth, test, and affirm the gifts within individuals for the common good. Idealistically, there would be such total attuneness to the Spirit that there would never be tension between the Church and the individual. Realistically, we are a pilgrim people who have not yet arrived at such perfection. The Church, organized as institution and as servant for mission, is necessary and to be respected. As Karl Rahner has pointed out, however,

> Provision has to be made that bureaucratic routine, turning means into ends in themselves, rule for the sake of rule and not for the sake of service, the dead wood of tradition, . . . and other such dangers, do not extinguish the Spirit.[7]

"The Spirit blows where it wills" (John 8:3), and at times in the past, as Rahner puts it, this Spirit has frequently overlooked the "usual channels" of the Institution.[8] Though most Christians affirm the need for some means of authorization to preach in the name of the Church, there is a growing number of individuals today who question the criteria for such authorization. In the Roman Catholic tradition, for example, preaching the homily within the eucharistic liturgy is restricted to male ordained clergy which, in the opinion of Sandra Schneiders, is a "a betrayal of the gospel."[9] These regulations, says Schneiders, "enshrine an anti-evangelical sexism and clericalism," and "they silence many who are gifted and trained to preach, at a time when there is truly a famine of the Word of God in the land."[10]

Rahner again reminds the hierarchy that they ought not be "surprised or annoyed if there is stirring in the life of the Spirit before this has been scheduled in the church's ministries." Rahner goes on to say:

> And subordinates must not think they have nothing to do until an order is handed down from above. There are actions that God wills even before the starting signal has been given by the hierarchy, and in directions that have not yet been positively approved and laid down officially.[11]

When choosing to act without the Church's official approbation, however, it would behoove the individual to examine frequently whether or not there is evidence of the fruit of the Spirit in one's actions: "Love, joy, peace, patience, kindness, goodness, faithfulness, gentleness, and self-control" (Gal 5:22-23).

Preachers need to be aware of the primacy of their own openness to the living word and God's transforming Spirit. The noted Protestant preacher Charles Spurgeon once said: "It were better to speak six words in the power of the Holy Ghost than to preach seventy years of sermons without the Spirit."[12] The evangelist Luke tells how Jesus read from Isaiah 61 in the synagogue service one Sabbath; he sat down to address the assembly and said: "Today this scripture has been fulfilled in your hearing" (4:21). The most perfect one-liner ever recorded! What a goal for preachers! Most preachers have experienced that the mastery of all the exegetical tools, hermeneutical helps, and how-to's do not have the same impact as the unleashing of the power of God's Spirit when words and life correspond. St. Paul put it well when he said: "You are a letter from Christ delivered by us, written not with ink but with the Spirit of the Living God, not on tablets of stone, but on tablets of human hearts" (2 Cor 3:3). Schillebeeckx asserts that "The mission to preach the message is justified insofar as, and on the condition that, the proclamation is both a part and an expression of the imitation of Jesus."[13]

Spirit Overshadows the Hearers of the Word

As preachers experience the power of the Spirit in their own lives, there ought to follow the realization that it is not the preacher alone, but the work of that same Spirit in the preaching event that enables the word of truth and love to be heard by the rest of God's people. The Spirit abiding in the preacher of God's word is the same Spirit present in the hearer, enabling the hearer to resonate with truth spoken and, hopefully, moving the hearer to a response.

Just as the preacher is called to pray over a text, enter into the life of the text, and study the commentaries on the text, so now is the preacher called to do an exegesis of his or her congregation. The preacher prays for the people of God that they might be open to hearing the word of God for their lives this day. The preacher enters pastorally into the lives of the people, and studies the commentaries of newspapers and television to know and understand the social realities that are affecting their lives. The people need to experience a preacher who knows their fear and frustrations, their hungers and hurts, their confusion and challenges, and then tries to throw the light of God's word on their darkness.

To give this concrete expression, for example, one preacher, Fr. Bill, goes over to his church during part of his homily preparation time and sits in varied pews. He tries to get into the skin and stories of different parishioners. In his imagination he sits with the teenager Tom in the back row and asks: "What is God's word here for Tom struggling with the awakening realization that he is gay?" Fr. Bill moves to the middle of the church, and sits with Jim who just lost his job. Next to Jim is his dad who is grieving the death of his wife after forty-nine years of marriage. The preacher moves to the front left pew where Mary usually sits with her four children. Mary's husband walked out on her for a younger woman. In the right front pew is Betty, frightened, going for cobalt treatments for cancer.

Were it not for the assurance of God's Spirit to be with him, Fr. Bill and all other preachers, in face of such an awesome task, might easily despair. What these people ask is not a simple answer to their questions or problems; they know that our words cannot change most situations. "What our words can do is help people to make connections between the realities of their lives and the realities of the Gospel."[14]

Many preachers today are encouraging a group of parishioners to gather one day or evening early in the week to share how the next Sunday's readings spoke to them. Believing in the work of the Spirit in the community, the preacher listens, questions, ponders their insights. The people understand that the preacher must be true to the work of the Spirit in him or her, and is not expected necessarily to pursue the direction established by the discussion. Such a listening session, however, has often proved helpful for both preacher and people. "If a minister takes seriously the role of listeners in preaching," says Fred Craddock, "there will be sermons expressing for the whole church, and with God as the primary audience, the faith, the doubt, the fear, the anger, the love, the joy, the gratitude that is in all of us."[15]

In spite of all the preacher's efforts to enable God's word to be heard, the hearers bring their own baggage and blockage at times to such hearing. If there is to be conversion, as is the goal of all preaching, it will come about by the work of the Spirit and the openness of the person to that Spirit. The preacher must embrace the truth that Paul knew: "I planted, Apollos watered, but God gave the growth" (1 Cor 3:6). The preachers' enthusiasm for their awesome task must not depend on experiencing positive strokes and seeing conversions happening before their eyes. The preacher's task is to proclaim the truth in love and leave the results to God's Spirit and the individual's free response.

Jesus knew the pain of watching the rich young man walk away. I believe, however, that Jesus trusted that God's Spirit would continue the pursuit down the road. Today's preacher is called to maintain the same respect, and the willingness to let go of seeing tangible results. The preacher's task is to "preach the word, be urgent in season and out of season" (2 Tim 4:2) and leave the rest to God.

Spirit Overshadows Dynamics of Word, World, People

This chapter began with the opening words of Genesis, speaking of the Spirit of God moving over the face of the waters and giving life. This chapter now ends with some of the closing words of Revelation: "The Spirit and the Bride say 'Come.' . . . let him who desires take the water of life without price" (22:17). From the beginning to the end, the word of God attests to the promise of the Spirit of life for all peoples; so the preacher has the courage to respond: "Yes, send me." But to enflesh the living word and to enable it to go forth to the people of God to do its saving healing thing is a complex and awesome task. The mandate to "Go therefore and make disciples" is accompanied by the promise "I am with you always" (Matt 28:19-20). Jesus promised to send the Spirit (John 15:26) whom the scriptures reveal as vivifying, enlightening, energizing, enabling, unifying. Every preacher can trust that promise and that gift to be present as the preacher gives birth to the word anew for a people and a world so in need. "Thus through the Holy Spirit, God's love now becomes a gathering love leading the whole creation back to the Father. The goal of history will be reached when Christ hands over the kingdom to the Father and God will be all in all."[16]

David Buttrick summarizes the mystery of it all, and expresses the "wonder-full" task of the preacher when he says: "We may be two-legged little human beings, but we stand before the mysterious Presence-in-Absence and, through Christ mediate understandings of God to a being-saved community in a most mysterious world. Good heavens, what a vocation!"[17] And the gift of the Spirit enables all this to come to pass!

Notes

1. All scriptural references throughout the text are taken from RSV.
2. *The Critical Meaning of the Bible* (New York: Paulist, 1981) 1.
3. Ibid.
4. Paul Achtemeier, *The Inspiration of Scripture* (Philadelphia: Westminster Press, 1980) 141.
5. *Overhearing the Gospel* (Nashville: Abingdon, 1978) 74.
6. *The Divine Mother: A Trinitarian Theology of the Holy Spirit* (Lanham, Md.: University Press of America, 1984) 158.
7. *The Spirit in the Church* (New York: Seabury Press, 1979) 44–45.
8. Ibid. 61.
9. "New Testament Foundations for Preaching by the Non-ordained," in *Preaching and the Non-ordained*, ed. Nadine Foley (Collegeville: The Liturgical Press, 1983) 76.
10. Ibid.
11. Rahner, 61.
12. As quoted by Marshall, Morgan, and Scott, eds., in *Twelve Sermons on Holy Spirit* (Baker, 1975) 122.
13. "The Right of Every Christian to Speak in the Light of Evangelical Experience 'In the Midst of Brothers and Sisters,' " in *Preaching and the Non-Ordained*, 36.
14. The Bishops' Committee on Priestly Life and Ministry, National Conference of Catholic Bishops, *Fulfilled in Your Hearing* (Washington: United States Catholic Conference, 1982) 10.
15. *Preaching* (Nashville: Abingdon, 1985) 85.
16. John J. O'Donnell, *The Mystery of the Triune God* (New York: Paulist, 1989) 84.
17. *Homiletic* (Philadelphia: Fortress Press, 1987) 457.

Chapter 10

The Spirituality of a Preacher

EDWARD M. RUANE, O.P.

Introduction

"Without a vision the people perish" (Prov 29:18). This is as true today as it was for the sages of Israel. In describing our own day, one might easily conclude that people are perishing for lack of a life-sustaining vision that enables them to move forward, to ennoble their lives, to struggle for new possibilities, to mobilize and direct their energies. A lack of vision causes individuals and a community to drift aimlessly, to jump from one thing to another, to flounder before social and cultural currents, and to lose hope. Western culture has become increasingly secularized and compartmentalized.

It is difficult to know how to speak of God and the life of the Spirit in a society which is increasingly unaware of its spiritual malaise and its divorce from transcendental insight and values. Much of society's faith has been co-opted by apparent material substitutes while, at the same time, the interpretation of life's demands, disappointments, and sufferings in light of Jesus Christ is often mocked and denied. Further, the social concept of the common good or community well-being is clearly relegated to the back seat. Yes, the common good, but situate it behind the individual good. "Me" and "mine" tend to dominate over "us" and "ours."

Does not this lack of vision exist now? Is there not a profound urgency for men and women who proclaim Christ's vision of God's reign to become a burning reality in our world? One can hear the cry of Paul VI in *Evangelii Nuntiandi*: "In our day, what has happened to that hidden energy of the Good News, which is able to have a powerful effect on human conscience?"[1]

Yet at the same time, people hunger for meaning; they hunger for meaning in community. As never before, one sees shelves filled with self-help books, the multiplication of twelve-step programs in response to addictions of every description, and crowds flocking to Enneagram and Myers-Briggs workshops. Cults have flourished, and fundamentalism is clearly the faith-movement on the rise. Even with a spiritual hunger gripping the land, the Roman Catholic Church has rediscovered the centrality of the word of God in its ordinary daily existence. Beginning with the liturgical reform of Vatican II, through its use of biblical images in describing the Church, and its *Dogmatic Constitution on Divine Revelation*, to the development of the Lectionary, the restoration of the liturgical homily, the Rite of Christian Initiation of Adults, and various bible study groups, the role of scripture has definitively been restored to the daily life of the Church. Although the Church is not yet quite at home in this rediscovery, nevertheless this is the moment to proclaim a vision. It is a moment of danger indeed, but far more a moment of opportunity. This is the moment for gospel preachers. For this opportunity to be seized, it demands a spirituality that can sustain a vibrant preaching geared to this moment in history.

As the reflections of a preacher, this chapter is descriptive rather than definitive and reflective rather than systematic. It presupposes that preaching is a distinct, necessary, and privileged gift.

> There is a variety of gifts but always the same Spirit; there are all sorts of service to be done, but always to the same Lord; working in all sorts of different ways in different people, it is the same God who is working in all of them. The particular way in which the Spirit is given to each person is for a good purpose. One may have the gift of preaching with wisdom given by the Spirit; another may have the gift of preaching instruction given by the same Spirit; . . . (1 Cor 12:4-8).

All the gifts enumerated by Paul are from the Holy Spirit, and all are given for the benefit of the community. The first three chapters of First Corinthians and the greetings offered in his letters demonstrate that Paul understood his vocation strictly as a preacher-apostle. What was the spirituality that sustained Paul? What is a spirituality of the preacher? I use the term "spirituality" as meaning a particular and consistent experience of grace that constantly supports any movement of the Spirit. What is this particular and consistent experience of grace that characterizes and sustains the life of the preacher at this particular moment in history? Five inter-penetrating dynamics characterize the spirituality of preaching.

Sense of Urgency

Whether changing the social situation of the Hebrew nomads at the time of Moses and Aaron, or the crucial moments surrounding the exile at the time of the prophets, one can discern a common thread: a sense of urgency in the face of crisis. So too, throughout Church history, great preachers are called forth in light of a critical historical moment. One need only recall the periods that generated a Chrysostom, Augustine, Bernard, Catherine of Siena, Savanarola, Luther, de las Casas, Sojourner Truth, Martin Luther King, and Oscar Romero. Each of these great preachers was formed by a sense of urgency to speak God's word at a critical time. According to the Gospel accounts, the same kind of moment was perceived by Jesus. His scathing condemnation of the Pharisees and religious leaders of his day showed that the people were like sheep without a shepherd, hungering for someone who spoke with authority. This aimless wandering of the people moved Jesus' heart with pity, causing him to leave his "lonely spot of prayer" and feed those who were hungry, weak, and outcast. Human need drew forth Jesus the preacher whose words effected what they said. Need, addressed by Jesus, manifested the *Dabar YHWH*, the same *Dabar* spoken over chaos in Genesis 1: "God said . . . and so it was." "Jesus said . . . and so it was."

The preacher's sense of urgency is perceived in relationship to God's urgency. Without preaching, there will be no faith. Without preaching, the word of God becomes dormant. People suffer, and their spirits die. Without preaching, the people's liturgy becomes formality and loses its power. The memory of what God has done is lost without preaching. And when memory is lost, no identity is possible. Yves Congar made this rather startling observation as early as 1968:

> I could quote a whole series of ancient texts, all saying more or less that if in one country Mass was celebrated for thirty years without preaching and in another there was preaching for thirty years without Mass, people would be more Christian in the country where there was preaching.[2]

For a Roman Catholic theologian to make such an observation goes against what had been commonly believed since, at least, the time of the Council of Trent. Perhaps many Catholic priests find preaching difficult precisely because preaching's ability to transform history has not been emphasized nor the power of the word appreciated. Today many scramble to improve their preaching with neither a grounding in the theology of preaching nor an understanding of those qualities which enables the word to become a vehicle of transformation.

A quick glance at a variety of biblical texts portrays the clarity with which New Testament communities viewed the urgency of preaching. One need only remember Paul ". . . how can they believe in him unless they have heard of him, and they will not hear of him unless they get a preacher, and they will never have a preacher unless one is sent" (Rom 10:14). Recall Philip's question to the Ethiopian eunuch: " 'Do you understand what you are reading?' 'How can I,' he replied, 'unless I have someone to guide me?' " (Acts 8:30). In light of these passages, one can well understand why Paul quotes the exuberant passage from Isaiah 52: "How beautiful on the mountains are the feet of one who brings good news, who heralds peace, brings happiness, proclaims salvation. . . ." Jesus reflects this same urgency when he refuses to remain to do more healing: "Let us go elsewhere to the neighboring country towns, so that I can preach there too, because that is why I came" (Mark 1:38-39). The author of the letter to the Ephesians expresses anxiety for the Gospel by asking for prayers so as ". . . to be given an opportunity to open my mouth and speak without fear and give out the mystery of the Gospel of which I am an ambassador in chains; pray that in proclaiming it I may speak as boldly as I ought" (Eph 6:19-20). The urgency of the preacher flows from humankind's need for God's salvific word. Humbert of Romans, the fifth Master of the Order of Preachers (1254–1263), succinctly summarizes this biblical position: "Zeal for souls is the proper immediate source of preaching."[3] The seriousness of preaching is intimately connected to the salvation of the world. This radical need is nothing less than the concern of God. One who senses this kind of urgency may well be called to preach; yet urgency alone is not sufficient.

Touched by Grace

To preach is to receive a call, to discover a charism from God. The scriptures often refer to authentic prophets in contrast to false prophets. False prophets are self-proclaimed, or prophets designated by others to quiet consciences like the royal prophets of the Hebrew monarchy. They speak what people want to hear. In the New Testament as well, one can see false preachers both in the Acts of the Apostles and in Paul's letters (Acts 8:9-24; 13:4-12; Gal 1:6-10). An examination of the call to preach present in the Hebrew scripture, the call of Jesus, and his call of the disciples can offer insight into the nature of this call.

The authentic preacher in the scripture is one called and commissioned by God. This call is often described as a profound awareness of God having drawn close and touched the person, even argued and wrestled with him or her. As calls of preachers are described in the scriptures, we have images offered of a burning bush on holy ground, angel seraphs with burning coals, and scrolls to be eaten that are sweet to the taste. The prophet Amos says: "The lion roars: who can help feeling afraid? The Lord speaks: who can refuse to prophesy?" (Amos 3:8). Indeed, visions appear and strange commands occur. "When God first spoke through Hosea, God said to him: Go marry a whore, and get children with a whore. . . ." (Hos 1: 2). In their unique way, the prophets are claiming an experience with God, an experience that apparently overpowered them, an experience from which they had to live despite their resistance and reluctance. Moses stuttered; Isaiah was a man of unclean lips; Jeremiah was too young. Ezekiel speaks of his reluctance: "The spirit lifted me up and took me; my heart as I went, overflowed with bitterness and anger, and the hand of God lay heavy on me" (Ezek 3:14).

This same type of experience is described in the New Testament. Each of the synoptics precede Jesus' preaching ministry with two events: the baptism and the temptation. In the baptism of Jesus, the heavens opened and God's Spirit descended on him like a dove and a voice from heaven said: "You are my Son, the Beloved; my favor rests on you" (Matt 3:16-17; Mark 1:10-11; Luke 3:21-22). Following the baptism there is the account of Jesus' struggle with the call, the temptation in the desert. In Jesus, the human being, there is not the dramatic scene of God's overpowering him; rather we see his free, willing, and obedient response despite temptations and struggles to the contrary. Likewise, in the call of the disciples, the evangelist portrays this overwhelming experience of grace. In Luke's Gospel, Peter, after having fished all night and caught nothing, obediently drops the nets again at Jesus' command and they are filled to overflowing. Peter's response is to fall on his knees before Jesus saying: "Leave me Lord; I am a sinful man." And Luke simply states: "For he and his companions were completely overcome by the catch they had made. . . . Then bringing their boats to land, they left everything and followed him" (Luke 5:4-11).

The immediate following of Jesus by those whom he called, or the unusual experience of Paul being thrown to the ground and blinded, or the more subtle, though no less real, encounters like those of Nicodemus, Mary and Martha, and Magdalen bespeak an experience of grace out of which they lived. This is the key: the call of God is an encounter with grace that comes to a person in more ways than one can imagine. Not only the encounter with grace, but the recognition of this encounter as a grace-event constitutes a new way of understanding, seeing, and being. It need not be an extraordinary event, but it must have extraordinary significance. The drama of the encounter does not constitute the call by God. Indeed, the type of immediacy that characterizes the call of the prophets and disciples is the biblical authors' literary style of emphasizing the impact of God upon the person. A person is touched in the deepest part of his or her being and will not ever be the same again. One begins to live out of such an experience or experiences. Henceforth, the world and all human experience is interpreted from and referred to the significance of this grace-event. Paul could only interpret the world, human life, and human meaning from his experience of the Risen Christ. Jesus could only interpret the meaning of the world and human existence from his experience of Abba's reign. This does not imply that one lives perfectly and without sin. One need only look at the on-going tale of Peter and Paul and the other disciples to see that their response was imperfect at best. Sin continues to mark life, but the vision of the grace-event remains firm and true. Faith is not grounded on one's own faithful response, but upon God's gracious gift.

Karl Rahner refers to this experience as mystical. He states: "The Christian of the future will be a mystic, or will not exist."[4] The Christian is one who has experienced the touch of Jesus Christ and has consciously appropriated it so that it continues to be a present reality. The Christian is one who is aware ". . . of the fact that he (God) is not far from any of us, since it is in him that we live, and move, and exist. . . ." (Acts 17:28). In this historical moment a secondhand experience of God that derives from culture or family or church is insufficient. Though indeed these realities may mediate such an experience, the person must become actively invested and involved. To put on the "mind of Christ" requires purification and transformation that reaches the depths of the human personality. "But we are those who have the mind of Christ" (1 Cor 2:16).

Thus, when it comes to a spirituality of the preacher, there is no doubt that the call must come from God no matter how that is experienced. This call gradually colors one's entire being. It gets under the skin and into the very marrow of the bone like a two-edged sword (Heb 3:12). The preacher is not extraneous to the preaching, but becomes a witness to the power of the word proclaimed in his or her own life.

For the Sake of the World

By its very nature preaching is for the salvation of others. The grace of preaching is never only for the sake of the preacher. Jeremiah, after having resolved not to preach again, laments:

> You have seduced me, Yahweh, and I have let myself be seduced; you have overpowered me: you were the stronger. I am a daily laughingstock, everybody's butt. Each time I speak the word, I have to howl and proclaim: "Violence and ruin!" The word of Yahweh has meant for me insult, derision, all day long. I used to say, "I will not think about him, I will not speak in his name any more." Then there seemed to be a fire burning in my heart, imprisoned in my bones. The effort to restrain it wearied me, I could not bear it (Jer 20:7-9).

Jeremiah was compelled to speak the word of God, even though he vehemently resisted, because not to speak would destroy his very self. The spirituality of Jeremiah the preacher stemmed from an experience of the Spirit coupled with a sense of urgency for the cause of God in the midst of the world.

Edward Schillebeeckx has insisted that the world be taken with the utmost seriousness: "The world and the human history in which God wills to bring about salvation for men and women are the basis for the whole reality of salvation. There is no salvation, not even religious salvation outside the human world."[5] Is this not the very nature of the scriptures? The Hebrew scripture tells the story of a definite people. It is not abstract conceptions of God's dealing with people. Scripture is not only about real people; it also speaks of a God immersed in and united with this people at this time and place. So too, Jesus of Nazareth, the definitive revelation of God lived in one location, and dealt with a particular people at a given time. He performed certain actions, used particular images, lived in the flesh, had specific friends, and died in a vivid manner.

No one takes history more seriously than God. Thus, it follows that those who experience God and God's call in Jesus also become more and more profoundly united with their moment in history. One's place in the world is the moment and place where God dwells and life happens. The whole kenotic action of God in Jesus is an act of entering into the depths of human existence. This entrance into human joy and pain is precisely where the experience of God receives its interpretation. With the ability to name and see God in history, the experience of God becomes more deeply grounded and clearly refined. The story present in the biblical text becomes the paradigm of all stories dealing with God and God's people. A spirituality of the preacher that calls for the experience of a mystic can never infer an individualist interiority that is removed from life. The great mystics in the Christian tradition are those who have a passionate love and concern for this world with its joy and sorrows. Why? It is in the midst of concrete realities that they have experienced the intimate presence of God. God is always "God-with-us." The times are never a danger for the preacher called by God. What is dangerous is to be insulated from the times and removed from people. In the introduction, I described some aspects of our moment in history. To feel these tensions, to struggle with temptation, to anguish over the presence of God is the locus that reveals the Spirit's movement, God's presence leading us into a more complete future, "thy kingdom come." The preacher must be at this locus.

In the Midst of the Church

To say that the preacher lives in and exists for the world presumes that the preacher lives in and is a part of the Christian community, the Church. Just as a preacher cannot stand apart from the people, neither can the preacher merely repeat the Gospel story. The preacher must be a member of the household of faith. To live in the world with its pain and anguish and confusion, the preacher needs the community to sustain and affirm and strengthen that primordial experience of God. Though the experience of God is profoundly personal, it is always communal. For a preacher to consider his or her self above the Church or outside the Church is to forfeit the call to preach. This does not mean to say the Church cannot be challenged by the preacher. Indeed, it must be, but it does mean that one is always a part of and never separate from the body of believers. We need only to see that Jesus lived and died within the household of Israel in the tradition of all the prophets. Indeed, he challenged the manner in which Israel lived its covenant faith; yet his death, freely accepted, portrayed vividly his submission to Israel and at the same time his absolute fidelity to God. Israel's faith was the mediating experience that supported and even demanded Jesus' fidelity to the point of death. Jesus was a true Israelite.

Further, it is the preacher's life lived in the midst of the Church that is the acid test of whether the message proclaimed is ideology or genuine praxis. It is ideology if it remains only a wonderful and beautiful idea. Is the message becoming incarnate in the attitudes, values, and behaviors of the preacher? The early Church did not preach the Kingdom of God;

rather, it preached Jesus, for it was able to recognize in his life, death, and resurrection the kingdom of God as realized. Again, one hears the teaching of Paul VI: "Modern men and women listen more willingly to witnesses than to teachers, and if they do listen to teachers, it is because they are witnesses."[6] One could substitute the word "preacher" for "teacher." The preacher's life is a wordless witness, a radiation of the Gospel message he or she proclaims. The presence of the preacher as an equal member within a particular Christian community will demand of that preacher a quality of presence, sharing, and solidarity that will test whether or not the Gospel is incarnation or remains on the level of ideology. In a day and age that thirsts for authenticity, life in the Christian community is a condition without which there can be no truly credible preaching. Questions posed by Paul VI do more than imply this conclusion:

> Do you really believe what you are proclaiming? Do you live what you believe? Do you really preach what you believe? The witness of life has become more than ever an essential condition for real effectiveness in preaching. Precisely because of this we are, to a certain extent, responsible for the progress of the Gospel that we proclaim.[7]

The manner in which a preacher lives and acts determines, to a degree, the credibility and receptivity of the Gospel. The preacher lives in the midst of the Church for the sake of the world. Precisely because the message is greater than the messenger, the preacher is in a constant posture of openness to on-going conversion. For this reason preaching itself is a religious activity. It is closely related to prayer. The continual act of preaching, by God's grace and mercy, can convert the preacher.

Simon Tugwell, in his introduction to Humbert of Romans' *Treatise on the Formation of Preachers*, points out that Humbert's concern is to elucidate how preaching is "a legitimate nucleus for a whole way of life, a whole way of sanctity."[8] Preaching calls one to live at the heart of mystery—one's life woven together with God's. It is in this deep communion with God that the preacher remains in touch with the sustaining call of God leading the preacher from one moment to the next. If prayer is superficial, the personal witness to the preaching becomes obscure. If the preacher does not live what is preached, there is a sense among the people, over a period of time, that something is not right. Living in the midst of the world as one called by God demands a prayerful stance which empowers the preacher's life to become a transparent proclamation. Schillebeeckx says it more bluntly: "If you don't talk to God first, you can't talk about him.''[9] The liberation theologians, Leonardo and Clodovis Boff put it this way: "It is in prayer and contemplation, and intimate and communitarian contact with God, that the motivation for a faith-inspired commitment to the oppressed and all humankind spring and are renewed.''[10] Preaching, by its very nature, requires one to deal prayerfully with the mystery of God present in the depth dimension of the human. Indeed, preaching is a religious exercise of the highest order.

To Effect a Hearing

The final dynamic in a spirituality of the preacher is the constant preoccupation to effect a hearing. How can the word be heard? Humbert of Romans says: "Though a grace of preaching is strictly had by God's gift, sensible preachers still ought to do what they can to insure that their preaching is commendable, by carefully studying what they have to preach.''[11] Because of the preacher's preoccupation with the mystery of God communicated to this present world, there is a two-fold dimension to this study. On the one hand, the depth of God is pursued by a serious study of scripture and theology as the sources that animate and permeate all preaching. On the other hand, there is study of language and the manner in which it functions. Because the first is rather obvious, I would only like to refer to it briefly. Vatican II states:

> All the preaching of the Church must needs be nourished and governed by Sacred Scripture. . . . So remarkable is its power and force that the word of God abides as the support and energy of the Church, the strength of faith for the Church's children, the food of the soul, the pure and perennial source of spiritual life.[12]

Theology is the science that mediates our preaching, that enables us to interpret the scripture in such a manner that God's word continues to be spoken. William Hill, an American Dominican, in an article entitled: "Preaching as a 'moment' in Theology" states: "Proclamation arises out of faith, but to be effective it must come from a faith mediated theologically.''[13] Hill goes on to point out that preaching cannot be mere repetition of scripture but it must be a creative transformation; otherwise preaching becomes a mere rhetorical propagation of a tradition. This critical theology is what gives substance and relevance to preaching. Walter Burghardt, a famous American Jesuit preacher, states in his own inimitable fashion:

> True enough, it is not theology I preach; for the pulpit is not a classroom. But without theology I risk preaching platitudes. . . . Our homilies are rarely heretical. They fail, fall short, flounder rather because they are stale and flat, vapid and insipid, dreadfully dry and boringly barren. One reason? They are not pregnant with the inexhaustible riches that is Christ; they carry so little substance, so little sap to slake the parched spirit.[14]

The preacher's study is to know the word and to be able to proclaim it in such a manner as to effect a hearing.

Scripture and theology become objects of study, but there is also the study of communication as an act of theology itself. Referring to Lonergan's theological method, of which "communication" is the last specialty function, William Hill states: "Communication concerns itself with the effort to unleash God's word into the tissue of human life and society."[15] What is a word? It is a symbolic utterance by which the inner reality of one person is participated in by another. One can never say preaching is "only words" as though to dismiss their significance, as if symbolic words were anything less than effective vehicles of awesome realities, namely bearers of meaning. Words, being symbols, are intensely significant. A few powerful words spoken at a significant moment can help transform history, as, for example, Luther's "Here I stand" symbolized the division of the western Church, and Martin Luther King's "I have a dream" captured the civil rights movements. Burghardt writes:

> Words . . . can be weapons, and words can be healing. Words can unite in friendship or sever in enmity. Words can unlock who I am or mask me from others. . . . Words sentence to death . . . and words restore to life. . . . Words charm and repel, amuse and anger, reveal and conceal, chill and warm. Words clarify and words obscure. A word from Washington rained down atomic hell on Hiroshima; words from an altar change bread and wine into the body and blood of Christ.[16]

Because words have power they best be attended to, for they do nothing less than constitute reality. The feminist critique, for example, strongly calls attention to the construction of patriarchy by the very naming of God. Yet, without words, experience is never intelligently appropriated. For example, to know that one is a child of God, a temple of the Spirit, an heir to heaven, there must be more than the inner reality of the grace. Karl Rahner made this point powerfully:

> This inner world of grace alone cannot make it possible for human beings to have a developed, objectivated, fully conscious understanding of them-

> selves as the believing recipient of the divine self-communication. . . . The external, historical word expounds the inner one. . . . The inner word of grace and the external historical word come together *as* the mutually complimentary moments of the one word of God to humanity.[17]

Part of the asceticism, therefore, of the preacher is to be intentional about the words used. "What the preacher does when he or she preaches is mediate God's meaning,"[18] and in doing this constitutes the very reality of the proclamation.

One might ask how this is related to the spirituality of the preacher? If the preacher has been touched significantly by the grace of God and possesses a real passion to communicate this experience, "how" becomes a question. Preaching is an activity; it is a specific and public proclamation at a moment in time. The act of preaching is an act of incarnation whereby the preacher's words are assumed by God's word. The word of God becomes flesh in the word of the preacher. Story, images and metaphor enable one not only to remember, but also to re-experience the God of Jesus and so facilitate the operation of grace. Abstractions, while speaking to the mind, do not engage the whole person as a participant in the preaching event in the same way story does. One need only look at the preaching of Jesus and his style to see an example of this. The preacher-storyteller knows what to do with the listener. Through the sharing of story, the preacher's experience is participated in by the listeners. The homily continues to live on in the imagination of the hearers as part of their own story. The preacher labors to the best of his or her ability to incarnate the word, to enable God to be experienced as the most real of all realities in our world. Thus, the component of assiduous study whereby the human person becomes a participant in revealing truth is the ascetical activity of the preacher. The preoccupation with words is to effect a hearing of God's word.

Granted all of this, the preacher need not be eloquent as that term is commonly understood. The preacher with the help of God is to yield all the resources he or she has to the preaching event. Some of the most effective preachers were not humanly impressive; witness the apostle Paul for example. The resistance of the prophets based on this very point was referred to earlier. God's response to Moses demonstrates this vividly.

> "But, my Lord, never in my life have I been a man of eloquence, either before or since you spoke to your servant. I am a slow speaker and not able to speak well." "Who gave man his mouth . . .," Yahweh answered him,

> "Is it not I Yahweh? Now go, I shall help you to speak and tell you what to say" (Exod 4:10-12).

It is God alone who makes human words the vehicle of God's own word. This is the grace of preaching.

Conclusion

The Church once again has made the word of God central to its ordinary daily existence. The many biblical movements that characterize its life today are preparing the way for a profound re-evangelization. The world itself cries out in need. The very existence of the Church is to evangelize, that is to preach.

> We wish to confirm once more that the task of evangelizing all people constitutes the essential mission of the Church. . . . Evangelizing is in fact the grace and vocation proper to the Church, her deepest identity. She exists in order to evangelize, that is to say in order to preach and teach. . . .[19]

A perceived spiritual hunger has gripped the land; preaching feeds that hunger by offering a vision, God's vision. An aimless and destructive narcissism characterizes the present search for human meaning. Preaching presents the possibility of pointing the way to human fulfillment through human transcendence. An empty longing grips millions; preaching can enable that to became a desire for the holy, the infinite, the only reality that can fill the human heart. Therefore, preaching is not only a gift but a profound responsibility. St. Paul puts it this way: "Not that I do boast of preaching the Gospel, since it is a duty which has been laid on me; I should be punished if I did not preach it" (1 Cor 9:16). Paul VI makes an even stronger case. He asks:

> Can we gain salvation if through negligence or fear or shame . . . or as a result of false ideas we fail to preach? For that would be to betray the call of God, who wishes the seed to bear fruit through the voice of the ministers of the Gospel; and it will depend on us whether this grows into trees and produces its full fruit.[20]

If this is true, then God is raising up preachers throughout the world. It is not that the grace of preaching is lacking, but it may be that the grace is not always recognized, or worse yet, not permitted full expression. Realizing that the grace of preaching always comes from God, the spirituality that sustains this grace is present when a person, having been touched by grace in the midst of the Church, possesses a sense of urgency for the sake of the world to effect a hearing of the ineffable word of God.

Notes

1. Paul VI, *Evangelii Nuntiandi*, (1975) no. 4.
2. Yves Congar, "Sacramental Worship and Preaching," *The Renewal of Preaching: Theory and Practice*, Concilium 33 (New York: Paulist Press, 1968) 62.
3. Humbert of Romans, *Opera de Vita Regulari*, II, p. 381 as quoted by Simon Tugwell, *The Way of the Preacher*, Templegate Pub., 1979, 47.
4. Karl Rahner, "The Spirituality of the Church of the Future," *Theological Investigations* 20 (New York: Seabury Crossroad, 1981) 149.
5. Edward Schillebeeckx, *On Christian Faith: The Spiritual, Ethical and Political Dimensions* (New York: Crossroad, 1987) 8.
6. Paul VI, *Evangelii Nuntiandi*, 1975, #41.
7. Paul VI, *Evangelii Nuntiandi*, 1975, #76.
8. Simon Tugwell, ed., *Early Dominicans: Selected Writings* (New York: Paulist Press, 1982) 181.
9. *God is New Each Moment*: Edward Schillebeeckx in Conversation with Huub Oosterhuis and Piet Hoogeveen (New York: Seabury, 1983) 125.
10. Leonardo and Clodovis Boff, *Introducing Liberation Theology* (Maryknoll: Orbis Books, 1988) 64.
11. Tugwell, *Early Dominicans*, 205.
12. *Dei Verbum*, Vatican II, #21.
13. William Hill, "Preaching as a 'moment' in Theology," *Homiletic and Pastoral Review*, 77 (1976–77): 10.
14. Walter Burghardt, *Preaching: The Art & the Craft* (New York: Paulist Press) 59.
15. Hill, Ibid. 11.
16. Burghardt, Ibid. 6.
17. Karl Rahner, *Theological Investigations*, IV: 258–259.
18. Hill, Ibid. 13.
19. Paul VI, *Evangelii Nuntiandi*, #14.
20. Paul VI, *Evangelii Nuntiandi*, #80.

Chapter 11

Preaching and Pastoral Care

HARRY M. BYRNE, O.P.

If we are to focus our attention on preaching as pastoral care, a few distinctions need to be made. Preaching in the Catholic tradition is often associated with a particular liturgical service or experience of worship. What most immediately comes to mind is the homily at the Eucharist or other sacramental celebration or perhaps the preaching events of a retreat or some spiritual exercise. Those who proclaim to us the Christian message in such situations are easily identified as preachers and participate to some degree in the charism of preaching. This is the gift identified from the very beginning of the Church as a special charism given to certain members of the community to proclaim and explain the significance of the scriptural message to the contemporary Christian assembly.

From the time of Jesus, in the writings of Paul, through the great preachers of the early Church and down through history to the present, the aim of preaching was to be pastoral in content and to be a direct response to the realities of a particular congregation in light of their Christian faith. Preaching responded to the needs of the community from a pastorally aware perspective, guiding individual members with words of direction and inspiration. The charism of preaching has always been understood as a gift given to the community of faith through the favor of the Holy Spirit to proclaim the mission and message of Jesus Christ in the world. This same charism is given to members of Christian communities today as part of the ongoing revelation of God to God's people.

In a ministerial context, however, preaching must be understood from another perspective as well. Preaching is a primary means of offering pastoral care and, therefore, can be a central form of communication for those in the role of pastoral minister. Preaching is an essential form of pastoral communication in the ministry of the Church. This broadens our understanding of who may be called and given the charism to preach. In a variety of ways and in multiple settings, from small groups to large congregations, ministers are called to communicate pastorally by preaching. The challenge offered to those who are involved in pastoral ministry is to look more closely at the place preaching plays in their ministry, to deepen their understanding of the power of the preached word in providing pastoral care, and to incorporate this pivotal form of pastoral communication into their ministry. Further, it is a call to communicate directly to one's congregation.

The ordinary and regular preaching of the minister on an everyday basis is essential in providing pastoral care for the community. The charism to preach, therefore, is closely related to the vocation to pastor. It is too fundamental to the Church's mission to separate the charism of preaching from the call of an individual to be a pastor.

The pastor and the preacher must definitely become part of a community, involved in its life, struggles and celebrations, before he or she preaches to that community. The pastor cannot remain outside or aloof from the everyday happenings of the people being served. This involvement means taking time to listen to the members of the community and to their needs and desires. Often there is a common concern that arises from the community, one that is expressed in a variety of spoken and unspoken ways. Listening and watching carefully, trying to eliminate that which hinders one's hearing and piecing together what is communicated to us will give the preacher a fairly accurate reading of the pastoral needs of the parish community. To these needs comes a word of healing, the encouragement that sustains, a wise insight of guidance, and the communal prayer of reconciliation. Preaching from a pastoral perspective is the response to the community's message of need.

Preaching can be the usual way of providing pastoral care for large numbers of the faith community. It could easily become a primary means of communicating pastoral care between the pastor and the congregation. Pastoral preaching should obviously be community oriented although not exclusively so; it attempts both to address the needs of the community and carry a message which in some way touches the experience of each listener.

Those who are not directly involved in the particular need being addressed by the preacher can be invited to participate in the pastoral care process which calls on all in the community to minister to others. They may not be experiencing this particular need, and so they are asked to invest their supportive strength in the common good of the lives of their sisters and brothers. Those who are not in need are part of the body of

Christ helping to express communal pastoral care. Preaching, through the power of the word, builds up the community. The entire faith community reinforces the ministry performed by the pastor and cooperates in offering pastoral care from the rich resources entrusted to the people of God. Although the pastor may be the primary pastoral care coordinator and representative of the community, through preaching the entire assembly can be inspired and empowered to participate in the ministry of compassionate concern and care, thereby incarnating in its behavior the words of faith. The preaching of the Church becomes the praxis of the community as it witnesses the gospel lived in the world.

Preaching and the Four Functions of Pastoral Care

All pastoral care begins with a relationship between minister and individual or group. The quality of the relationship greatly influences the degree of effectiveness of the care received. Similarly, the quality of the relationship between the preacher and the congregation will have a direct bearing on the influence of the preacher's message on the listeners. The newcomer or stranger who preaches to the group may have an innovative attraction, but without the establishment of an actual relationship he or she will soon begin to diminish the impact of the message offered to the congregation. The preacher, like any good pastoral minister, must exhibit in the style and message of his or her preaching the qualities of one who truly cares. As in all pastoral ministry, it is the quality of the relationship that allows preaching to become beneficial and growth promoting.

It will be helpful at this point to look at the classical functions of pastoral care, those goals which have traditionally formed Christian ministry, and relate them to preaching in a pastoral setting. William Clebsch and Charles Jaekle in their book *Pastoral Care in Historical Perspective* describe the four pastoral functions in the Christian tradition as healing, sustaining, guiding, and reconciling.[1] These functions have focused the practice of providing pastoral care through the centuries, giving direction to ministers by establishing precise goals for service to the community.

The preacher can be the representative of the people and minister to the community as it deals with ultimate concerns and attempts to understand these meanings. To facilitate healing, to sustain life, to be a guiding influence, and to promote an experience of reconciliation are legitimate goals of all pastoral preaching. Although there may be especially troubled individuals in any community (those who need the concentrated attention of the pastoral minister) all members of the congregation continually need healing, sustaining, guiding, and reconciling. The preacher, through the ministry of the word, offers to the entire community the possibility of experiencing these four functions of pastoral care in a continuous, growth-promoting way.

Healing: The First Function

In the Christian tradition, to be a healer implies that the minister helps to restore an ill and "wounded" individual or community to health (physical, mental, spiritual) and wholeness (an integrated and unified equilibrium). To aid in the healing process is to reverse disintegration and fragmentation so that the individual can grow spiritually toward fulfillment and peace in a wholesome way. The preacher can foster this restoration by communicating a healing word that provides a curative insight that enables a positive change to take place. This turning point is the reversal of the "sickening" propensity which dominates the person's life, redirecting one toward healthy integration and future unity. The healing message of the preacher can both explore the spiritual significance of sickness and health and help bring about the listener's renewal.

A secondary goal of healing is to improve and enrich the quality of peoples' lives. The pastoral minister who is called to preach to a community whose membership has experienced the trauma of the AIDS epidemic needs to offer a healing and inspiring word of hope in the face of great sorrow and fear. In another congregation, the members of the parish community who have experienced the loss of a spouse listen to the preacher who speaks of the experience of human love and the healing power of God's love. The words of the scriptures explored in a homily with those who struggle with dark recollections of past traumas can begin to feel a healing of the memories. The practical goal of promoting and enhancing health and wholeness goes beyond the limits of medicine and psychology; its object is to touch the very spirit of the individual and the whole community.

Pastoral preaching can facilitate the type of spiritual development which will enable the believer to deal effectively with those obstacles which impede or prevent healthy integration. At an earlier time, pastoral care was known as the "care of souls" by which a pastor was called to heal or nourish "souls." Preaching which has healing as its objective can continue that ministry of Jesus which not only cured the body but touched the very life of the soul.

Sustaining: The Second Function

To sustain, a second function of pastoral care, has the goal of helping an individual or community endure and move beyond changes which are irreversible and potentially overwhelming.[2] It is that care and concern which helps the devastated go on with life and cope with the harsh realities which are part of the human condition. How can the pastoral minister help others adjust to the fact that restoration is not possible? Preaching encourages the listener to resist the tendency to become a victim of blind fate, voicing a spiritual challenge to grow through endurance. The preacher calls the congregation to look at the significance of an experience from a spirit-guided perspective. The preacher can express sustaining support to the bereaved and to others who have experienced loss in their lives. The funeral homily is an opportunity to minister to those who are dealing with the realities of separation and death of a loved one. In a variety of ways, the pastor can offer similar consoling and compassionate messages to those who experience other forms of loss and death in their personal lives. That the pastoral minister is there as a supportive resource in the time of extreme need and that there are other sources of personal and communal strength and life support, especially within the faith community itself, make a difference in a person's life of faith.

Guiding: The Third Function

Perhaps the function of guiding is the most compatible with the role of the preacher as the communicator of pastoral care. Here the goal is to aid the individual or the community in the decision-making process and to give prudent advice and wise counsel. Group guidance can be used effectively by the pastoral preacher to give direction to the common needs of a congregation with a similar concern. In guiding others, the pastoral minister can help alleviate the confusion that is often experienced in dealing with everyday problems, helping to clarify what is real and important, instilling self confidence in the hearer, and giving direction from a sound perspective. To the local church that is experiencing the racial integration of its neighborhood or a parish community trying to understand the resignation of its pastor from the ordained ministry to marry, a word of guidance regarding an uncertain future may be vital to both its spiritual and social life. Pastoral guidance communicated through preaching offers counsel to those who search for answers as they deal with the life choices that affect their mental and spiritual well-being. Pastoral preaching can offer the significant assistance which enables a person or community to make confident choices and decisions. The preacher as guide, then, provides direction in the ambiguous and confusing challenges of daily life.

Reconciling: The Fourth Function

The function of reconciling in Christian pastoral care is to mend fractured relationships, human and divine. Because of the significance of the community in Christian spirituality, each human being is seen to be essentially connected with others, our neighbor and God. Therefore, when relationships become seriously disconnected or disrupted there are repercussions for the individual, for the community, and for God. This vital balance of a healthy relational triad must be cared for and nurtured so that life and growth can be maintained.

The preacher is called to facilitate reconciliation so that the process of forgiving and being forgiven can begin and be developed. It is a time of vulnerability and humility, a time for sensitive words. This message can take place within the sacramental celebration of reconciliation in the community or in the context of the numerous preaching moments that are part of the ongoing faith life of the congregation. A word preached and flowing from the reconciling appeal of God can offer hope to reestablish a relationship previously broken. One who welcomes back, as the father does in the story of the prodigal son, symbolizes the role of the preacher who offers the reconciling word to those who have experienced the distance and loneliness of separation due to misunderstanding, anger, or selfishness.

The four functions of pastoral care, when used to inform our pastoral preaching, can work together integrating the word of God with present-day realities for the health and wholeness of both individual and community. To preach the good news of Jesus is to express in the name of the body of Christ words of healing, of sustenance, guiding direction, and hope-filled reconciliation. Proclaiming good news is what preaching and pastoral care are all about; this responds to the need of the individual listening for some hopeful instruction and by the entire congregation poised for some directive leadership. The four functions preached within the context of the scriptures blend together and bond in such a way as to enable preaching to become truly caring pastoral ministry. As the functions of healing, guiding, sustaining, and reconciling provide distinct activities, so the preacher's words should be a clear message about the particular situation for this unique group of listeners and their real needs and questions.

Preaching must continue to adapt contemporary means of communication to express pastoral care and to accomplish the goals of the four functions. This can best be done when the preacher is willing to listen and respond to the signs and demands of the times. Whenever we express ourselves pastorally we are able to enliven, restore, sustain life, and reunite and serve our brothers and sisters in helpful and necessary ways. We know, too, from our own experience that we begin to understand, are comforted, identify feelings, are stimulated to action, and are brought to new awareness by hearing words of "good news." Preaching serves this process well, especially when it strives to be practical and relevant. The preacher facilitates and fosters the life of the body of Christ when he or she remembers that pastoral care and pastoral preaching are for the sake of proclaiming the Gospel which serves God's people.

Because preaching is meant to be a primary and continuous means of communication by the pastor with the community, contemporary insights in the fields of psychology, sociology, and communication theory offer new understandings and methods that enable preaching to be an effective means of pastoral communication. Using this knowledge and creating modern and meaningful techniques for preaching will not only enhance ministry but can actually facilitate the ongoing pastoral care and counseling process taking place in the local church. The preacher of God's word as facilitator of healing, sustenance, guidance, and reconciliation is key to the success of the pastoral care ministry of the faith community to its own members and outward to the world.

The Preacher as Pastor and Prophet

It is not an easy task that has been set out for the pastoral minister. Besides being trained in the skills of good preaching, having a background of theological and spiritual knowledge which enables one to speak the truth, and making one's own the lifestyle of the preacher—a life of prayer and reflection, the minister is now further called to truly become a pastorally sensitive, caring preacher. This ministry demands dedication to a mission of service that will use the very word of God as the vehicle to communicate a pastor's care. Deeply rooted in this mission is the commission to be prophetic and to challenge the community to grow to a more profound level of committed life, to become authentic and holy and more fully Christian. It means helping those who listen to the message of the preacher to deal more hopefully with the realities of the human condition.

To be a pastoral preacher means to come face-to-face with one's sinfulness and the power of sin with which all humanity struggles. The pastor is expected to address sin-related concerns; this spectrum ranges from the selfishness of nations to the guilt of those who feel abandoned. Writers today speak of the "addiction" of sin, its overpowering attraction and that primitive tendency which is within each of us to sin. The pastoral preacher must address this reality of human nature in his or her communication with the community. It is easy for us to be so embarrassed at our own sinfulness that we become mute and afraid to speak. But the good news tells us of a God who seeks reconciliation, who offers both mercy and forgiveness, healing and support. That is the preacher's message too! It is grounded in that fundamental response of God who looked upon what had been created and saw that it was indeed good. Corruption and sin are part of what we have to deal with in life, but the divine blessing of the human condition pushes us to look more closely at that original goodness which continues to predominate in the personhood of each individual. The pastoral preacher must acknowledge that he or she is a sinful healer, one who can be tempted to condemn, to be hypocritical, and to use double standards. Allowing oneself to remember the purpose of the mission is to recall the preacher's own experience of God's repeated acceptance of our repentance and the liberating offer of God's loving reconciliation.

As the preacher has been challenged in his or her own relationship with God, in the graced exploration of oneself, the pastoral preacher calls others to change and grow. We can become complacent with ourselves; it is easier to maintain the status quo, not to "rock the boat." The message of the preacher is to awaken the congregation from its lethargy and to offer words of correction and challenge. Here, correction means to help put right, to enable one to get back on track, to give direction for self betterment. Challenging the community and individual members to change means to preach for repentance. There is always danger in this type of preaching in that we can make our words too general, not sufficiently direct and to the point, so that the challenge is misunderstood or easily dismissed. This often happens when the preacher addresses social justice issues; there is a "that doesn't have to do with me" attitude when the communication is presented in generalities. Sadly, the effort in this case is defused of its power to invite conversion. On the other hand, the particularized or overly personalized challenge can create unnecessary embarrassment or even animosity in the hearer's reaction. The message of the preacher should not end up being an attack on the reputation of an individual or group within the community. When this happens, again, the purpose of offering a stimulus to renew and grow is lost in negative reaction. The goal of the preacher is to offer a pastorally caring message which guides listeners to a reflective response to enhance both the life of the individual and that of the community.

The pastoral preacher is one who tells the truth, communicating the realities of life and inspiring human hope. This means that on some occasions the preacher is a reality check on the life of the Christian community, contrasting who the community is with who it is called to be. Those ignored facts of life which keep the community honest and responsible have to be voiced. The pastor is imaged in the prophet crying out and reminding the congregation of its call to holiness and witness. The preacher does not leave unvoiced those critical words which speak as conscience to the mind and heart of each listener. It is responsible leadership when preaching is formulated to say what needs to be said for the common good. The pastor uses different forms of expression, but has the single goal of raising the question that each person in the community needs to ask: "Is what the preacher says true?" If so, the challenge has been received and the pastoral preaching has become a catalyst for change. Jesus, speaking with wisdom and authority, did the same for the people of his day with his comments, stories, and questions. Today's preachers continue this tradition by making the good news they proclaim to the people of God a pastorally sensitive challenge to remain faithful in their striving toward wholeness and holiness.

Conclusion

The general goal for this chapter has been to share with those who are pastoral preachers some thoughts based on my study and practice of pastoral care and my experience as a preacher. Within this goal has been my not-so-hidden agenda urging all pastors who are called to preach the good news to the people of God to see their mission of communicating as pastoral care through graced words. The guidance and care of the pastor can reach out and touch many more lives to promote health, growth, and wholeness in the community of faith. Pastoral care can also be preventative and enriching rather than merely reactive and problem oriented, as it so often is today. Likewise, the preacher from this perspective can be relevant and at the service of the community offering prophetic leadership with a challenging message.

Our tradition tells us that when preaching is most effective it is truly pastoral communication. Those who today seek more inspiration and support from their pastor-preachers are at the very least asking for more direct and clear messages from their leaders. If the Church is to continue to develop its mission to a world hungry for good news of salvation, it will have to take seriously this call to pastor all people, to respond to their needs (especially the spiritual), and to preach this response from a strongly pastoral foundation. Preaching pastoral care, therefore, is not an option for the preacher; it follows the model of Jesus the preacher who commissioned his followers to communicate the message of God's love, in every place, for all people till the end of time.

Pastoral care, when forming the word to be preached, allows the care to take place in its proper context: the body of the community of believers. Here pastoral care becomes the shared responsibility of all the assembly, hearing the message and responding to it through service to one another. This has been our tradition from the beginning, and it is what we return to as we face the future. This also is pastoral care grounded in the word of God and the grace of preaching; communication from this source can indeed be blessed and life giving.

Pastoral care, when incorporated into our preaching, is an integral part of truly beneficial pastoral activity. There is an essential interplay between preaching and the multiple expressions of pastoral ministry. This interplay develops, reinforces, and enriches both pastoral care and preaching. Without this integrative approach to preaching and the various other types of pastoral activity central to the mission of the Church, the primary ministerial message of service is less powerful and therefore less effective. There is no need, however, for a new vehicle for pastoral communication to be found or invented. Preaching, the preeminent classical means of communicating pastorally, continues to be a most effective and efficient form when used with skill and enthusiasm. Pastoral preaching is a special and unique way of offering care to the community. We can neither ignore its vital need by the Church today nor replace it with some other form of communication. As pastoral ministers we need to accept the commission to bring the light of the gospel through pastoral preaching to the actual problems of our sisters and brothers in the community of the faithful, to the everyday needs and concerns of God's listening people.

The real challenge, in the final analysis, for each one of us called to be pastoral preachers is to say what we have been called to proclaim with our words and lives. We are to express God's care for the world; we are to communicate as pastors of God's people the good news which was there from the beginning, which is with us today, and leads us forth in hope into the future. God sent the word into the world that we might hear God's loving communication to us: "Listen to me, you are mine and I am the one who cares about you."

Notes

1. William A. Clebsch and Charles Jaeckle, *Pastoral Care in Historical Perspective* (New York: Jason Aronson Inc., 1975) 4–10.
2. Ibid. 8–9.

Chapter 12

Preaching the Social Gospel

EDWARD J. VAN MERRIENBOER, O.P.

I. Introduction

During the last twenty-five years, there has been an impressive development in social thinking and commitment among Catholics. The Second Vatican Council and modern popes have succeeded in translating the message of the gospel into a set of moral principles and spiritual orientations for the development of one's social conscience. Yet, preaching this aspect of the gospel message still offers great challenges to the preacher. Why does this form of preaching present such a challenge?

I have experienced two great concerns after many years in the social apostolate: the complexity of social issues and the witness of the preacher to the values preached. There are other issues that could be raised at this point, such as the excessive guilt often associated with social preaching or the simple inability of people to change unjust situations. However, complexity and witness seem to be the greatest reasons for reservations about social preaching.

Before addressing these two challenges, I think it would be productive to clarify what I mean by the "social gospel."[1] The social gospel can in no way be compared to an ideological stance because it does not offer a blue-print for a particular social or economic system. It expresses for our times the reflection of the Church on social realities, assessing them in light of the Gospel and offering guidelines for practical behavior in society. It is basically an application of theology, and especially moral theology, to the ethical questions raised by human societies.

Preaching the social gospel is a service which can enable the People of God to become active builders of a more just and peaceful society. "With the support of rational reflection and of the human sciences, the Church seeks to lead people to respond to their vocation as responsible leaders of earthly society."[2] If the preacher can have a greater clarity about the goal of social preaching many of the problems associated with this form of preaching can be overcome. All that will be said in this chapter will be guided by the goal to form the social conscience of the People of God.

The challenge of complexity can be approached within the context of this goal. The modern world is, in fact, very complex in every aspect of human experience. Part of this complexity is rather new to human history because new systems of economics have emerged with advances in technology. The developments in communications technology have made us very aware that our world is complex. It is now possible to view world events in our home while they happen. The Gulf War is one recent example of how we can experience the complexity of living locally while being aware of global events. Within our North American culture there is a strong need to understand our lives, and when this is not possible we avoid knowledge about things beyond our control.

The truth of the modern world is that no one person or even a group of people can understand the world fully. It is not possible for a human person to be well versed in everything; therefore, the need for specialization is imperative. The preacher is one of many world actors who has specialized in one area of human experience; namely, morality. It is on the level of moral values that the preacher makes a contribution. The preacher does not have to understand global politics, cultural systems, or economic theory to know what is morally desirable. In particular, the preacher's expertise is rooted in the preaching of Jesus of Nazareth who proclaimed the reign of God in history.

The second challenge associated with social preaching is directly related to the preaching of Jesus. When the disciples of John the Baptist asked Jesus if he was the Promised One, he gave these words, "Go back and tell John what you have seen and heard, the blind see again, the lame walk, lepers are cleansed, the deaf hear, the dead are raised to life, and the Good News is proclaimed to the poor. . . ." (Luke 7:22). It is in his actions that the truth of his words find authority.

As we preach social values, we must be aware that our life-style will enhance or detract from the authority of our words. The personal witness of the preacher and that of the institutional expression of the Church will be at issue when we proclaim social morality. Often, I have heard in various forms the words from the musical, *My Fair Lady*, ". . . don't talk at all, show me!" Moral preaching involves conversion, and the preacher must realize that this dynamic will involve the preacher and the congregation.

Later in this chapter, I will return to these two challenges as part of an integrated approach to social preaching, but first I would like to develop further the meaning of the social gospel. What are the values which are the content of social preaching? Where do we locate them in the preaching of Jesus and in the social teachings of the Church? How can these values guide the social behavior of a particular church in a given culture? What is their significance for today's societies?

II. What is the Social Gospel?

The first key to understand the social gospel is to realize that it represents an element of continuity, flowing from the teachings of the gospel regarding the love of each human being, the defense of the poor and the oppressed, the denunciation of injustice and greed, the spiritual destiny of humanity and its universal dignity, the loving service of all brothers and sisters. These are the basic and constant principles, which present church teachings express in different forms. These values are the content of our preaching. They are the measure by which Christians are called to make moral judgements about social behavior.

The origin of these values is located in the public ministry of Jesus. The preaching ministry of Jesus was shaped by the task to proclaiming the reign of God. We find this theme in the first public preaching of Jesus:

> Now after John was arrested, Jesus came into Galilee, preaching the gospel of God, and saying, "The time is fulfilled, and the reign of God is at hand: repent, and believe in the gospel" (Mark 1:14-15).

Throughout his preaching Jesus does not give us a definition of the reign of God, since he preferred to speak about it in parables. There is an element of mystery and uncertainty about it. In brief, we can say that the reign of God is the ultimate goal of the preaching of Jesus, ultimate in terms of its value and destiny for human history.

For the purposes of preaching, I would offer the excellent working definition of the reign of God given by Benedict Viviano, when he writes:

> . . . The kingdom is political, it is social (that is, it includes peace and justice without which there is not true holiness), it is personalistic, giving eternal meaning to the individual person, and it is universal, embracing all men and women and the entire cosmos. These are essential components of the kingdom, which is not pie in the sky by and by but God's future for humanity. . . .

> To attempt to define the indefinable, we could say that the kingdom of God is a future apocalyptic divine gift not built by human beings directly but given as a response to hopeful prayer, longing and hastening struggle. It is the final act of God in visiting and redeeming his people, a comprehensive term for the blessings of salvation, that is, all the blessings secured by that act of God.[3]

The preacher's objective is to enhance each Christian's ability to participate in that "hopeful prayer, longing and hastening struggle" in the context of their given vocation. In summary, one can say that we are about the reign of God when we pray and live the values found in the preaching of Jesus. Let us now examine each of the elements present in describing God's reign.

A. UNIVERSAL HUMANITY: THE IMPACT OF AN IDEA

Few ideas in history have exerted such an impact on societies as the Christian concept of universal humanity. This idea emerged progressively in the Hebrew scriptures from the teachings of the prophets, for whom justice and mercy appeared as central values in social relations. An attitude of universal friendship expressed in hospitality and compassion grew out of the conviction that no human being can be denied help, especially the poor, the stranger, the widow, the orphan, the suffering.

Jesus rooted his preaching in these teachings of the prophets and enriched, widened, and deepened them. Love and charity became the norm of social relations.[4] Not only friends and one's own people are to be loved but also strangers, enemies, persecutors. The love preached by Jesus knows of no restrictions such as race, social status, sex: there is "no more Jew or Gentile, no more slave and free individual, no more male or female. You are all one person in Jesus Christ" (Gal 3:28).

Jesus proclaims that God is the norm for such new relations because God is the cause of all creation. God's care extends to even the birds and flowers, indeed all of creation, but is even greater for humanity. The preacher must find methods to express this profound truth about humanity so that it becomes a cherished value for all.

As we grow in awareness of the great social sins of racism, sexism, classism, etc., we find a new urgency to preach the universal dignity of all people. Attitudes and behaviors which deny this idea must be confronted in our preaching. We must denounce any idea or practice contrary to this truth. The Second Vatican Council makes this point strongly when it says:

> True, all are not alike from the point of view of varying physical power and the diversity of intellectual and moral resources. Nevertheless, with respect to the fundamental rights of the person, every type of discrimination, whether social or cultural, whether based on sex, race, color, social condition, language, or religion, is to be overcome and eradicated as contrary to God's intent.[5]

Christians from the early centuries have been convinced that their faith in this truth could change society.[6] The universalism of humanity, including its universal call to salvation, is a radical principle for social transformation.

One can only dream about what our nation and our world would be like without social divisions. In faith, we do not believe that this aspect of the gospel is an idealized utopia, but a challenge to a profound conversion in order better to understand and practice the gospel in ever new situations.

B. THE PREFERENCE FOR THE POOR

A second value of the social gospel which will shape our preaching is Christ's preference for the poor. The historical impact of Matthew 25:31-46, in which Jesus identifies his presence in history with the "least" among us can hardly be overestimated. This conviction has lead saintly men and women to act on the belief that to show mercy to the hungry, the prisoner, the sick, the stranger is an act of love for the Lord himself. Even if its effects cannot be assessed with precision, this belief in the special love of the poor has and is changing social relations.

When we realize that the option for the poor is an option for Christ we link our social action with the mystery of salvation. It is our actions toward the poor and oppressed which will be the standard for God's judgment regarding our personal and collective salvation. When that moment comes when God will judge the nations, it is our active concern for the poor which will be the source of our belonging to Christ. In this sense, the option for the poor is not optional; it is an imperative.

In recent years, some concern has been expressed within the Church that this gospel value could cause Christians to become exclusive in their love. This exclusion could even lead to a type of class hatred of the non-poor. Rightly understood, this preference for the poor cannot lead to such an exclusion; rather it should enhance the universal character of humanity, because it is the poor who are considered less human or less worthy of our concern.

Since the Second Vatican Council, there has been an increasing awareness that living out this gospel value must include changing the situations which create poverty and injustice.[7] Poverty today has, in fact, worsened and become more widespread in many parts of the world. The increased speed of social change has made the inequality between human beings even more appalling. Millions of human beings today live without hope because of their poverty. A fresh moral evaluation of the type of poverty that oppresses so many of our brothers and sisters is needed, and its implications for moral living assessed. There exists in the world a material indigence, or the lack of essential goods to such a degree that life is reduced to a subhuman level.

In addition, in recent thinking a new poverty has been noted which is caused by violent denial of the elementary rights of social, cultural, and religious freedom. This poverty can be extremely serious and can cause suffering of a new type. Therefore, the option for the poor is not limited to countries of the Third World, but all countries in which men and women are physically, culturally, and spiritually oppressed. This is valid even within the most wealthy countries.

A very realistic analysis of the present forms of economic underdevelopment recognizes that various types of poverty have their roots in political factors and, in the final analysis, in a moral ill brought about by sins of many people. Pope John Paul II speaks of "structures of sin."[8] This concept calls us to a deep collective conversion. Each person, but more importantly each social group, is called to a generous examination of his or her own moral behavior in the face of today's dramatic situation of mass poverty and underdevelopment.

The concept of structures is derived from the social sciences to describe human behaviors which become so fixed over time that they limit social choices to such a level that consideration of alternative behaviors seems unthinkable. The present Pope shows an awareness of this fact of human behavior and reminds us that these structures are of human creation and can be changed. One example of a social structure is the economic system of capitalism. For North Americans, capitalism has become "our way of life" and we are hard pressed even to imagine an alternative way of providing for economic well-being. It has been pointed out that even liturgy is influenced by our capitalist mentality.[9]

The challenge of the option for the poor is as a call to universal solidarity. This solidarity as a virtue, redefines the place of the poor in society. It makes true progress in establishing the basic right of the poor to human dignity. It enables us to reject economic objectives, such as the accumulation of material goods as our sole aim. Solidarity creates a type of happiness which is satisfied with enough goods to meet one's needs and to share our surplus with the poor.

The culture of consumerism, oppressive ideologies, and simple resignation in the face of the poverty of the masses must be transformed through a culture of solidarity with the poor. This culture is already a renewed source of hope to many people. This hope, rooted in the Gospel, is an essential condition for the liberation of the poor from every type of material, political, and spiritual oppression.

C. THE COMMON PURPOSE OF CREATION

Closely associated with the gospel value of the option for the poor is the purpose of all of creation. "God intended the earth and all it contains for the use of every human being and people,"[10] declared the Second Vatican Council. This value has shaped the Christian understanding of the nature of ownership, distribution, and economics throughout church history.[11] Even the value of private property has derived its role in Catholic thought within the context of the communal purpose of earthly goods. Without a notion of the social nature of creation, behaviors of greed and maldistribution can be justified. If through a narrow understanding of the nature of work we can make exclusive claims to our property, we have rejected this truth.

New knowledge concerning the ecological relationships to economic development and distribution has expanded this gospel value to a new consciousness of the ecology. The wastefulness and ruthless destruction of the ecosystems are deeply rooted in many values of western thought and behaviors. The ideology of constant growth and expansion has become a type of cultural doctrine which must be challenged.

Even social leaders seem at times prisoners of the mentality that "bigger is better." In spite of much good will, there is still an absence of alternative models to meet the material needs of humanity and respect the ecology. This absence is rooted in a lack of moral purpose to make the hard changes in our way of life so that the earth has a future. It is important to recall in the face of such a gigantic task that the present social system was a product of human will. Also the source of a new way of life will find its origin in the will of people to find another way to live in harmony with nature.[12]

An egotistic person cannot even be touched by the threat of the ecological catastrophe which the world already experiences. Cherishing the truth that the world has only been given to us by God for our use can be a great step in the reconciliation of humanity with the ecology. The question is no longer my survival but the survival of humanity. Our present notion of economic freedom must be modified by a true humanism.

Any proposals on how to resolve the distributive and ecological problems of the present age must be assessed in light of the truth that the world was given to everyone by God. We must renounce that "freedom" of competition and profiteering that threatens disaster for the earth. It should be clear to every believer that Christians cannot be "salt for the earth and light for the world" unless they know and make known to others by word and example what creative freedom is and what it means for human ecology. To conserve creation and share it is to acknowledge that it is a gift from God.

D. THE LOVE OF ENEMIES

A fourth social value found in the preaching of Jesus is love and respect for one's enemies. This teaching reflects a development in morality because Jesus even requires that we forgive injuries (Matt 5:43-44). Respect and love ought to be extended also to those who think and act differently than we do. In Catholic social thought, this ethic has been applied to interpersonal relations and relations between states. But both ethics are rooted in this radical teaching of Jesus that we must forgive. Because of this teaching, Christians have a moral obligation to work for world peace.[13]

Peace is not the mere absence of war; nor is it to be established by force. It is the result of observing God's moral order, which is an order of justice and love. Catholic social teachings recognize the right of nations to self-defense but often in the discussion of self-defense the primary value of peace is forgotten. War is a result of the failure of the People of God to live the value of peace.

Preaching peace can prove almost impossible during times of war, because it is often thought to be unpatriotic or political. Because of this reaction, it is imperative that peace preaching be an on-going experience within the community. During times when emotions are not strong, the community can integrate peace as a Christian virtue and understand the different aspects of Catholic peace teaching.

Preaching on the just war ethics which finds its origin in the writings of St. Augustine can enable us to understand that even the right to defense has limits and conditions. The central idea of this ethic is an argument for peace. In times of international crisis Christians should be able to make a moral decision about the morality of national policies by using this moral framework. The just war theory was developed in our tradition to enable nations to integrate the command to love one's enemies within the complex reality of international relations.

Since the use of nuclear weapons against Japan at the close of the Second World War, there has been a strong debate among moral theologians if just war ethics can be used. The criterion of proportionality seems almost impossible to apply to a nuclear, biological, or chemical war.[14] This aspect of the social gospel is undergoing development in light of the present reality of global nuclear warfare.

Pacifism as a legitimate moral option for Christians should be included with any preaching about war and peace. The fact that faith can lead a person even to suffer an injustice rather than resort to violence must be respected even in civil law.[15] To reject all use of force is an act of courage rooted in the gospel truth that we must love those who hate us. Pacifism has the value of making people think of alternatives about the use of violence in resolving conflicts.

Peace as a gospel value is possible. The recent great shift in relations between the superpowers can offer the world a new opportunity to reduce the need for war to resolve conflicts. The Roman Catholic Church has been a leader in exploring the need and function of some form of world authority to resolve conflicts but our preaching on peace should not limit itself to present and future political organization. The personal ethic of peace should also be explored within our interpersonal life.

Homilies on family harmony, interpersonal forgiveness, and respect for those who do not have our values are part of peace preaching. Hate is the same human experience between people as it is between nations. To link the two levels of peace can be a step toward the development of a greater spirituality of peace.

III. Social Readiness for Social Preaching

Not all people will welcome the social gospel as good news. In fact, some preachers fear this responsibility because it might arouse active and violent opposition. Anger, misunderstanding, and denunciation may sadden the preacher but they should never surprise him or her.[16] One good thing to recall at such moments is that the people must care about what is preached if they have such a reaction. They are listening! Yet, preaching social values need not always lead to such conflicts.[17]

Some of this opposition results from the fact that the preacher does not know the congregation's social situation. Just as Jesus adjusted his message to his audience, so must we. Jesus spoke to the poor in a tone and in words of compassion. His tone and words shifted to confrontation with the religious leadership of the Jewish community. Jesus knew his people, but do we?

There are levels of responsibility for society and people vary in their ability to respond to social issues because of their socio-economic position. Some groups are the actual victims of an injustice and will find courage in the preached word. Others can be the direct or indirect cause of social sin. Increasingly in the Church's ministry social analysis is a tool to understand people's social values in relationship to their social class.

This type of analysis enables the preacher to understand why people express hostility to the poor or certain racial groups. In working class parishes, the people often find themselves in competition for jobs with racial and ethnic minorities or fear that they will lose their investment in their home if their neighborhood becomes racially integrated. These situations do not justify their prejudice but social values must be preached with an awareness of the social pressures that the congregation has in daily life. It is a particular group of people that must learn how to live out the gospel's social values concretely.

If the preacher does not consider the social context of the congregation, a sense of alienation can develop. Feelings of rejection or lack of concern from the church can become real blocks in the conversion process. Also, this understanding helps the preacher select examples which are nearer to their experiences and make moral recommendations which are possible.

For example, when preaching on the need to share our goods with the poor, the preacher might recommend that the people try to live more simply so that there will be more goods to share. To recommend to working class people that they eat less steak and more meatballs will illustrate that the preacher has little understanding that most working class families today find it hard to afford meatballs, much less steak, while trying to educate children and provide for their own old age.

An awareness of the social situation of the congregation enables the preacher to express a sensitive concern for them and present them with challenges for growth which are possible. When the preacher recommends actions which do not respect the social context of the congregation there is a real danger that the social values of the gospel will be rejected. The key to success is to form a bond with the people by noting your understanding of their life struggle.

When preaching to congregations which do have influence on social policy, a firm effort must be made to confront those behaviors which are contrary to the gospel. Corporate executives, professionals, political leaders are all actors on the social stage of the nation and the world. Their policies regarding wages, hiring, production, etc., have direct relationship to the common good. The preacher must clarify in such congregations that they have a grave moral responsibility in their workplace. It is imperative that they understand morality to be a wider concern than sexuality and interpersonal relations.

Preaching among poor people should take on two dimensions. There should be a clear expression of the preacher's solidarity with them in their struggles and a challenge to live social morality within the context of their poverty. An overly romantic notion of the poor might cause us to forget that all people are called to live the ethics of the reign of God.

Respecting the social readiness of each congregation allows the preacher to adjust the homily to the people hearing the word. The preacher knows the story of their daily lives better and avoids simple stereotypes such as "our parish is middle class or poor." Values vary among groups and the challenge of the gospel will take shape within that context.[18]

A great amount of attention has been given to the development of liberation theology in Latin America. This theology finds some of its originality in the fact that it is being developed within the context of the poor.[19] At present, theological projects in North America are learning from this experience and are attempting similar projects within our context. The professional reading of the preacher should include socio-cultural analysis of North Americans.

Without a social awareness the word is preached in an ahistorical context. It will not find the right earth in which to be planted unless the preacher is willing to till the soil first through social analysis of the congregation.

IV. Models of Social Preaching

To give some direction for application for what has been said above, I would like to offer three models for preaching justice and peace. These models might help you determine when and how to preach social values.

The first model of social preaching I shall call informational. This type of homily might be preached on a national holiday or on the occasion of the publication of a social statement by church authority. A charitable appeal such as the Campaign for Human Development or the missions can also be an occasion to preach on social values. Lastly, an exposition of the gospel on an ordinary Sunday when the connection to concrete human needs is evident, such as the parable of the Good Samaritan, could be a time to preach an informational homily.

The behavioral goal of this type of homily is to inform the congregation of the wealth of social thinking and action which is part of the life of the Church. Examples of people past and present who are living these values can be illustrative. This homily is an opportunity to affirm social values and offer people a positive alternative to the many social sins of our time.

The second model for preaching social values is dialogical in nature. This type of preaching is occasioned by some public event which challenges social values. It might be the outbreak of war or some legal decision which violates human rights. This homily is suggested for those times when it is clear that some moral value is involved but the way to respond is not clear to the preacher. A call for community discussion on these social issues is made in order to discern some concrete way in which the community can respond to it.

The preacher describes the social issue which is the cause of the problem and articulates the values which are found in the scriptures and church teaching relating to this problem. Personally, I believe that it is good for the preacher to take a position on the issue but express an openness to hear other viewpoints. To admit that there could be other interpretations of the situation does not weaken the preacher's moral position.

This model respects the fact that the same faith can lead various Christians to different responses.[20] When a legitimate pluralism does exist this should be noted so that the people form their conscience accordingly. The underlying point that this issue is of common concern to all Christians will be enhanced. By way of suggestion, an informal meeting could be organized after such a homily to give people the opportunity to discuss the issues beyond their family and friends.

The last model that I would like to propose is the action homily. This preaching contains a clear call for a specific action in response to an injustice. Some events seem so contrary to the gospel imperatives of justice and peace that Christian involvement in specific action to bring about change is demanded. Emotions will always be running high around such issues; some people may resent any attempt by church people to assume moral leadership.

Some examples of this type of situation are euthanasia, violence against racial groups, making of laws which deny human rights, the use of military against non-combatants. Often the guilty use moral arguments to justify their actions. For example, the national policy of repression of Black people in South Africa is often justified from biblical texts but that does not make the policy moral. These occasions are the most demanding moments for social preaching.

In the development of the homily, I would suggest that a description of the issue be made which includes the clear gospel value which is involved. Explain calmly why and how this problem conflicts with the clearest interpretation of the gospel and church teachings. Finally, indicate to the people who are the responsible parties in the conflict, e.g. politicians, and sketch specific actions to take. The goal of this type of preaching is the acting on gospel values in an effective manner. When the issue is clear, and not to act would be a breach of our gospel commitment some action must be taken recognizing that "action on behalf of justice is a constitutive dimension of the preaching of the gospel."[21]

V. The Witness of the Church

The Church is a visible structure and is obliged by the teachings of its founder, Jesus Christ. We cannot find within the Christian experience a notion that there is one gospel for the world and another for its members. When preaching social values, we must be aware that the witness of the Church toward these values will be at issue. Part of preaching the social gospel is the conversion of the Church to its mission.

The bishops of the Second Vatican Council wrote that, "the Church, embracing sinners in her bosom, is at the same time holy and always in need of being purified, and incessantly pursues the path of penance and renewal."[22] When applying this to preaching, the preacher must acknowledge that the institutional Church too is in a struggle to be faithful to these values. The preacher is a person who is one with the people in their sin rather than someone set apart from them. The Church does not always offer the best example in regard to wages, the role of women, the freedom of expression of thought, its use of material goods, etc. The preacher might feel it would be better not to raise these issues because of possible divisions being created within the Church. My question is this: did the preacher create the division or did the preaching bring to awareness what was already there?

A false division between the clergy and the laity can be destructive in the Church's life. But it is a fact that some of us have a special role in making Church policy. The greater burden of witness does fall on the preacher and the church leadership. To make social gospel preaching effective there must be some acknowledgement of the need for institutional conversion on the part of the Church. Without this admission, social gospel preaching could become a source of alienation of the faithful from the Church. The preacher will share in the redemptive suffering of the Church in order to be more faithful through the preaching process.

VI. An Afterward

The death of Jesus was the clearest and most conspicuous case of prophetic suffering. His death has comforted and supported all who experience prophetic suffering by the consciousness that they are "bearing the marks of the Lord Jesus" and are carrying forward what he began in the proclaiming of the reign of God.

The cross and resurrection of Jesus contribute to strengthening the prophetic power of religion and the redemptive forces of the reign of God. This truth directly concerns social gospel preaching, because the social gospel is the voice of prophecy in the modern world.

Notes

1. The term "social gospel" is often applied to the nineteenth-century Protestant Social Movement but in this chapter it is used as the social mission of the church in general.
2. John Paul II, *Sollicitudo Rei Socialis*, December 30, 1987, no. 1.
3. Benedict T. Viviano, O.P., *The Kingdom of God in History* (Wilmington: Michael Glazier, 1988) 29.
4. Second Vatican Council, *The Church in the Modern World*, no. 32, as found in Joseph Gremillion, *The Gospel of Peace and Justice* (Maryknoll: Orbis Books, 1976) 268.
5. *The Church in the Modern World*, no. 29.
6. Letter to Digognetus, *Patres Apostolici*, ed., Funk, 1901, 336.
7. John Paul II, *On Social Concerns*, no. 36.
8. *On Social Concerns*, no. 37.
9. C.f. Empereur, James and Christopher Kiesling, *The Liturgy That Does Justice* (Collegeville: The Liturgical Press, 1990).
10. *The Church in the Modern World*, no. 69.
11. Paul VI, *The Progress of Peoples*, nos. 22–24.

12. C.f. Carol S. Robb and Carl J. Casebolt, eds., *Covenant for a New Creation: Ethics, Religion, and Public Policy* (Maryknoll: Orbis Books, 1990) and Donald Dorr, *The Social Justice Agenda: Justice, Ecology, Power and the Church* (Maryknoll: Orbis Books, 1990).

13. I would recommend *What Are They Saying About Peace and War?* by Thomas A. Shannon (New York: Paulist Press, 1983) as a good resource for preaching peace.

14. C.f. Angie O'Gorman, ed., *The Universe Bends Toward Justice: A Reader on Christian Nonviolence in the U.S.* (Philadelphia: New Society Publishers, 1990).

15. *The Church in the Modern World*, no. 79.

16. C.f. Alvin C. Porteous, *Preaching to Suburban Captives* (Valley Forge: Judson Press, 1979); Earl S. Johnson, Jr., "Preaching Peace in a Military Community," *The Christian Ministry* (July 83): 22–24; Elizabeth Schüssler Fiorenza, "The Silenced Majority Needs to Come to the Word," in Frank J. McNulty, ed., *Preaching Better* (New York: Paulist Press, 1985).

17. Kelly Miller Smith, *Social Crisis Preaching* (Georgia: Mercer University Press, 1984).

18. Kevin Phillips, *The Politics of Rich and Poor* (New York: Random House, 1990).

19. Robert McAfee Brown, *Unexpected News: Reading the Bible with Third World Eyes* (Philadelphia: The Westminster Press, 1984).

20. Paul VI *Octogesima Adveniens*, no. 50; and John Paul II, *Message for World Day of Peace*, 1991.

21. Rome Synod 1971, *Justice in the World*, no. 6.

22. Second Vatican Council, *On the Church*, no. 8.

Chapter 13

Authentic Preaching on Moral Issues

CHARLES E. BOUCHARD, O.P.

Introduction

Whenever I teach a class on "moral preaching" I always begin by asking students whether they have ever heard a homily preached on a moral issue (some have); I then ask them if they have ever heard a good homily preached on a moral issue (practically none have). Preachers generally avoid moral topics altogether, and when they do attempt to preach on them, they generally do it badly. There are a number of reasons for this.

First of all, preachers may not understand what "morality" means in the Roman Catholic tradition, nor what the rationale is behind certain Church teachings. Second, they may not understand what the purpose of morality is, or what kind of response authentic morality asks of believers. Third, preachers may not understand the relationship between scripture and moral norms which are derived from philosophy, or the relationship between faith and reason. And finally, preachers may not have a clear grasp of the preaching act itself. Depending on whether one sees preaching as exhortation, promulgation of law, or formation of moral character, moral preaching can assume very different shapes, each contributing to the dearth of moral preaching in the Church today. I would like to treat each of them in turn.

I. The Greatest Obstacle: Fear of Moralizing

When someone says, "Don't preach at me!" the tone is unmistakable. It conveys a hostile rejection of judgmentalism. The assumption is that the "preaching" is based on lack of knowledge, understanding, or sympathy, that the person being "preached at" is being judged unfairly or harshly, and that the person preaching is trying to impose his or her values on someone else without regard for that person's integrity or intelligence.

One of the greatest fears of preachers and congregations alike is *moralizing*. Although different people might disagree on just what this term means, nearly everyone would agree that it carries negative connotations. The great Protestant theologian Reinhold Niebuhr, in an article written over fifty years ago, says that moralizing is a failure of nerve characterized by

> holding up high ideals of brotherhood and love . . . on the supposition that nothing more than their continued reiteration will ultimately effect their realization. . . . Moralistic preaching, praising ideals, identifying ideals with Christ and Christ with ideals, comparing ideals favorably with the brutal realities of life and exhorting congregations to be true to the highest ideals—this is the thinnest kind of preaching. . . . What is missing in moralistic preaching is a proper sense of contrition, a realization of the fact of sin.[1]

Niebuhr identifies a common temptation for preachers—the temptation to stand aloof and fail to engage the world as it is. This is born of a fear that blending the world with grace will end up tainting or compromising God's word. Yet many theological traditions (including the Catholic one) insist that grace and nature are inherently compatible and that they need not be kept at arms' length. The preacher must constantly try to draw grace and nature together; idealizing which separates the two of them is inherently fallacious, and leads people to anxiety and despair.

We also find moralistic preaching wherever we find a preacher who stands above his or her congregation and scolds them for disobedience, selfishness, narrowness, bigotry, or a host of other sins:

> Moralizing is inimical to the gospel and debilitating to both the pastor's relationship with the people and the goal of Christian preaching. Whether the behavior being urged upon people is the avoidance of the old individualistic smoking-drinking-cursing sins or the new racism-sexism-nationalism sins makes no difference. It's all the same: the preacher is attempting to scold and berate the congregation by drawing some simple moral inference from the biblical text.[2]

The problem here is that the preacher presumes these sins on the part of the congregation and fails to take account of one's own sinfulness. The preacher's words are rejected because they are seen as *only* the preacher's words, because they are seen as words not born of a real knowledge of the congregation, or because they are not full of the spirit of compassion and healing which must always characterize preaching.

For Catholics, moralistic preaching often takes the form of exhortation to obedience (to the pope or to church teachings). But if the hearers do not have a corresponding awareness of the reason or values behind these teachings, they become frustrated and distant from the preacher who appears to be speaking an arcane and arbitrary language.

The first thing the preacher must remember is that preaching is not simply a delivery of what is "out there." If the preacher tries to present preaching on moral issues to the congregation as a packaged set of rules, instructions, or prohibitions, a conscientious hearer will certainly reject them. Although preaching is often understood as "bringing down" the good news, it is really "naming grace"[3] as it already exists in the world. This is not to deny the reality of sin, but to place it in the perspective of a promise of redemption for which we have already received a down payment. Grace in this case is not an ethereal, heavenly reality, but a profound inclination to moral good and to human fulfillment.

II. What is Morality?

There are a number of different ethical "systems," or paradigms for understanding morality. Each of them has implications for moral preaching.

MORALITY AS OBEDIENCE TO THE LAW

There are different ways of understanding the term "morality." For many people, it is a legalistic matter. Being moral means obeying the law or doing what the lawmaker or authority says. This kind of approach is apparent in those who give ultimate authority to the Word of God and take it as a literal guide for moral behavior. In this view, it is wrong even to question God's commandments; they are received complete and demand absolute obedience. This presupposes an unmediated view of revelation which is inconsistent with Catholic tradition. Charles Curran sees *mediation* as one of the most characteristic features of Catholicism. Whereas other Christian traditions view God's action and grace as relatively immediate, that is, not effected through the agency of someone or something, Catholicism tends to mediate grace through human actions and words in the sacraments, and God's authority through sociological and ecclesiological structures.[4]

MORALITY AS FEELING OR INTUITION

Others equate moral judgments with what they feel. In this view, a moral statement is nothing more than an expression of pleasure or repugnance. One might say, for example "Stealing is wrong," but that statement is really like saying, "I do not like stealing," or "stealing is ugly."

It has no rational foundation and cannot be explained or justified any further. Similarly, some moral judgments are mostly intuitions, that is, based on knowledge which may be true and correct, but inexplicable and unable to be conveyed to anyone else. "I just *know* that course of action is wrong, but I don't know why." Social taboos are often based on this kind of moral knowledge. Although pure intuitionists or emotivists are rare, elements of intuitionism or emotivism are common, especially in the young and morally immature.

MORALITY AS FULFILLMENT

These views of moral decision making are partial and inadequate because they are rooted in parts or "faculties" of persons rather than in the entire person. In the case of the legalist, morality is purely a matter of the will. One is either moral (obedient) or immoral (disobedient). Emotivists and intuitionists only use part of their personal potential—the feelings or the intuition—to make moral decisions. Adequate morality relates to the whole person, and must thus draw on as many parts of human potential as possible.

Although it comes as a surprise to many, Catholic morality is based on happiness. This means that rather than saying that morality is doing what an authority tells us, or following an arbitrary law, or simply identifying a feeling or emotional preference, morality must flow out of a search for long-term happiness and fulfillment. This fulfillment is found through the use of common sense (reason), emotions, intuition, memory, community (consultation with others), and consideration of consequences of proposed courses of action. Catholic morality, through the work of Thomas Aquinas, appropriated an Aristotelian approach to ethics. This approach is based on seeking long-term happiness or fulfillment rather than obedience to the law.

This kind of morality aims at the development of persons rather than just acts. Don Saliers points this out when he speaks of the reciprocal relationship between liturgy and ethics:

> Human persons are formed in myriad ways. But in the Christian life, the mystery of redemption in the death and resurrection of Christ is the basis and source of the formation of the person. The orientation and process of maturation is therefore never a matter of adopting right behavior or conforming to *a priori* systems of ruled actions. The qualities of formed character and the exercise of the virtues require the on-going deliberate rehearsal of the identifying stories and actions of God.[5]

While it might be possible to ask, "Is this act right or wrong?" an authentic Christian morality also asks, "What effect will this act have on me?" Christian morality aims at the formation of virtues—qualities of persons that become second nature—rather than just conforming acts to a rule. And eventually one's moral character begins to shape one's acts. Morality is no longer imposed from without by the will of a lawmaker, but has become a durable personal quality. This is why we are able to say of someone we know well, "She would never steal" or "I *know* she would always tell the truth." Moral character, or virtue, establishes a pattern of behavior which is consistent but flexible enough to be able to respond to unusual or ethically demanding moral situations. It arises from repeated virtuous acts and then begins to shape actions.[6]

If one operates out of a legalistic understanding of morality, obedience to the law becomes the purpose or end of morality. In a character model, however, law is not the end of morality but an important tool or guide. It helps us identify human values and goods much like a roadmap helps us discover the way to a destination.

III. The Use of Scripture in Moral Preaching

Another crucial area is the question of how scripture relates to morality, or how morality "uses" scripture. This is particularly important in the Roman Catholic moral tradition, in which moral norms tend to be philosophically rather than scripturally based.

The Second Vatican Council encouraged moral theologians to make fuller use of scripture so that morality might be more fully nourished by the word. As we have already hinted above, there are a number of ways in which scripture might be used as a foundation for morality.[7] We might summarize these by saying that there are four levels at which scripture is useful to us in morality:

A. The level of *rules and specific decisions*. At this level, we would seek guidance for specific questions or decisions, such as "is it moral to build nuclear bombs, seek a divorce, or take interest on a loan?" While scripture does address some of these specific questions, it is silent on many others. In addition, some of the answers it gives are historically conditioned and may not be readily applicable to our cultural or economic situation.

B. The level of *norms*. This level is slightly more general than the preceding level. Here, scripture is seen as a source for "guidelines" or general norms such as "respect life." Obviously scripture yields many norms of this type.

C. The level of *values, goals, and ideals.* More general still, scripture is seen as providing purposes or directions for human actions rather than rules or guidelines.

D. The level of *stance and attitudes.* While the previous three levels try to derive guidelines for actions, this fourth level aims at the formation of the *person.* It asks "What kind of person should I be?" and looks to scripture for the answer. It is at this level that scripture is most useful as a source for moral guidance, since the Gospel is clearly oriented to the conversion of persons—not apart from a change in their actions and choices, but more than that. Jesus repeatedly makes it clear that he has come to save people, to make them new, to convert them. He is not interested only in changing actions, goals, norms, or rules.

In his most helpful article, "Parable and Narrative in Christian Ethics," William Spohn outlines the importance of narrative to Christian theology today and describes how biblical narratives "guide moral reflection and action more directly." He notes how biblical events and narratives can serve as "lenses" for interpreting some current experiences, and how they can "inform and inspire dispositions or virtues." He says that the common denominator for these and other uses of narrative and symbol in moral reflection is *analogy*, since "in moral discernment we do not treat the story or images as raw material from which a general principle can be extracted and then can be held in reserve until the appropriate cases reappear, ready for the principle's application."[8] This approach represents an authentic understanding of the place and purpose of scripture in moral preaching: it shapes character more than specific actions, and it is most useful if used analogically, in concert with moral norms derived from other sources.

TEXT OR TOPIC?

Given the centrality of scripture, one of the obstacles to preaching on moral issues is the dilemma of whether to begin with the text, and let that determine the message, or to allow the congregation's initial need to be addressed by the text. Gerard Sloyan asked recently whether church teaching is neglected when the lectionary is preached.[9] He is skeptical about the possibility of using the pulpit to teach, noting that the homily should be geared primarily to "worship and praise which is also thanksgiving and petition, like the total liturgical act."[10] This should lead the preacher to be skeptical of shaping homilies according to topics, rather than according to the word. The fullness of the three-year cycle of readings should provide ample opportunity to treat many moral dilemmas: "One need not be too inventive to see a real relation, not a forced one, between what is written on the sacred page and a factory closing, a brutal murder in the parish, a tense educational situation in the school district. The preacher who consistently thinks biblically will have no problem in making the relation."[11]

Every scriptural passage, because it is the word of God, has within it the potential to illumine any topic. I have experimented with classes, giving them different topics, but the same set of readings. I was amazed by the diversity of excellent homilies on topics as disparate as abortion, nuclear arms, the economy, racism, and personal sinfulness that emerged from a single set of readings, without violating the integrity of the text.

Gerard Sloyan thinks it unlikely that over the course of a number of years the occasion to preach on any important moral topic will be lacking:

> The preacher who genuinely fears, after having preached the three-year cycle four or five times, that certain doctrinal or ethical developments of the centuries are getting short shrift—from him, that is—should sit down and carefully plot a correction of the omissions over the next few months. This cannot be done, of course without serious study of the upcoming text. None should be forced into a disquisition it is totally unrelated to. People are not stupid. They may not be able to articulate the principles of a liturgical homily, but they certainly know which preachers cavalierly set aside God's word just proclaimed to interrupt the flow of the worship service with a word of their own.[12]

While there will be special occasions (e.g., a highly publicized execution, an abortion protest, an arms summit, or the beginning of a penitential season like Lent) which will provide the context for the preacher to introduce a particular moral issue, others will have to be planned. The preacher can do this by making a list of topics that he or she feels should be related to the scripture over a two or three year period. Texts which treat of life, freedom, sin, justice, marriage, or sexuality will each, in turn, provide the preacher with an opportunity to preach the scripture's moral message on issues of import.

For Catholics, church teachings on morality play an especially important part in moral decision making. Encyclicals, catechisms, and pastoral letters are all important ways in which our moral wisdom and tradition are conveyed, and they must have some role in shaping the preached word.

This can be a difficulty, since preachers want to remain faithful to the word and should avoid "preaching" on church documents or making the Sunday pulpit a place for catechesis. In addition, many Catholics see church teaching on moral matters as intrusive and even irrelevant to their lives, and do not welcome its introduction into the Sunday homily.

It is important for the homilist to see church teachings on morality as an important resource for preaching, because these teachings try to articulate in a rational way the same values which the biblical word presents to us. The homilist must "look behind" the teaching to the human and gospel values which the teachings articulate, and see them as aids to preaching.

The preacher should also remember that there are various levels of church teaching which require different kinds of assent. Teachings which are infallibly proclaimed (such as the christological doctrines found in the Nicene Creed) obviously relate to the core of Christian faith and could only be rejected with great risk. Most others, however (including all moral teachings) are what are called "non-infallible but authentic." This means that they are important Christian truths, but that they are more tentative or incomplete—either because of lack of empirical data (as is the case in teachings on the personhood of the early embryo) or because they touch on practical matters of human behavior which are always affected by circumstances and situations. In these latter cases, teachings must necessarily remain somewhat general because they cannot reach to every case.[13]

When Christians "assent" to teachings on matters of faith such as Christ's divinity or the resurrection of the dead, they assent to speculative truths which have been revealed to us, and which we struggle to articulate in theological language. The assent we give is first to particular theological formulation and then to the full truth behind it, even though that full truth (of the mystery of Christ's combined humanity and divinity, for example) is not fully within our grasp. In moral matters, we are not assenting to a merely speculative truth, but to a truth about human behavior which moral norms try to protect. Thus, for instance, the church's teachings on the conditions for a just war do not exist only for their own sake, but for the values of human society, justice, national sovereignty, and the dignity of human life which they seek to reconcile and protect.

We might conclude by saying that the preacher's job in preaching on moral issues is five-fold:

1) to illuminate and explain the scriptural text and the values it presents;
2) to relate the text to some human ethical dilemma or concern;

3) to help the text to illuminate the values or goods to be sought;
4) to bring the congregation to the act of appropriating these real human goods in their own lives;
5) finally, to bring the congregation to thankful praise for these goods and for their call to realize them.

Preaching has been described as "naming grace";[14] preaching on moral issues is no less since it names and illuminates the most integrated, fulfilled, and happy kind of Christian life and calls us to help create it. It begins with the existing goods of human life and bathes them in the light of the Gospel, making them all the more appealing and desirable. This, in essence, is what the old Thomistic axiom "gratia supponit naturam" really means: grace does not supplant or destroy or distort human nature, but perfects and completes it. The preacher helps believers discover that, by helping them to savour human moral goodness and develop a deeper taste for it.

IV. Liturgy and Morality

Since for Catholics most preaching takes place in a liturgical context, it is important to ask how liturgy relates to morality and vice versa.

Liturgy and morality are often seen as discrete activities having little to do with one another. However, if we see morality as a process of shaping Christian personality and moral character, it is clear that liturgy and morality are two sides of the same coin. As moral theologian Enda McDonough notes:

> The liturgical link between celebration, remembering, identity and mystical experience has profound significance for Christian understanding of morality. These four elements themselves occur in varying forms and degrees in the responsible and responsive life called moral. Celebration of people, of human events and achievements, forms an important part of human living, whose moral significance has been much neglected. In such celebration we honor, render our due, give thanks and express our love for people. In that realization of moral value and virtue we are ourselves enriched and extended. We achieve a fuller self-understanding, self-appropriation, and self identification. In both celebration-liturgy and celebration-morality, remembering, sharing, identifying and responding may be characterized by an awareness of experience of mystery and presence which evokes awe, self-transcendence and ecstasy.[15]

This underscores the interrelatedness of liturgy and the moral life, a fact which is particularly important given the usual liturgical context of preaching for Roman Catholics.[16] It also reminds us of the non-rational dimension of ethics. While it is true to say that for Catholics moral theology is rational and not primarily intuitionistic, there is clearly a non-rational dimension to moral knowing. Even though they must be scrutinized reasonably, moral intuitions are a starting point for our moral deliberations (e.g., I "feel" repulsed by a proposed course of action, but I must "think it through" to see if my feelings are on target). Further, the best moral decisions are those that are felt as well as reasoned. We often dismiss emotions as "irrational," but in fact they can enhance the quality of a moral act.[17] Similarly, while our moral life cannot be based solely on moral intuition, some kinds of non-rational knowledge do play a part in how we "know" moral truth. Don Saliers alludes to this when he points out that the relationship between liturgy and ethics is based on the fact that both shape the affections:

> the relations between liturgy and ethics are most adequately formulated by specifying how certain affections and virtues are formed and expressed in the modalities of communal prayer and ritual action. These modalities of prayer enter into the formation of the self in community.[18]

Like any other preaching, preaching on moral issues aims at "naming grace," at discovering the hand of God in human life and activity. Preaching on moral issues, however, has an added dimension because it aims at revealing graced personhood and a graced lifestyle. For this reason, moral preaching is really more akin to "spirituality" than to what most people understand as moral theology. In fact, many writers today maintain that spirituality and moral theology are really a single discipline and should never have been separated.[19] Even though moral theology (in the Catholic tradition) is based heavily upon natural law (which may be defined as "moral knowledge derived solely from the use of reason"—as distinguished from revelation), this "natural" knowledge is enhanced and illuminated by revelation so that the preacher may be confident that there will be no contradiction between what scripture says and what seems "reasonable." This makes it possible for morality to be at once based on *imitatio Christi* and on the natural law.[20]

The preacher must also remember that it is not merely moral norms that he or she preaches, but the real, concrete values behind the norms. Moral norms are essential as guides and waymarks, but they are not the same as morality. So the preacher must always ask, "What human goods are at stake here? What values or avenues of human fulfillment is this norm trying to protect?" Just as we aim at the ultimate truths *behind* doctrinal formulations about the divinity of Christ when we preach, so when we preach on a moral issue, we aim at the moral value *behind* the formulation. In a sense, it is the preacher's job to lead people through norms and formulations and to bring them as close as possible to the goods and values themselves. The preacher can never stop at merely pointing to a value by saying "Do this." He or she must draw these values out of human existence and display them, make them attractive and desirable, and illuminate them with the scriptural word.

V. Moral Preaching: A Method

The questions above, while preliminary, are vitally important to good preaching on moral issues. Having seriously considered them, the preacher may move on to ask, "How does one preach on moral issues?"

In one sense it is false to dichotomize "personal" and "social morality," since they are of a piece. But for the sake of discussion we can isolate a number of issues which bear directly on our life together in community and only indirectly on our personal lives; we shall call these "social morality." There are others which are identified primarily with our personal moral lives, but which have important, if indirect, bearing on our public and social lives.[21] Let us begin by discussing the social questions.

PREACHING ON SOCIAL ISSUES

In one of the very few articles which deal with preaching on social morality, Bryan Hehir tries to relate parish preaching to the public ministry of the Church. He notes first of all the distinction between the Church's call to sanctify its members through preaching and the Church's public role vis-a-vis the rest of the world. The Church must enter this public arena "not because it has specifically political gifts, but because decisions taken in the political, economic, social and legal sectors of society have direct bearing on the dignity of the human person. There is therefore no division between a deeply personalist conception of the church's ministry and its public engagement on secular questions." The parish, he says, is the place where "a link is to be forged between the national posture of the church and the personal faith of the community."[22]

Because preaching ministers to personal faith, it must seek the conversion of Christians, as we have described above. But in its public dimension, preaching must somehow

> draw the community of the church and the wider civil community into a dialogue about the moral content of public policy. In a time when the moral content of issues is the link between religion and public politics, the church most effectively exercises its public ministry to *creating space* in the public argument for explicit moral analysis. (Italics my own).[23]

The preacher must always be conscious of this two-fold purpose of preaching. Preaching aims at the perfection and happiness of Christian believers and endeavors to draw them more fully into the saving power of Christ. But because these believers are part of a larger society which is also concerned about a certain kind of perfection and happiness—the kind which is built upon honesty, integrity, justice, and personal dignity—there is an overlap of values, and preaching should try to "create space" in the congregation for consideration of how these basic human values can be sought by believers and non-believers alike. This does not mean that the preacher would "water down" preaching to accommodate even those who do not believe the Gospel; it means that Gospel values are human values as well, and that the Church cannot achieve them nor even make room for them in a pluralistic society without the cooperation of many others.

Abortion is often considered to be a question of personal morality, yet I would like to place it in the social category. In preaching about abortion, the preacher knows that the sacredness of human life and the primacy of conscience are both biblical values. Yet as the political struggles in our country show, they are values which simply cannot be achieved or protected without at least the non-interference of those who do not share our beliefs. And usually, at the level of such basic moral goods, they can only be achieved with the active cooperation of many different kinds of people in a diverse society, each of which understands the goodness of, say, a position which asserts that human life is a fundamental value which must be protected by the society if we are to live in peace. It is not always clear how much correspondence there is between morality (which aims at personal perfection) and public policy (which has a more modest goal and aims at social order);[24] but the preacher must always address these social issues with one eye on the congregation before him, and the other on the wider society outside of the church doors.

In preaching on social issues such as nuclear arms and deterrence, gun control, abortion, access to basic human goods such as health care, housing, and education, capital punishment, taxes and economic and fiscal policy, busing, or discrimination, the preacher must ask two questions: 1) What does scripture have to say about these issues to these believers?

and 2) Where does this message intersect with the broader interests of society? In this way, preaching does not wither away during the communion meditation, but is carried out the doors and into the world by those who have heard it. Preaching must aim first a personal conversion, but must always have some relevance to the world without.[25]

PREACHING ON PERSONAL MORALITY

The fear of moralizing is especially prominent with regard to personal moral issues, precisely because they are more personal than social issues and people often resent others "judging" moral choices which have to do with sexual morality, health care decisions, or marriage or family. Yet since such decisions are so crucial and often fall so close to the core of what it means to be human, they "shape persons" in a way that many broader, societal decisions do not. And since preaching and scripture are primarily concerned with shaping persons in the image of Christ, it seems entirely appropriate that scripture should address these questions of personal morality as well as those in social morality.

It is true that preaching must always be kerygmatic and soteriological, i.e., derived from the basic, saving message of the Gospel. Sometimes, however, we see this message in a dualistic way that makes it seem as though salvation is purely eschatological and other-worldly. For this reason, preachers sometimes fear preaching morality and prefer to focus on "heaven." Yet all Christians, and especially Catholics, believe that we preach not only the *promise* of salvation, but its partial realization here and now. This means that when we preach on moral issues we are not only preaching a "reward for good behavior" which will be collected in the heavenly kingdom, but the fact that virtue is its own reward, as well. The kerygmatic message of the Gospel, when applied to personal morality, must reveal what a graced, gospel life "feels like" here and now. This experience is not extraneous to the word of the Gospel, but is its affective, psychological, and even physical manifestation.

VI. Specific Textual Cues

To this point, we have spoken about how one might "use" scripture to address moral issues. I would now like to go further and to offer some more specific suggestions for how the preacher might draw a moral message from scripture. In each of a number of areas, I will discuss "cues" which emerge from scripture passages found in the three-year Sunday cycle.

I will then try to suggest how they intersect with Catholic moral teaching and the values that teaching upholds.

SEXUAL MORALITY

The most fundamental texts to deal with sexual morality are the creation accounts (Genesis 1 and 2). The fundamental message these narratives present is that God created sexually differentiated beings as part of the plan of creation, and that through this gift of sex, humans are able to share in God's creative power.

God's covenants with Noah (Gen 9), Abram (Gen 15), and Moses (Exod 20) affirm this message by making procreation and sexual responsibility part of God's great covenant with us.

The Pauline injunctions bearing on sexual morality (e.g., 1 Cor 6:15-19; ch. 7) make it clear that sex should not be excluded from our spiritual lives, but should be an intrinsic part of them. They also make it clear that sexual conduct is not a personal matter, but has social and ecclesial ramifications. Paul knows that sexual immorality has destructive social consequences and warns the Corinthians to be on guard. When Paul reminds his listeners not to "live in sexual excess and lust," (Rom 13:13) he is emphasizing that the flesh points to the spirit, and that our yearnings must lead beyond physical gratification. Similarly, in referring to the instrumentality of our bodies (1 Cor 6), he stresses the sacramental nature of sexuality. Far from being evil, it is a great power which actually communicates God's spirit to us.

Luke's account of the Annunciation (Luke 1) once again shows how God uses our reproductive capability to further God's own plan. When Mary conceives, she is aware that God has used this human capability to save us—so that sexuality is in some way salvific. Not a means of selfish gratification, sexuality and childbearing become ecclesial realities which mediate God's grace and mercy.

Finally, in the gospel episode of the woman caught in adultery (John 8:1-11), or the prodigal son (Luke 15:11-31), the gospel writers tell us that although sexual sins are a perennial part of life, they are not necessarily worse than other sins, and they can be powerful occasions of grace and regeneration.

LIFE/DEATH/MEDICAL ETHICS

Although the Deuteronomic writer exhorts us to "choose life," modern medical advances have often made that a difficult and complicated process.

Healing is often connected to extended suffering, pain, and expense, and there is considerable controversy about just which procedures actually "heal" and which merely prolong physical life. Simply choosing life becomes a complicated and refined process requiring great prudence and discernment.

Yet despite the complexity of medical technology, most bioethical questions can be seen as aspects of the following six basic questions:

a) What is "ordinary," or morally obligatory treatment?
b) How much suffering is a Christian obliged to accept?
c) When does life begin?
d) When does death occur, and our duty to preserve life end?
e) How can medical care, as one of humankind's fundamental goods, be justly allocated?
f) Who makes these choices?

The preacher will find it easier to address medical ethics if he or she bears these six areas in mind and relates them to key scriptural passages.

One of the most important texts here is the passion narrative (John 18-19; Matt 27-28) and related Christological texts (e.g., Phil 2:6-11) which describe the salvific nature of Christ's suffering. Christ's suffering and death, real though they were, bore great fruit for the rest of us. Because in baptism our sufferings are "bound up with those of Christ," they are not completely futile and not necessarily to be avoided at all costs. This does not mean that Christians should be masochists, but that they can see some unavoidable suffering as a valid part of human experience and as a way of entering into Christ's death, as Christians must.

These texts lead us to question choices for euthanasia which might be the "easy way out," and instead to see suffering as a mysterious and paradoxical way of illuminating God's love and the deeper values of human life.

When Paul tells us to "give God glory in our bodies," or says that he would "rather be away from the body and with the Lord" (2 Cor 5:1), he says that our physical lives are not ends in themselves, but means to glorify God. This is pertinent to disputes today about the possibility of withdrawing life-sustaining treatment like artificial hydration and nutrition. Were physical life the end and purpose of creation, withdrawing such treatment would never be permissible. But since we were created "to know, love and serve God, and to be with him forever in heaven," (as the Baltimore Catechism so clearly taught us!) when physical life permanently loses its ability to mediate our relationship with God, Christians can look beyond that human life to the purpose of life itself, viz., union with God.

Abortion is related to these medical questions. It is particularly difficult because it touches on a number of areas outlined above (the beginning of life, who decides, what is equitable distribution of health care), and because there is fundamental disagreement in society about the status of the embryo. Because of this, there is basic conflict about what kind of moral act abortion is: is it murder or something else? The matter is further complicated because it is intertwined with questions of subjective culpability as well as with vexing social problems like racism, poverty, and the relationship of morality to civil law. Despite the complexity of the question, there are still some important texts which will be fruitful for the preacher. Paul's instruction about widows and orphans (Jas 1:27, 1 Tim 5:3-16), as well as Jesus' own concern for the poor and marginalized, (Matt 5:3, Luke 6:20, 14:15) will provide a basis for the preacher to address the Christian's obligation both to the embryo (which, even if it is not fully a person, is certainly the "least" of the human community), as well as to the mother, who is often isolated by poverty or fear.

Other texts which bear on the centrality of the community of believers (Acts 3–4) will remind us that such crucial moral choices must always be made in the context of a community rather than under the illusion that we act as isolated and totally individualistic moral agents. This emphasizes the social dimension of abortion and enhances the congregation's awareness of its responsibility to provide for pregnant women as well as for their children.

THE ECONOMY

The life of the earliest Christian communities (Acts 3–4) highlights the communal nature of our life together and suggests the mutual responsibility that members of the Christian community have for one another. While it would be naive to extrapolate from these descriptions to contemporary economies which are global, pluralistic, and market-driven, it would be fruitful for the preacher to explore what implications this kind of mutual responsibility has for twentieth-century Christians. At the very least, these accounts draw Christians to accountability for the needs of all members of society and for just distribution of society's goods, even if they do not specify exactly what economic mechanism might accomplish this best. At the same time, Jesus' words about taxes due to Caesar acknowledge the important role of civil government even when it is distinct from the community of faith.

The parables of the rich young man (Mark 10:17ff) and the unjust steward (Luke 18:8ff) remind us that our buying, selling, and possessing must have an eschatological dimension. This means that ownership and possession of goods, while not evil, must always be transparent and penultimate. They cannot be ends in themselves, and must somehow contribute to our final goal and purpose as Christians.

WAR AND PEACE

Although the scriptures in some places suggest pacifism as the only acceptable stance for Christians (Matt 5:38-42), tradition has modified this radical position in favor of one which recognizes the good of civil authority and the need to protect it, even by violent means. It sets up secular government as a necessary structure which provides order and the possibility of human community (cf. Paul in Thessalonians to civil leaders), but also urges circumspection and care in exercising that kind of authority. War, unfortunately, will occur ("nation will rise against nation"), but Christians see it as a last resort and let their hearts be formed by Christ's promise of peace. ("My peace I leave you. . . .")

The scriptures will not normally provide answers to specific political or strategic questions; these must be left to the prudence of governments and policymakers. However, by its emphasis on universal salvation and God's promise of peace, scripture does restrain myopic nationalism and tries to put interests of individual nations in the context of broader, international goals.

Conclusion

In this chapter I have tried first to suggest why we hear so little good preaching on moral issues. I hope I have also described why such preaching is vitally important. I then outlined a number of preliminary questions which must be answered before one can undertake moral preaching in the Catholic tradition, viz., the nature of morality itself, the use of scripture, the relationship of morality to liturgy, and the fact that we live in and must cooperate with a world which is not always receptive to the Gospel message.

Finally, I have suggested the outline of a method which uses lectionary texts, properly studied, as "cues" for preaching on moral issues. The passages I have cited are by no means exhaustive, but they do suggest a way in which biblical texts can shed light on important moral questions. As in all preaching, it is the preacher's job to imaginatively explore ways in which both text and topic can be blended into a homily suited to the needs and context of a particular congregation. Nor should these textual cues be understood as an invitation to proof-texting, since the scriptural texts must always be the basis and the ultimate inspiration for preaching. The preacher must be careful to begin and end with the word of scripture, but to allow it to work with other sources (such as philosophically derived norms taught by the Church), and to function primarily at the level of character building and growth in virtue.

In this way, the preacher allows the word, "rich as it is," to unfold and penetrate our lives and even to touch the sometime cynical world in which we live.

Notes

1. Reinhold Niebuhr, "Moralistic Preaching," *The Christian Century* (July 15, 1936): 985–87.
2. William Willimon, *Integrative Preaching: The Pulpit at the Center* (Nashville: Abingdon Press, 1981) 76–79.
3. M. C. Hilkert, "Naming Grace: A Theology of Proclamation," *Worship* 60 (1986): 434–49, at 441: "Perhaps we can take a clue from contemporary Christology and try to understand the mystery of the word 'from below' rather than 'from above.' Rather than beginning with the power of God's word as something totally other and beyond our experience, why not begin with the revelation of God which is to be discovered in the midst of—in the depths of—what is human? Can we reflect on the mystery of preaching as the naming of grace in human experience?"
4. See Curran, "Moral Theology in the United States," in *Toward an American Catholic Moral Theology* (Notre Dame, 1987): 21–51, at 34: "Catholic ethics appeals not immediately to the will or word of God, but rather to the human that mediates the divine will and word."
5. Don E. Saliers, "Liturgy and Ethics: Some New Beginnings," *Journal of Religious Ethics* (1979): 173–189, at 187.
6. Craig Dykstra, in *Vision and Character* (New York: Paulist Press, 1981), argues against "decisionalism" which neglects the formative nature of morality.
7. William Spohn, *What Are They Saying About Scripture and Ethics* (New York: Paulist, 1984), provides an excellent overview of various models for using scripture in morality.
8. *Theological Studies*, 51 (1990): 100–114, at 111.
9. Gerard S. Sloyan, "Is Church Teaching Neglected When the Lectionary is Preached?" *Worship* 61 (1987): 126–141.
10. Ibid. 131.
11. Ibid. 138.
12. Ibid. 139.
13. Aristotle makes a fundamental distinction between "speculative" truth (which deals with science and mathematics so that two plus two is always four to anyone who understands the terms) and "practical" truth, which deals with behavior. See Aristotle, *Ethics*,

1103b26–1104a11, "In a practical science, so much depends on particular circumstances that only general rules can be given." *The Ethics of Aristotle: The Nichomachean Ethics*, trans. J. A. K. Thompson (New York: Penguin Books, 1982) 93–94.

14. See note no. 3, above.

15. Enda McDonough, *The Making of Disciples* (Wilmington: Michael Glazier, 1982) 40.

16. See Frank Quinn's chapter on the liturgical context of preaching in this volume.

17. See St. Thomas on how the emotions can make a bad act worse or a good act better, *Summa Theologica* 1-2, q. 24, a. 3.

18. "Liturgy and Ethics," 175.

19. John Mahoney, S.J., in his book *The Making of Moral Theology* (Oxford: Clarendon Press, 1987), describes the preoccupation with sin, the concentration on the individual, and the obsession with the law which characterized moral theology since the advent of auricular confession. See Chapter 1, "The Influence of Auricular Confession." For another example of a similar approach, see Servais Pinckaers, O.P., *Les sources de la morale chretienne*, (Editions Universitaires, Fribourg, 1985), especially chapter X, "La theologie morale au declin du Moyen Age: la revolution nominaliste."

20. See Benedict M. Ashley, "Scriptural Grounds for Concrete Moral Norms," *The Thomist* 52 (January 1988): 1–22.

21. This distinction is based upon Jacques Maritain, who notes in his *Man and the State* (Chicago: University of Chicago Press, 1951): "For human life has two ultimate ends, the one subordinate to the other. An ultimate end in a given order, which is the terrestrial common good, or the *bonum vitae civilis*; and an absolute ultimate end, which is the transcendent eternal common good. An individual ethics takes into account the subordinate ultimate end, but directly aims at the absolute ultimate one. Whereas political ethics takes into account the absolute ultimate end, but its direct aim is the subordinate ultimate end. . . ." (62).

22. Bryan Hehir, "Preaching and Public Policy: The Parish and the Pastorals," *Church* 4 (Fall 1985): 3–7. See also, David Hollenbach, "Preaching and Politics: Consistency and Compromise," *Church* (Summer 1987): 11–15; and John Keating, "Parishioners and Politics: The Christian Citizen," *Church* (Fall 1992): 8–12.

23. Hehir, 6.

24. See John Courtney Murray, *We Hold These Truths: Catholic Reflections on the American Proposition* (New York: Sheed and Ward, 1968) 286; and Charles Curran, "The Difference Between Personal Morality and Public Policy," in *Toward an American Catholic Moral Theology* (Notre Dame: 1987) 194–201, on the distinction between morality and public policy.

25. Hehir, p. 7, offers four suggestions for joining public ministry and preaching ministry: a) follow the democratic model of the pastorals, to "draw the congregation into a process of reflection and decision making." b) balance the sociopolitical with the personal-sacramental conception of discipleship; c) open options for people: help people know what steps they can take; d) offer other forums, since the time in the pulpit is too limited.

Chapter 14

The Primordial Word: Preaching, Poetry, and Pastoral Presence

LOUIS T. BRUSATTI, C.M.

Introduction

> The words of the poet are like gates, good and strong, clear and sure. But they are gates into infinity, gates into the incomprehensible. They call upon that which has no name. They stretch out towards what cannot be grasped. They are acts of faith in the spirit and in eternity; acts of hope for a fulfillment which they can never give themselves; acts of love for unknown goods. . . . The poet is driven forward by the transcendence of the spirit (Rahner, 316).

The Word of God is interpreted by life and proclaimed with faith. The preacher stands ready to break open its meaning and power as the assembly listens to the call to conversion addressed through word and preaching. That word addressed by the preacher is a primordial or foundational, and poetic word. It is a word driven by the transcendence of the Spirit.

Exploring the ministry of proclaiming and preaching the Word of God in the assembly takes into account a number of dimensions:

1) the ministry of proclaiming the Word of God in the assembly;
2) the proclamation of the Word as the immediate context for preaching;
3) a definition of the primordial word spoken by the poet-preacher; and,
4) an exploration of the meaning of the pastoral word as poetic word.

The final section of the chapter outlines one process of creating the pastoral and poetic word by presenting a pastoral and theological reflection on a specific ministerial experience.

The Proclamation of the Word: Context for Preaching

"This is the Word of the Lord. . . . This is the Gospel of the Lord . . ." announcements echoing throughout the assembly and indicating the proclamation of the Word is finished. There is silence.

Pick up a lectionary and look at it; touch it and flip through its pages. Look at the words and notice, simply notice what is before you. It could be any book with a fancy cover, yet it is not. We name this book scripture, and declare that it is the living word of our God.

This collection of words on a page represents nothing more than dead and dried-up bones, bones like those Ezekiel saw spread over a lifeless valley. There is nothing living about the word of God as it sits printed on a page.

To proclaim the word in the assembly, a word formative to the one proclaiming it, to the preacher, and to all believers, is to ask some questions: Can a breath of the Spirit enliven the dead bones of these words to become the living word? Is there a story to be found among the word-bones that can stir the human heart? Can the word of God stand enfleshed among the assembly of the faithful?

The answer is YES! The Hebrew scripture reminds us "Dry bones I am going to make the breath enter you and you will live" (Ezek 37:5). Breath entering the word-bones and bringing forth the living word is proclamation. The word is given life through the ministry of proclamation, a ministry proper to the laity. Proclamation is a ministry in its own right. Faith-filled proclamation of the readings at the eucharist is essential to the preached word. The ministry of word proclamation creates the context for the preached word.

To proclaim the word is to breathe into and draw out from, to discover life within the word-bones. To proclaim the word is to walk the valley as Ezekiel, to listen to God and respond, to put sinews and flesh on the word-bones. It is to breathe life into the word-bones and watch them walk into the lives of those who listen.

To proclaim the word is to risk the self, to be as clay in the hands of the very word delivered. To proclaim the word is to be powerful and powerless, to be naked and clothed as royalty, to be food in the world and food to believers, to be servant and leader.

To put flesh on the word-bone is to engage in a ministry of service. It is not a task for anyone. It is essentially a lay ministry calling for adequate training in the skills of oral communication, regular and prayerful preparation, and ongoing dedication to the word. It is a ministry for those who want to become immersed in the word of God.

To stand before the eucharistic assembly is to become the story teller of our tradition. The story must be told well and with great care, for in the telling the word takes on the flesh of the one proclaiming it. In the listening the assembly is transformed into the living tradition and recognizes again that it is the Body of Christ present in our world.

Authentic proclamation of the word must emerge from the way the preacher lives as a believer and as one filled with the life of the risen Christ. The preacher's proclamation betrays his/her spirituality, the way he/she struggles to live out the pattern of Christ present in our world. The preacher's daily encounter with the word of God will be reflected in the manner of his/her proclamation. If the preacher is deeply touched by the word as it penetrates his/her heart, that encounter will be reflected concretely in its proclamation. The way the preacher speaks the word will reflect his/her encounter with the word. The two go hand in hand.

Proclamation is foundational to preaching, and affirms or supports that which calls the preacher to speak the word from his/her heart. The preacher can do this only after it has rested in his/her heart through daily reflection and prayer. A spirituality of proclamation challenges the preacher to allow the word-bones to take on flesh and life as they echo in his/her heart calling the person to conversion and transformation. The preacher's life as one who proclaims the word is an intermingling and intertwining dialogue with the word of God, the word-bones of scripture.

Proclamation of the heart emerges from an integrating habit of praying over the word which becomes a still point of the preacher's life. The word-bones of scripture live because the preacher lives; the word is active because he/she is being transformed. The flesh on the word-bones proclaimed is the flesh and heart of the preacher.

The word of God proclaimed from the heart of the preacher touches through Christ the heart of the listener as together they are moved to live their redemption more fully in Christ. The proclamation of the word of God is authentic when the Word is alive, as the preacher is alive. The proclamation is ministry because through the preacher Christ is present to the hearer in and through the assembly of faith.

The proclamation of the word is the task of those men and women whose lives serve the reign of God taking shape in the world. It is the task of those whose lives are touched as the word interfaces with our world. Proclamation is a lay task.

Authentic proclamation, the enlivening of the word-bones of Scripture creates the foundation for preaching the word. It is the task of the preacher to interpret the proclaimed word.

The Word and the Poet-Preacher

What word is spoken? Listen to Vaclav Havel, former poet-president of Czechoslovakia:

> In truth, the power of words is neither unambiguous nor clear-cut. It is not merely the liberating power of (Lech) Walesa's words or the alarm-raising power of (Andrei) Sakharov's. It is not just the power of (Salman) Rushdie's clearly misconstrued book. The point is that alongside Rushdie's words we have Khomeini's. Words that electrify society with their freedom and truthfulness are words that are harmful, lethal even. The word as arrow.
>
> What a weird fate can befall certain words. At one moment in history, courageous, liberal-minded people can be thrown into prison because a particular word means something to them, and at another moment, people of the selfsame variety can be thrown into prison because that word has ceased to mean anything to them, because it has changed from the symbol of a better world to the mumbo jumbo of a doltish dictator. . . . The selfsame word can at one time be the cornerstone of peace, while at another, machine-gun fire resounds in its every symbol (*U.S. News and World Report*, Feb. 26, 1990, 38).

The word is entrusted to the poet who then enfleshes that word and breathes life into it. It is the task of the poet to call us into the mystery and power and depth of what Rahner calls primordial words, "words that evoke the blinding mystery of things" (Rahner, 296). These are the words that spring up from the depth of the human heart and hold us in their power. These are the words that hold us under their enchanting spell because they open to us worlds beyond that which we know. These are the words that transcend the limits of definition; they cannot be defined. It is to such primordial or foundational words Havel draws our attention. "The primordial words always remain like the brightly lit house which one must leave behind, 'even when it is night'. They are always as though filled with the soft music of infinity. No matter what it is they speak of, they always whisper something about everything" (Rahner, 297).

Light	Earth
Darkness	Water
Death	Fire
Vigil	Breath
Blood	Star
Wind	Kiss

Primordial words open us to the depths of human experience. They are the words of the poet, words that lead us to that which is incomprehensible, words that touch reality and point beyond reality as we experience it today. Each of these words has a powerfully concentrated meaning needing no explanation. Such words are also words of longing that point to the infinite; they are words that save as they are crafted together in sentences. They are sacramental words, pointing to and revealing, while shrouding and concealing.

These words then become the domain of the poet. They are entrusted to the poet. Rahner again reminds us, ". . . the primordial word, before all other expressions, is the primordial sacrament of all realities. And the poet is the minister of this sacrament" (Rahner, 302).

When the poet is preacher, primordial words become the efficacious word of God. The preacher's word is the word of God enfleshed for a given faith assembly. The preacher extends the proclamation of the word of God in contemporary time and space.

Who then is the poet-preacher? The poet-preacher is one who is immersed in the word preached. What the preacher says cannot be mere talk; it is the word of one who struggles to live faithfully what is preached. Thus, to preach about resurrection is to experience in daily life the resurrection of Christ. To preach about sin and forgiveness is to know one's sinfulness and stand in need of reconciliation. To preach the stories of exodus means letting go of slavery and embracing God's freedom in the present moment.

Preaching suggests the reality of what is proclaimed in the word while pushing that reality into contemporary life. The God-message is interpreted clearly for today, by the realities of today and presented in the name of the assembly. The poetic proclamation points to the creative action of God among us and between us as we together journey in faith.

The poet-preacher is a human instrument communicating primordial words in the name of God—those words that evoke the lurking mystery of God's reality. The poet-preacher expresses personal existence when preaching, for he/she is one with a philosophy of life, specific perspectives and personal beliefs, a unique life experience and a given style. These realities ultimately enrich the words preached. They add flesh and blood to the word-bones. They speak the word of God from the perspective of a human being.

The task of the poet-preacher is to create a local scripture for the gathered Church, a scripture flowing from the dialogue of the proclaimed word of God, the ongoing tradition, and the realities of our day. Preaching articulates the word of scripture for today's pilgrim people and tells our living story and our response to the risen Lord. Preaching bridges the table of the word and the table of the eucharist as it calls us to enflesh the word and become the eucharist, to become signs of our sharing in God's life. The poetry of preaching reminds us that we are one. It calls and invites, enables and affirms, challenges and uproots, plants and invests. It calls the people of God to be the presence of Christ in our world today. It invites us to live this reality more and more.

The Pastoral Word

What happens when the poet-preacher stands before the assembly of faith? What is the meaning of the pastoral word spoken in the name of the transcendent God? What relationship exists between the preacher and the assembly?

The word spoken in Jesus becomes flesh again in the person of the poet-preacher. This word-made-flesh becomes a word mediated to the community by the one preaching. In turn, the poet-preacher becomes the word of response and thanksgiving that the community addresses back to God. The poet-preacher becomes the mediating and transforming word of poetry. He or she becomes the guardian and interpreter of the story, and the leader of the poem.

The pastoral word or word finally spoken, concerns itself with experience, significant human experience interpreted theologically. Pastoral presence is essential for the creation of pastoral reflection. Because the pastoral word is poetic, it is packed; that is, it is a word that says more and says it more intensely than ordinary language. Preaching is language that synthesizes the scriptural and human stories as it creates new meaning. It is language concentrated and organized so we can imaginatively participate in it and thus live the word more deeply.

The pastoral word spoken well broadens or deepens the personal experience of those listening. It is condensed and concentrated, saying the most in the fewest words. It captures the poet-preacher's interpretive process and theological method. The pastoral word transforms and interprets everyday experience in light of the proclaimed word. It thus moves us toward conversion.

> The poetic and pastoral word represent theological reflection at its best. Theological reflection recalls that we are born into a world of insensitivity, tears and cruelty, of narrow loyalties and strife, of bitterness, self-striving, pride and competition. But it knows equally a world full of sisterly and brotherly

> love, forgiveness, joy and compassion. In short we are born into a situation of sickness and health, of decay and growth, of despair and hope (Gariboldi and Novotny, xi).

It is here that the relationship between the poet-preacher and the assembly of faith is specified. The process of theological reflection is concerned with identifying God's saving power and presence in the events of life and interpreting that power and presence to the faith community. The preacher speaks in the name of the community and helps the community better understand itself and the issues it confronts.

This happens when the poet-preacher is attentive to the word of God proclaimed, the experience of the people, and his or her own experience. This attentive listening represents a form of prayer appropriate to the ministry of preaching. In short, reflection on personal and communal experience, and the proclaimed word of God is foundational for poetry and preaching.

The Pastoral Word: A Series of Reflections on the Living and Dying of Stephen

INTRODUCTION

"Pastoral theology is a systematic and scientific reflection upon the concrete situation of the Church; that is, on the Church as it is emerging in the actual experience of its ministry" (Collins, 12). Pastoral theology emerges when theological reflection is an ongoing discipline of the poet-preacher. The creation of the pastoral word presumes that the poet-preacher is one nourished by the word of God, and deeply invested in the lives of those whom the individual serves.

The following reflections are offered as an example of the poet-preacher's process and art. They are an attempt to concretize the material presented thus far. They are theological reflections based on one ongoing pastoral experience. Taken together these pastoral words journal a process, a process of discovering meaning, of interfacing human experience with the word of God, and of coming to recognize God present in the midst of the life and death struggle. They are offered here so that the reader might enter into the mystery of proclamation, the power of primordial words, and the pastoral word of the poet-preacher. They encourage the reader to discover his/her own process and methodology for creating the pastoral word.

THE PASTORAL CONTEXT

One of the great gifts of ministry is the ability to enter the unfolding story of persons and families. For four years I walked with a young man named Stephen and his family, as together they struggled with a cancer named Hodgkin.

Stephen entered the Vincentian college seminary at St. Mary of the Barrens in September 1983. "The Barrens," the oldest college west of the Mississippi, is located in Perryville, Missouri. Steve entered as a freshman, having completed two years of Vincentian high school formation at Saint Vincent's in Cape Girardeau, Missouri and two years at Saint Vincent's in Lemont, Illinois. When Steve came to the Barrens he was finishing his first round of chemotherapy.

By September of the following year, as Steve was beginning his sophomore year, the cancer was no longer in remission. He was given four to six months to live unless he underwent a very radical form of chemotherapy in conjunction with a bone-marrow transplant. He chose this treatment program, knowing that it might well kill him.

From late November 1983 until mid-March 1984 Steve was in the hospital. He was often at the point of death during this time. Miraculously he left the hospital alive and returned to the Vincentian formation program that summer.

September 1984 saw Steve begin—for a second time—his sophomore year of college. While his health seemed rather fragile, he was gaining strength and confidence. At the end of the academic year Steve decided to leave the college seminary program. It was a good decision. A native of Perryville, Steve moved to his family home a short distance from the seminary. Shortly thereafter he began working at the seminary and worked there until Christmas. He had intended to move to Houston, Texas to begin school again. His Hodgkins had other plans. It was no longer in remission. Steve entered the hospital for a third round of chemotherapy and a second bone-marrow transplant. He did not survive.

On the evening of March 12, 1986, Steven died. He was twenty-two years old. His family surrounded his bed during the course of Steve's last day and evening. I was able to be with Steve for the last ten hours of his life as we know it. It was a graced moment to be with him when he died.

ONE BEGINNING OF THE STORY: THE KINGDOM OF GOD ON AN OCTOBER AFTERNOON—1983

It was a sunny October afternoon. The trees were beginning their glorious dance into fall color, a dance leading to winter's death. I sat at my desk looking out the window at an elm tree dating back to the Civil War. I was anxious as I waited, experiencing a sense of dread as I faced my last appointment of the day. It was an anxiousness and fright I don't ever remember feeling.

Stephen appeared at the door with that typical college look of being imposed upon. After all, it was Friday afternoon; there were many better things to do than talk with the Dean.

Steve had gone to the doctor a week before for a routine check-up. Prior to the check-up, a number of the faculty had been rather worried. He seemed to be losing weight and had developed a persistent cough. He was not looking well, and there was always the wonder in the back of my mind—is the cancer active again?

I had talked with Steve's parents the day before, and I knew the cancer was indeed active again! It had progressed further than the previous occurrence, and the prognosis was not good—four to six months to live without further treatment. I also knew that it was my task to tell Stephen the life-threatening news.

Steve and I went into my sitting room. After some uncomfortable small talk I began. "Do you have any idea what the doctor is going to tell you next week?" Of course, he had no idea—at least none he wanted to share with me or anyone else, for that matter. Steve did not talk about his cancer. "I want to tell you what the doctor knows." There was a look of surprise on his face—why would I be telling him what the doctor knew; how did I know anyhow? He began to look the way I was feeling. "The cancer is back and is more serious than the last time. It had spread further than before and is now more deadly." I will never forget that line. I will never forget the look on his face. It was as if I had sentenced him to death—and perhaps I had!

There was a long silence. It all seemed like a bad dream to me. Steve seemed lost or perhaps captive to his interior world. I could see and feel the pressure building in him to the point of explosion. Steve was not a very verbal person. Lots of feelings happened in his interior world, feelings known to very few people. After what seemed an eternity, I broke the silence. "Do you want to tell me what's happening inside you?" I knew he would need an invitation if he was to share anything, if he was to let another inside his torment.

For the next hour a flood of tears came forth. There was anger and denial, floor pacing and chair pounding. An absolute refusal of any further treatment was his first response—denial at its best. I worked hard to give him as much freedom and control as possible, for he seemed to have none and desperately needed some. I wanted to let him feel and experience his pain and disappointment. I wanted him to "hit bottom" so he could begin to rebuild his hope—or at least have a base from which to begin. I encouraged the tears and shouts of anger. They came, and we talked.

It was a time of intimacy and vulnerability for both of us. I saw a side of Stephen that I had never seen—so weak and frightened by the future. I saw a frightened little boy needing to be held and comforted. I saw a young man feeling victimized by forces beyond his control. I saw a young man of faith wondering if God existed.

Finally, there was a period of calm and silence. It seemed to me that the task of the moment was complete—at least for this moment. By a previous arrangement with Steve's parents, I was going to drive Steve home once I had broken the news, so that he could be with his family for the evening. Another priest and I would join them later in the evening for a family gathering. I wanted to end this painful day by celebrating the sacrament of the sick with Steve and his family.

I asked Steve if he was ready to go home. He hesitated and then asked me a question: "Will you be there when I die; will you say my funeral mass?" I must have looked rather shocked. He looked me straight in the eyes and said, "The chances are good that I'll be dead in two years." Steve knew the gravity of the situation more than I or anyone else. I promised to do my best to "make good" his requests. We ended with a long and tearful embrace. Then I drove him home. In many ways, Stephen's passion story began.

A PARADIGM OF DYING AND DEATH: THE FINAL MOMENT OF GROWTH

[*based on Mark 9:14-29; 15:33-39; and 15:46*]

They brought the boy to him and as soon as the spirit saw Jesus, it threw the boy into convulsions . . .

Stephen was young when he left us—a mere twenty-two.

How long has this been happening to him?

The demon he struggled with for four years
has been exorcised twice before.
The strong demon of cancer was now in control.

It has often thrown him into the fire and into water in order to destroy him . . .

Stephen's life was one of unfulfilled hope,
and dreams that could only be dreamed.
Unfinished is a word that fits
when one stands on this side of eternity,
on this side of the kingdom come.

The father of the boy cried out, "I do have faith. Help the little faith I have."

Steve's was a life of faith,
often expressed through his snide laugh.
Like many his age,
his faith seemed hidden more often than not.
Perhaps, a faith in absence,
a faith in an empty tomb.
He was so consumed with the demon
that it was difficult to know this young man.
What imagination and life;
what laughter and playfulness
lived beyond the demon?

His eyes occasionally spoke this life
and when someone caught the moment with him
the curtain of the demon would cover him from sight.

This kind can only be driven out by prayer . . .

And then the last day . . .

When the sixth hour came there was darkness over the whole land . . .

The vigil began:

Stephen dying;
His family supporting;
I standing and being with;
All touching and holding . . .

['Tis the task of the shaman and poet to do these rites of passage.]

The hope of technology was taken away.
  Those for whom death is failure were not amused and in typical form stood by amazed at what they saw of love.]

The vigil continued—
  it was a waiting at the tomb of the kingdom to come.

Jesus cried out in a loud voice . . .

While the demon cancer would kill Stephen,
  it would not die itself—for demons never seem to die.

He was conscious.
His eyes became glazed with the oncoming curtain of death.
He tried to talk now and then—
  his fluid-filled lungs made him more and more difficult to understand.
  He cried out toward the end: "Forgive me . . ."

My God, my God why have you deserted me?

He struggled to say: "I love you . . ."

A peacefulness came over him.

[If I had not been watching, I would have missed his last breath,
the breathing forth of his spirit.]

Jesus gave a loud cry and breathed his last. The curtain of the Temple was torn in two from top to bottom.

The curtain was torn and Stephen could see
  what he was now to become.
He left us finished and resolved.
He continues on without us.

. . . It was now evening. . . . And they rolled a stone against the entrance of the tomb . . .

MASS OF CHRISTIAN BURIAL: THE HOMILY

[*based on Wisdom 4:7-14; Revelation 21:1-7; John 12:23-36*]

For a fleeting moment our imagination ponders and the tears flow
  for the unfulfilled expectations of Stephen's life;
  for all the hunting and fishing that will never happen;
  for the dream of a future that will never be lived out.
The deepest questions of the heart are spoken in wonderment:
  Why?
  Why Stephen?

Why the young?
Why now?
Our tears and questions and imagination invite us
to let go of what can no longer be;
to let go so that the memory of Steve—
his often flip sense of humor,
his penetrating quietness,
his unique way of saying just about anything,
most of which can't be said in public—
to let go so that he can be remembered into our future,
and be carried with us as we hear the word of God today:
"See I make all things new . . ."
"See, Stephen is my son and I am his God."
It is our simple faith in this Jesus Christ
who is Alpha and Omega,
life and resurrection to eternal life
that lets us move beyond our questions and tears.

It is our simple faith that Jesus is alive with us right now
that enables us to let go
and realize that in life,
the gospel planting for death takes place.

Steve's short life and all of our lives
are about seed planting for resurrection.
The grain of wheat must fall.
The grain of wheat must die so that it might grow to greatness.

That is Steve's story;
that is our story.

The moment of conception saw Steve's planting in love begin:
the love of parents,
the love of brother and sisters,
the close bonds of the extended family—
grandparents, brothers-in-law, nieces
and nephews.
This is the planting into life as we know it.

There was a growing in faith
and a struggle few knew to keep faith in light of
his cancer and the questions it raised for him.

His was a faith supported and nurtured by his family,
a faith interpreted and given meaning
by a sacramental life.
This is the planting into faith
and ultimately into faithfulness.

There were the movements to school
and the childhood desire and dream to explore priesthood and Vincentian life—the people here from the community today testify to the seriousness of his exploration.

The movements to school spoke of developing independence
and the search for his identity as a unique
person.
No one will ever deny the marvelous uniqueness of Stephen!
This is the planting into adulthood—the becoming of the
"just man who pleased God . . ."

And interwoven in the normal struggles of youth and adolescence
was the unexplained and unexpected, yet deadly cancer.

Tough decisions, pain and hospitals were a permanent part
of Steve's life the last four years,
as he grew toward personal integrity and completeness,
as his faith in a God
who would ultimately care for him grew,
as his tough-guy image became less
and his gentle side grew.
This was the planting into struggle and deeper faith.

Wednesday night the planting was into the mystery of Christ.

Stephen let go into his God.
He had put up the fight of someone
who loved life as we know it.
He let go while his family,
amid tears and hugs and grief encouraged him.
He let go into the mystery of his own being,
fully forgiven as he asked forgiveness;
fully loved as he struggled to say,
"I love you . . ."

He let go and became one honored now
by the Father in kingdom glory.
He made the final leap of faith into faithfulness.

The uniqueness of Stephen's life speaks the dynamic of our lives
as a people of faith.
The angels have led Stephen into paradise.
The martyrs have welcomed him into the new Jerusalem.

Steve is now a sign for us,
a sign living in the fullness of the risen Christ.
We encounter him in memory.
We encounter him in eucharist.
for here we know the fullness
of the Body of Christ in mystery.

The poet Stephen preached the passion and death of Jesus
by living it each day these past four years.
He now lives the resurrection with Christ.

THE GRAVE AND FINAL REFLECTION

Stephen's grave is the silent reminder
of a life once lived,
now known in memory.

Flesh no longer alive;
Blood no longer pumping;
Breath no longer creating the rhythms of life;
Smiles no longer given;
Struggle and pain no longer shared.

Dirt over the spot where he "rests in peace."
[What a curious way to describe eternity—peaceful rest!]
Grass struggling to live,
seeks to blot out the violence of the open grave,
and the reality of what it now covers.
A marker with a name and dates—birth and death.
A small picture jars memory.

Is life not counted more than birth and death dates?
Is memory not more than a picture?

I watched him die for four years
and prayed each day that he would not.

It was a long and uneven death march—
full of hope and joy today,
full of doubt and despair tomorrow.
There were days when everything was so right;
and days when the possibilities of death were all consuming.

To share the last ten hours of his life
with those who "cheered" him to kingdom life
was a great blessing.
The time came and he let go into the arms of a loving God.

He was ready to let go.
He was at peace with himself
and those around him.
I believe he was at peace with God—
the end was too right for him not to have been.

And now the Stephen stories are told
and the memory is re-membered.
Flesh is strong.
Blood is life-giving.
Breath becomes Spirit.
Smiles are given.
The struggle and pain continue.
The grave is only one silent reminder of ultimate transition.

the life gospel of Stephen
and all those before us continue to live among us
and call us into a kingdom future.
Amen!

A FINAL NOTE

Emerson reminds us, "There is in all great poets a wisdom of humanity which is superior to any talents they exercise. The great poets make us feel our own wealth and then we think less of his compositions. His best communication to our minds is to teach us to despise all that he has done" (Sculley, 638).

The poet-preacher is needed only until Christ is fully formed in us. Preaching those primordial, poetic words creates new poets who will continue to refresh and renew the Church.

Resources

Collins, Raymond F. *Models of Theological Reflection*. Lanham, Md.: University Press of America, Inc., 1984.

Emerson, Ralph Waldo. "The Over-Soul." Found in *The American Tradition in Literature*, edited by Sculley Bradley, Richmond Beatty, and E. Hudson Long. A W. W. Norton Book published by Grosset and Dunlap, Inc, New York, 1967.

Gariboldi, Ronald G., and Novotny, Daniel. *The Art of Theological Reflection: An Ecumenical Study*. Edited by Jean S. Novotny. Lanham, Md.: University Press of America, Inc., 1987.

Perrine, Laurence. *Sound and Sense*, 6th edition. New York: Harcourt Brace Jovanovich, Inc., 1982.

Rahner, Karl. *Theological Investigations*, volume 3. Baltimore: Helicon Press, 1967.

United States Catholic Conference. *Fulfilled in Your Hearing*. Washington: Bishops' Committee on Priestly Life and Ministry, 1982.

US News and World Report, vol. 108, no. 8, February 26, 1990.

The **Aquinas Institute of Theology** faculty contributors:

Charles Bouchard, O.P., president of Aquinas Institute and assistant professor of systematic theology, teaches moral theology.

Thomas Brodie, O.P., formerly taught Hebrew scriptures at Aquinas Institute and now teaches in the theologate for the Province of Ireland.

Louis Brusatti, C.M., formerly a member of the faculty, now teaches at De Paul University in Chicago.

Harry Byrne, O.P., is assistant professor of pastoral theology.

Joan Delaplane, O.P., professor of pastoral theology, teaches preaching courses.

Mary Catherine Hilkert, O.P., associate professor of systematic theology, is a Schillebeeckx scholar.

Mary Margaret Pazdan, O.P., is associate professor of biblical studies and specializes in Christian scriptures.

Frank Quinn, O.P., professor of systematic and pastoral theology, is a liturgist.

Edward Ruane, O.P., assistant professor of pastoral theology and director of field education, also teaches preaching courses.

Benjamin Russell, O.P., the former dean of the school, is now pastor of St. Vincent Ferrer Church in River Forest, Illinois.

Regina Siegfried, A.S.C., is assistant professor of historical studies and concentrates on United States spirituality.

Carla Mae Streeter, O.P., is associate professor of systematic theology and a Lonergan scholar.

Samuel Torvend, O.P., a liturgist, is assistant professor of historical and liturgical theology.

Edward van Merrienboer, O.P., adjunct instructor of pastoral theology, is Promoter of Justice and Peace for the Dominican Generalate in Rome.

Ronald Zawilla, formerly of the Aquinas faculty, a medieval scholar, works in liturgical arts.